D1260252

Imagination Transformed

THE EVOLUTION OF THE FEMALE CHARACTER IN KEATS'S POETRY

Karla Alwes

SOUTHERN ILLINOIS UNIVERSITY PRESS
Carbondale • Edwardsville

PR
4838
.W6
AA5
1993

Copyright © 1993 by the Board of Trustees,
Southern Illinois University
All rights reserved
Printed in the United States of America
Edited by Robyn Laur Clark
Designed by Duane E. Perkins
Production supervised by Natalia Nadraga
96   95   94   93   4   3   2   1

Library of Congress Cataloging-in-Publication Data

Alwes, Karla.
Imagination transformed : the evolution of the female
character in Keats's poetry / Karla Alwes.
p.   cm.
Includes bibliographical references and index.
1. Keats, John, 1795–1821—Characters—Women. 2.
Women in literature. I. Title.
PR4838.W6A45   1993
821'.7—dc20   92-23190
ISBN 0-8093-1835-0   CIP

The paper used in this publication meets the minimum
requirements of American National Standard for Information
Sciences–Permanence of Paper for Printed Library Materials,
ANSI Z39.48-1984. ⊗

26216571

For my daughters, *Bronwyn and Emma*

Contents

Acknowledgments

My gratitude and appreciation go to Robert Bagg, who first instilled and encouraged my love of romantic poetry; Jack Stillinger, whose early reading of this work furthered that love; Leon Waldoff, for allowing me to be a part of his Wordsworth and Keats seminar, and for the encouragement I drew from that experience; and to John Marciano, whose love of the beautiful in all things, like Keats's, continues to influence my work and my life.

I thank also the women friends in my life—Signia Warner, Paula Drake, Sherry Imanaka, Lise Anderson, and Nancy Weaver—who were there at the beginning of this project as well as at its completion, and whose capabilities gave me the courage to recognize my own.

Thanks also to Curtis Clark, acquisitions editor, for believing in this work, and to Robyn Laur Clark, copy editor, who played a major role in making that belief a reality.

An earlier version of chapter 7 is reprinted from *Nineteenth-Century Literature* 43.2 (September 1988): 195–219, by permission, © 1988 by The Regents of the University of California Press. An earlier version of the discussion of "La Belle Dame sans Merci" (chapter 4) appeared as "Romanticizing Misogyny: The Woman as Symbol in the Poetry of John Keats" in *Misogyny in Literature: An Essay Collection*, ed. Katherine Ackley (New York: Garland, 1992) and is reprinted by permission.

A Note on Documentation

     All citations in text to Keats's poetry, unless otherwise noted, refer to *The Poems of John Keats*, ed. Jack Stillinger (Cambridge, MA: Harvard UP, 1978). The citations all include line number(s). Citations to Keats's letters refer to *The Letters of John Keats*, ed. Hyder Edward Rollins, 2 vols. (Cambridge, MA: Harvard UP, 1958) and are referred to as *Letters* followed by volume number and page number (2:301–3).

Imagination Transformed

Introduction

A reader of Keats's works cannot help being struck by
the abundance of female figures. Every major poem involves
at least one feminine character—often more than one—and
almost always as the controlling metaphor. She serves alter-
nately as a means of preservation and as an agent of destruction
to the poetry's male heroes, the she who must be both embraced
and denied in order to acquire masculine identity. As Keats
enacts it in his poetry, the power of the female is both primor-
dial and transcendent, and by identifying her with his own
often recalcitrant imagination, he exploits the female not only
as an ideal to be achieved but as an obstacle to that achievement.

The romantic female persona is a poetic contrivance to her
male creator. She is, as Elizabeth Janeway observes of the earli-
est images of goddesses from the Stone Age, a "fetish," a "lucky
piece" for a "desperate man . . . to thumb in time of need" (3).
Janeway comments that the Stone Age figures have neither
faces nor feet, are not characterized as individuals or as women,
but portray instead, like the figure of romantic poetry, "man's
need for her. . . . She is the Great Mother, feared and adored,
both mediator with and representative of necessity" (3). From
the Stone Age to the romantic era and beyond, the woman as
symbol is created in order to be the index by which the male
measures his identity. She is, as Simone de Beauvoir says, "all
that man desires and all that he does not attain" (223). The
misogyny that lies behind romantic poetry places the onus of
responsibility for the male's creative survival, and thus his cre-
ative identity, squarely on the self-representation he derives
from the woman as metaphor for both.

Marilyn Gaull remarks that Keats "depicts women either as
silly and self-deluded, or as goddesses who preside over painful

1

initiation rites" (222). The silliness and self-delusion, as well as the magnificence of the later goddesses, originate with the development of the creator himself, and it is through the dismissal and acceptance of the successive female figures that Keats personifies the changes that occur with his growth as a poet. From the mortal maidens of 1817 to the omnipotent goddesses of 1819, the females portray the salvation and destruction, passion and fear that the imagination elicits. The "yearning Passion I have for the beautiful" that Keats describes to his brother and sister-in-law (*Letters* 1:404) is combined, in the later poetry, with a fear of the unknown, especially of the female, and consequently a fear of the new elusive imagination that will delineate her, the product of an increasingly tragic vision of experience.

As symbol of the imagination itself—both creative and errant—Keats's women represent both the joy of creativity and the fear that Keats often felt over its possible loss. More than that of any of his contemporaries, Keats's poetry represents the feminine figure as symbol of the poet's own fears of alienation and loss of masculine (creative) identity. Thus the figures in his works serve as lovers, guides, and nemeses to the male heroes. The portrait that emerges at the end of the collective works is of a supremely androgynous figure who becomes a "close bosom-friend" to the male figure, one who represents both the creator and Apollo, "the maturing sun" ("To Autumn" 2). The journey to this point is dangerously littered with women who taunt and intimidate the male, however, and who are anything but a "friend" to him.

Marlon Ross refers to the "anxious self-consciousness that pervades all Romantic poetry, . . . the persistent effort of the Romantic poet to find in his own voice an aboriginal self that re-creates the world" ("Romantic Quest" 26). And when men attempt to recreate the world, to reproduce self-meaning in their literature, they must take into account the feminine (and primal) principle of creation. They must either provide for or dismiss the idea of procreativity, symbolized by the adult, or fully evolved, woman, who inspires the man with horror that is "the horror of his own carnal contingence, which he projects upon her" (Beauvoir 167). Strictly speaking, there are no "adult" females in Keats's poetry. He chooses to dismiss the mortal female once she comes of age, and when she is abandoned, her successors are mythologized into the timeless, and thus ageless, figures of goddesses. It is a difficult task to attempt to create constancy through a symbol whose very nature is perceived, by the male, as inconstant, deriving from her status as alien to the male. How to reconcile her creative powers that will ensure his status as poet with those perceived as destructive is the raison d'être behind Keats's greatest works.

Having completed "Isabella" and "The Eve of St. Agnes," and "half-finished" "Lamia," Keats tells his friend Benjamin Bailey that he "look[s] upon fine Phrases like a Lover" (*Letters* 2:139). Through his status as lover to the imagination, the poet may be able to exert better control over the increasingly problematic relationship that develops between himself and his work, certainly apparent in "Lamia," the poem only half-finished in need of a resolution, with the seemingly unresolvable characteristic of a serpent/goddess whose power, Keats facilely asserts, "smote, [yet] still guaranteed to save" (1.399).

For the poet who sees himself as "lover" to the imagination, a natural (and troublesome) correlative of the female as a metaphor of the imagination is the concept of sexuality. Whether mortal or immortal, the relationship between Keats's females and the male personae is frequently characterized by a cluster of sexually connotative terms, such as "enthrall," "entrammel," and "ensnare," which convey the magic and subversive power of the female and give an impression of simultaneous attraction and repulsion on the part of the male—present in both Keats the poet as well as Keats the man, as evidenced by the various letters he wrote that concurrently impugn and elevate the nature of women.[1] The network of metaphors enacts and animates Keats's own relationship with his often contrary imagination that will become, in the crucial odes, his "demon Poesy" ("Ode on Indolence" 30). Nina Auerbach comments that the demonic female figures of literature, traditionally characterized as alien to the male, exude "a power that withers patriarchs . . . [and] find their greatest triumphs in displacing male authorities" (8). It is thus evidence of masculine survival when the male writer is able to create and subdue the female in her demonic form. Male authority, and the authorship that lies within it, derives its power from his gendered identity and inherent difference from the female. The female muse is distinctly separate from the male writer: while she is the imagination, he is the energy that gives it life, purpose, and, when necessary, limitations.

The female is a convenient symbol for the male imagination precisely because she is traditionally characterized as fragmented into the nine individual Muses and can thus be so easily dehumanized into a "spiritual object" (Gilbert and Gubar 403), while at the same time offering sexual solace to the masculine identity. But "that which is creative must create itself" Keats says of the imagination (*Letters* 1:374). The object must become the subject, and as Keats journeys from the naive poet of "Imitation of Spenser," a poem that, as its title makes clear, attempts nothing beyond imitation of his male predecessor, to the tragic poet of "The Fall of Hyperion," who had watched his eighteen-year-old brother Tom die of the family disease tuberculosis, the poetry's females evolve from the early dormant mortal maidens to the mythic goddesses of the later poetry, with a humanizing power that distances them from their own objectification and reintegrates the nine fragmented voices of the Muses into a whole.

The sexual enthrallment that binds Keats to his creations will change, too, from one of benign attraction to one of inextricable possession, because the female is, by necessity, more than a lover to Keats—she is the gauge of his own search for identity. Multidimensional and mysteriously protean, the females provide a complete portrait of the growth of the imagination, of both the potentialities and the disappointments that the poet discovered in it through them.

Another more traditional figure is central to much of Keats's poetry—the dashing and misogynous Apollo, god of the sun, of poetry, of medicine, and sundry other masculine realms, whose sexual pursuits are legendary. The mythic war between the Titans and the Olympians that constitutes the narrative events of the "Hyperion" poems is a battle between the arche-typally feminine earth and the masculine heaven. With the triumph of the Olympian Apollo as sun god, all feminine power is in danger of being supplanted.

The myths of Apollo that Keats embraced and integrated into his poetry as early as February 1815 ("Ode to Apollo") demonstrate the poet's own conflicting need of and fear of the female. The fears will become impossible to resolve by concentrating solely on the god of the new order of Olympians as metaphor for the imagination, as Keats's early poetry at-tempts to do,[2] because the myths of Apollo deny the power, often the very existence even, of the earth goddesses who pre-ceded him. Keats's own need for the maternal goddesses, how-ever, will eventually outweigh his need for Apollo.

Several of the stories about Apollo focus on or allude to his misogynist traits, as he frequently chases down and often causes the death of fleeing mortal women or lesser goddesses. *Lem-prière's Classical Dictionary*, to which Keats himself often turned for knowledge of mythology, notes that Apollo's "amours with [different females] are well known, as are also the various shapes he assumed to gratify his passion" (67). It will be Keats's own creations who assume "various shapes" to gratify their own pas-sion within the poems, an interesting counterpoint to Apollo's description, as noted by Lemprière, which is more androgynous than virile, a fact that Keats certainly would not have ignored: Apollo is "generally represented with long hair, as a tall beardless young man, with a handsome shape, holding in his hand a bow, and sometimes a lyre; his head is generally surrounded with beams of light" (67). Holding a bow and a lyre, two objects of feminine shape and proportion, without the phallic arrow any-where in sight, and sporting what amounts to a halo, like that which crowns both Madonna and the Christ child, Apollo seems less threatening a figure to women than does Cupid, who is al-lowed a quiver of arrows. Yet he is mythologized as the andro-centric god who replaces feeling with intellect, that is, the femi-nine with the masculine, and attempts, as the newly born Olympian, to deny the earth's existence altogether, an attempt that will become evident in much of Keats's poetry.[3] While his females, in their own progressively frightening shapes will seem like caricatures of Apollo, Keats will imbue the masculine sun god with a passivity, especially apparent in the first "Hyperion," that helps produce the final androgynous figure of "To Autumn," an androgyny that will define the figures of both Apollo and the season. After the first great flourish of the sun god in the early poetry, Keats will invoke him only infrequently because the later poetry is directed toward a reconciliation between the violently severed earth and heaven (the outcome of the mythic battle) that goes beyond the Apollonian ideal and into the poet's own realm of salvation—the human heart. The desired reconciliation will degender both earth and heaven by creating the androgyny that will supplant both the frightening female and her vulnerable male prey.

The work in which the male is seen as most vulnerable is "La Belle Dame sans Merci," the startling little poem that serves as both turning point and critical link between an imagination that resides with the feminine earth, which Keats will now eschew, and an imagination that attempts to leave the earth for the Apollonian realm of timelessness. Probably the most controversial of his works, it is one of a handful that is most closely associated with Keats's life and his own sexuality. Not surprisingly, feminist critics have discussed la belle dame as an archetype of the female who knowingly and willingly emasculates the male.[4] Written in April 1819, after the death of Tom Keats and during the early months of the poet's tragic relationship with Fanny Brawne, the poem apotheosizes a female who while powerful enough to abandon the earth—the poetic goal—is unwilling (or unable) to reconcile the two realms, to repair the schism between the earth of the fallen sun god, Hyperion, and the heaven of his successor, Apollo. She is the symbol and the example of the imagination "brought / Beyond its proper bound, yet still confined,— / Lost in a sort of Purgatory blind" so that she "cannot refer to any standard law / Of either earth or heaven" (*Letters* 1:262). "La Belle Dame" is the harbinger of the period of Keats's career most defined by his frightening uncertainty about the imagination.

Her immediate progeny will be the female symbols in the

odes of 1819, in which Keats tries to diffuse the destructiveness of the female by splintering her persona into discrete symbols that seem, at first, to convey compassion toward the mortal speaker who seeks possession of their power through union with them. The attempt will ultimately be futile, however, because the female symbols of the odes are still incapable of identifying with the mortal state (the nightingale, for example, has "never known / The weariness, the fever, and the fret" [22–23] of mortality), and these symbols finally become, as "La Belle Dame" had, representatives of an imagination "brought / Beyond its proper bound."

Moneta of "The Fall of Hyperion" is the final goddess, more powerful than any of her predecessors, to appear in Keats's poetry. Because she understands the power and beauty of both realms, earth and heaven, her power extends even beyond that of Apollo. At the final stage of the development of the female, Moneta combines the wisdom of the Apollonian realm with the compassion of the feminine earth and defines the poet, who will not recognize both realms, as a "dreamer," one who "venoms all his days, / Bearing more woe than all his sins deserve" (1.175–76). Through her reclamation of the power of the maternal female, Moneta transforms the dreamer's identity into that of a poet. The restoration that the dreamer-poet discovers possible in "The Fall" is fully enacted in the final ode, "To Autumn." The poetic process reaches fruition in exquisite testimony to the season of ripe abundance. In this poem of restoration, all transcendent powers lie in the temporal beauty of the earth. The imagination that had consistently attempted to leave the earth gives the earth itself the suggestion of timelessness, where "summer has o'er-brimm'd" the bees' "clammy cells" (11) and they believe the "warm days will never cease" (10). For the first and only time in the poetry, timelessness becomes a characteristic of earthly beauty, if only to the bees. The figure that presides over this apotheosis, along with the sun, is timeless as well, for it is a figure finally degendered and neutralized into a process of procreation rather than a female who, by virtue of her gender, could be either docile or dominant to the male but never simply equal.

Although many critics have discussed the poetry's females and female symbols, the discussions have generally been tangential to the exegesis of the poetry itself. And even some of the critics who focused on the changing female figure often failed to include the process by which change occurs within the vision of the poet himself. These critics thereby incorrectly (and perhaps a bit patronizingly) concluded that the females of the middle and late poetry are little more than "femmes fatales," an epithet that denies rather than validates the process of change, for it reduces the poet's enthrallment to self-imposed destruction rather than to a relationship expressive of the anxiety with which Keats consistently delineated his imaginative powers.[5]

The female as literary object is, of course, nothing new to writers. Caroline Heilbrun argues, for example, that in creating female personae, women writers are articulating their own pain (72). But the process retraced here is that of a male writer who exploits the female as an object so that he can transcend his fear of her as a symbol of his own creative limitations. Thus the object takes on the characteristics of the subject as Keats creates a dialectic that denies and embraces, in order to, as Ross says, "establish rites of passage toward poetic identity and toward masculine empowerment" ("Romantic Quest" 29). Because romanticism is, as Ross observes, "historically a masculine phenomenon" (29), women, even women writers, "become anchors for the male poets' own pursuit for masculine self possession" (29). Real, flesh and blood women did not particularly interest Keats as poet, but the ideal woman whom he strived for in his poetry to create and possess would, if controlled, ensure his own place among the male romantic poets. For male writers, empowerment is valid only when the specter of the objectified female becoming subject is subverted. The threat of masculine dissolution looms especially large for Keats, whose poetry becomes progressively more androcentric as it delineates and cherishes an ideal female whose origins lie in the perceived paradoxical nature of her gender. Keats can subvert this outcome finally by degendering the female into a figure as androgynous and passive as the diluted Apollo from "Hyperion."

This study will allow the poems themselves to dramatize Keats's account of his struggle to come to terms with his ideas regarding women and poetry, so intrinsically bound to each other in his mind because they both represent consummate ideals to him. Such representation ultimately verifies Keats's belief that, as he said of his most revered predecessor, Shakespeare, "a Man's life of any worth is a continual allegory . . . his works are the comments on it" (*Letters* 2:67). A man's works, the issue of his imagination, will be what finally identify him as a poet. And this identity, to Keats, is procreative and can be found only through the enjoined powers of the female. It is through her that Keats's own allegory emerges.

"A Leafy Luxury"
Poems of 1817

A study of Keats's career must give more than cursory attention to his very early poetry. Had Keats died after writing "Sleep and Poetry," for example, he would be remembered today as little more than a protégé of Leigh Hunt. But precisely because Keats lived to write such cornerstones of English poetry as "The Eve of St. Agnes" and "Ode to a Nightingale," his germinal poetry demands much critical attention. Poems such as "I stood tip-toe upon a little hill," "Calidore," "On the Grasshopper and Cricket," and "Sleep and Poetry" contain the rudimentary images, symbols, and metaphorical language that in a phenomenally brief span of fewer than four years would become the legendary workings of the mind of a major poet.

Keats's later works assured his immortality, of course, but the question is how he got there. Morris Dickstein sees the early poems as most "vulnerable to the charge of escapism" (26), but by what route did he go from the poems published in 1817, which do indeed evoke a fledgling poet who seeks to escape the earth, to "The Fall of Hyperion," in which that same poet is admonished to "think of the earth"?[1] How is the poetic journey from "Ode to Apollo" (1815), which celebrates quintessentially masculine attributes, to "To Autumn" (1819) and its eternal presiding figure of quiet androgyny mapped out? That is, how does a poet who seeks inclusion in the realm of "English poets," all male, become one who recognizes the limitations of his own masculinity?

Keats's statement that he "look[s] upon fine Phrases like a Lover" is not a particularly new idea for male writers, but Keats takes the simile further than most by enforcing a closeness between his own "coy muse" ("To George Felton Mathew" 32) and himself in an attempt to discover his poetic identity through intimacy with the female.

It is an intimacy that in reality frequently causes an alienation of oneself from another, rather than a union, even though a love relationship is second only to one's childhood in the acquisition of identity. The shared intimacy between lovers evokes epithets for the beloved that refer back to the self; the lover is a mirror in which we see ourselves duplicated. But for the male who surrenders his nascent identity to the female as lover, he risks that she will be the "Fatal Woman," as Mario Praz calls her, an archetype that borders on the cliché in romantic poetry (191). Keats wants not only the traditional inspiration from his muse but, as the following lines from his first volume of poetry show, an intimacy that, if successful, will ensure his own identity as a poet:

> O Mathew, lend thy aid
> To find a place where I may greet the maid—
> Where we may soft humanity put on,
> And sit, and rhyme and think on Chatterton.
> ("To George Felton Mathew" 53–56)

In "Sleep and Poetry," Keats describes the desired feminization of the ideal imagination:

> A drainless shower
> Of light is poesy; 'tis the supreme of power;
> 'Tis might half slumb'ring on its own right arm.
> The very archings of her eye-lids charm
> A thousand willing agents to obey,
> And still she governs with the mildest sway:
> But strength alone though of the Muses born
> Is like a fallen angel: trees uptorn,
> Darkness, and worms, and shrouds, and sepulchres
> Delight it; for it feeds upon the burrs,
> And thorns of life; forgetting the great end
> Of poesy, that it should be a friend
> To sooth the cares, and lift the thoughts of man.
> (235–47)

The female described in this early poem bears much resemblance to the final figure of "To Autumn," foreshadowing the great figure of the earth who sits "careless on a granary floor, / Thy hair soft-lifted by the winnowing wind" (14–15). The "friend" that the poet hopes to find in his imagination will be realized in the final great poem, but for now the message is that the Muse's power alone, without the intimacy and friendship she can offer the poet, despite the ancillary risk of her becoming a "Fatal Woman," is a "darkness" delighted by "worms, and shrouds, and sepulchres." The lack of intimacy between poet and imagination is, in short, death—a state that offers neither poetry nor identity nor the transcendence that these poems seek.

The muse that Keats invokes in his early poetry is indeed a friend—docile, maidenly, and undemanding. She inspires poetry that remains primarily serene and, more important, largely imitative and illustrative of the past and current male poets, a reliable gauge of poetic achievement to a new poet with no identity of his own. In the later poetry, the female, empowered by Keats's doubts over his own masculine identity, will become a means by which Keats must confront, rather than escape, the pain that his poetry acknowledges. Here, though, the pain of darkness is easily overcome in the facile acknowledgment of beauty as a transcendent and ameliorative power. In these early poems, salvation is an option rather than a question.

In the volume of 1817, the female figure serves as an inseparable part of nature itself. The dichotomy between earth and heaven, nature and the imagination, which epitomizes the later poems, has not yet occurred. Rather, the poems of 1817 depict an earthly paradise, "a leafy luxury," as Keats calls it ("To Leigh Hunt, Esq." 13). Nature is the vehicle to beauty and imagination, and the poet is a "removed spectator" to the scene, stationing himself "outside yet near" the described scenes, indicating the "disembodied nature of chameleon speculation, the poetical character's need to escape self-consciousness" (Rzepka 170). The need to escape, so prevalent in Keats's early poetry, enforces a confined mortality on the female figure, who is as disembodied as the speculative poetics. Characterized by the feminine traits of prettiness and passivity, she is frequently seen only as a smile, a blush, or a glance of a hesitant eye, and she is easily dismissible because of her mortal state. Not autonomous, as she will eventually become, she is childlike in and obscured by her dependence on the natural surroundings, her beauty contingent on the correlation between nature and herself:

> Were I in such a place, I sure should pray
> That nought less sweet might call my thoughts away,
> Than the soft rustle of a maiden's gown
> Fanning away the dandelion's down;
> Than the light music of her nimble toes
> Patting against the sorrel as she goes.
> How she would start, and blush, thus to be caught
> Playing in all her innocence of thought.
> O let me lead her gently o'er the brook,
> Watch her half-smiling lips, and downward look;
> O let me for one moment touch her wrist;
> Let me one moment to her breathing list;
> And as she leaves me may she often turn
> Her fair eyes looking through her locks aubùrne.
> What next? A tuft of evening primroses,
> O'er which the mind may hover till it dozes.
>
> ("I stood tip-toe" 93–108)

This passage views the mortal female as part of the "leafy luxury" that surrounds the poet, and from which he remains distant, no more (or less) important than the "tuft of evening primroses" that follows as the next scene in the imaginative panorama to which he turns. The early female, disempowered by the same state of mortality that infects the poet who seeks escape, plays, like nature itself, the role of object to his voyeurism. It is here, in the first volume of poems, that Keats's "tendency to class women in [his] books with roses and sweetmeats," a statement he made in a letter to Charles Brown (*Letters* 2:327), is most obvious. Keats went on to say, though, that women "never see themselves dominant" in his poetry, a statement that Brown himself took issue with, and one that certainly cannot

be considered valid by any scholar today.[2] The only poems of
Keats's career that are not dominated by women, in fact, are
those under present consideration. The fear that Keats unwit-
tingly acknowledges in such a disclaimer, fear of the imagina-
tion and the woman who both symbolizes and animates it, keeps
her confined within nature and mortality so Keats may escape
her becoming the "Fatal Woman," who, Praz writes, is more
common to poets "during times in which the springs of inspira-
tion [are] troubled" (189–90). Because Keats's poetic career
and the direction it will take are unknown to him at this point,
his is indeed a "troubled" imagination. His attempt to allay
concerns is one that cannot give women full poetic process
at this point, despite their representative connection with the
imagination.

Thus, whenever women appear in these early poems, they
are indeed classed "with roses and sweetmeats," or, as in "I
stood tip-toe," with "dandelion's down" and "evening prim-
roses." While the poet stands away from the scene, attempting
to peer into the poetic future, the unnamed maiden appears in
as dreamy a state as the scene itself, "playing in all her innocence
of thought." Unlike Madeline in "The Eve of St. Agnes," this
maiden's innocence is never disturbed by either a rush of con-
tradictions between reality and appearance or by Porphyro.
Furthermore, this maiden looks "downward," unlike Madeline,
who, as the first feminine personification of the problems inher-
ent in the attempt to flee reality, will look to "heaven with
upward eyes for all that [she] desire[s]" ("St. Agnes" 54).[3] The
"leafy luxury" of the earth is all that is visible to the mortal
female who loses herself to it because it is all that is desirable
to Keats at this point, making the female herself both subordi-
nate and coincidental to her surroundings. The luxuries of
nature in these early poems, reiterated to the point of near
redundancy, threaten to swallow up both the poet and the
female. While the poet stands tip-toe, he cannot find the means
of flight, and the female is mired with no means of elevation.

It is Keats's desire to imitate his predecessors in these poems
that allows nature to obfuscate. In "Imitation of Spenser," na-
ture is "so fair a place [that] was never seen" (23). Escape lies

in a beauty that is tenuous because it circumvents, through illusions, the process by which it may be sustained—a process that must include the reality, as well as the beauty, of the earth. And the goddess Psyche appears in "I stood tip-toe," but, unlike that of the great ode to come, she is not the raison d'être, for Keats does not yet exploit the female as an exclusive channel to the imagination. Psyche, like the mortal maidens, appears in this poem only coincidentally. Keats's real interest lies in Apuleius, the creator of her tale—a poet who, to Keats, illustrates the function and meaning of poetry as well as the importance of the role of predecessor to his own identity:

> And when a tale is beautifully staid,
> We feel the safety of a hawthorn glade:
> When it is moving on luxurious wings,
> The soul is lost in pleasant smotherings:
> Fair dewy roses brush against our faces,
> And flowering laurels spring from diamond vases;
> O'er head we see the jasmine and sweet briar,
> And bloomy grapes laughing from green attire;
> While at our feet, the voice of crystal bubbles
> Charms us at once away from all our troubles:
> So that we feel uplifted from the world,
> Walking upon the white clouds wreath'd and curl'd.
> So felt he, who first told, how Psyche went
> On the smooth wind to realms of wonderment.
>   (129–42)

Keats finds "safety" in an already-told tale, and in his close association with the male creator. The "pleasant smotherings" in which he loses his soul are similar to the pleasant confines of nature. Psyche, the goddess with whom the poet will eventually have a significant relationship, is here simply a vehicle for the poet whom Keats wishes to emulate. The relationship Keats seeks at this early stage in his poetics is more one with his male predecessor than with the female figure who will eventually define them. Risk at this point lies in the failure to imitate others rather than the failure at creating anew.

The moon is a cherished symbol in virtually every major poet's lexicon, and thus appears in "I stood tip-toe" as well:

> O Maker of sweet poets, dear delight
> Of this fair world, and all its gentle livers;
> Spangler of clouds, halo of crystal rivers,
> Mingler with leaves, and dew and tumbling streams,
> Closer of lovely eyes to lovely dreams,
> Lover of loneliness, and wandering,
> Of upcast eye, and tender pondering!
> Thee must I praise above all other glories
> That smile us on to tell delightful stories.
> For what has made the sage or poet write
> But the fair paradise of Nature's light?
>
>   (116–26)

Light is consistently inspirational to poets, and Keats is no exception. As "maker of sweet poets," however, the moon can be seen here as Keats's first attempt, albeit a minor one, at creating a matriarchal figure, which in being procreative as well as creative, illuminates the dominant roles of the later females.[4]

Unlike the mortal maiden, who is permitted to be only a part of nature, the moon as deity is seen presiding over both nature and poets. She has limitations, however, for unlike the sun, who will appear as Apollo in "Hyperion" to hold sway over heaven, the moon's domain in these early poems is only that of the earth. Heaven is never mentioned in these lines, in fact; the earthbound Keats cannot yet soar with Apollo because he has not reached full creative, that is, masculine, power. The supreme figure in the poetry of the earth, therefore, is the moon, traditionally the lesser of the two heavenly deities because it is associated with the female.

Apollo, who will briefly become Keats's poetic alter ego and through whom Keats will unsuccessfully attempt to find an identity, remains in the background of "I stood tip-toe," playing a secondary role to the earth and moon:

> Ye ardent marigolds!
> Dry up the moisture from your golden lids,

> For great Apollo bids
> That in these days your praises should be sung
> On many harps, which he has lately strung;
> And when again your dewiness he kisses,
> Tell him, I have you in my world of blisses:
> So haply when I rove in some far vale,
> His mighty voice may come upon the gale.
>   (48–56)

Apollo's voice here, like the nightingale's in the ode to come, is one that the poet hopes to find "in some far vale." It is a voice that will assure Keats's identity as a poet and his place in the male lineage. The contradictions that the nightingale will pose, as female symbol of the errant imagination, are absent here, for the poet remains content in the "leafy luxury" he has created, and Apollo is merely a visitor who does not yet represent the dichotomy between earth and heaven that will characterize the later poems. But here, with Apollo's visit (or at least his voice), a temporary fusion of the two realms exists, a fusion that Keats will seek in vain throughout the rest of his career.

In this period of serenity before the dilemmas posed by the greatest of Keats's poetry, the moon "exceed[s] all things in [her] shine" (207) because it is a poetry that does not imbue the female with a power that lies beyond the earth. Even the goddesses of the early poems are as mute as the nature that silences them. They are objects rather than subjects, and their sensuality is borrowed from the earth rather than inherent in them. The female's power as symbol (and as subject) will increase with the later emergence of her own sensuality. But for now the moon, because it is the feminine representative of the nature Keats celebrates, is superior to all else. And the female, who does not yet possess the sexual destructiveness that will eventually define one side of her, can exist on the mortal level as unnamed maidens and immortally as Psyche and Cynthia, two supremely benevolent deities to Keats.[5]

The connection between poetry and sexual love produces the state of highest imaginative activity in the early poems before "La Belle Dame sans Merci" and "Lamia" reveal the deadly extremes of this combination, yet, as Dickstein observes, "erotic activity in [Keats's] early poems often shades off into harmless and innocent play, such as biting the white shoulders of nymphs" (38). There is little sense of physical eroticism in the early poems because the female is not yet a completely sexual being. True eroticism frequently involves a sense of physical and emotional risk, and there is nothing frightening about the early virginal females. Their dominion, and that of the poet, is of the earth, and the primary sensation is one of comfort, produced in large part by the limitations the poet exercises upon his imagination at this time.

In "Calidore," nature and the earth are again the setting. It is Keats's first fragmentary poem, a romantic theme in itself (Levinson, *Fragment* 6), and it ends where "Sleep and Poetry" will begin, with the "happy mortals" (158) entreating sleep. A young knight, Calidore "turns for calmness to the pleasant green / Of easy slopes, and shadowy trees that lean / So elegantly o'er the waters' brim" (9–11). But the beauty of nature in this poem quickly gives way to the superior beauty of woman as Calidore experiences the joys of courtly romance:[6]

> What a kiss,
> What gentle squeeze he gave each lady's hand!
> How tremblingly their delicate ancles spann'd!
> Into how sweet a trance his soul was gone,
> While whisperings of affection
> Made him delay to let their tender feet
> Come to the earth; with an incline so sweet
> From their low palfreys o'er his neck they bent:
> And whether there were tears of languishment,
> Or that the evening dew had pearl'd their tresses,
> He feels a moisture on his cheek, and blesses
> With lips that tremble, and with glistening eye,
> All the soft luxury
> That nestled in his arms.
>
>   (80–93)

The "leafy luxury" of the earth, the focus of the majority of the volume's poems, is converted here into the "soft luxury" of a woman whom Calidore "nestled in his arms," a major step toward the poet's apotheosis of the female herself rather than of her earthly surroundings. The soul is again "lost" here, as in the "pleasant smotherings" of "I stood tip-toe," but in this poem the soul is gone into a sweet "trance" of erotic desire. The sexuality, though, like the female herself, is tentative.

This poem introduces a favorite word of Keats that he will use throughout his career to denote the idea of simultaneous attraction and repulsion, especially with regard to the female: "thrall" (103). This word takes on further significance when Keats's later and more renowned knightly figure, the woebegone knight-at-arms, meets la belle dame sans merci, denounces the earth, and loses both the "leafy" and the "soft" luxury that Calidore experiences here.[7]

In this poem, however, the attraction, and thus the thrall, is benign because no denunciation of the earth occurs, and Calidore is free to simply draw his "warm arms, thrilling now with pulses new, / From their sweet thrall" (102–3), an appropriate analogy to Keats and his current imagination as well.

One of the obvious reasons for the significant difference in both meaning and outcome of the thrall here and later is that all of the characters in "Calidore" are mortal. Keats has not yet attempted to "burst [his] mortal bars" ("I stood tip-toe" 190), as he proposed doing, so these early poems do not yet pair a mortal with an immortal, as virtually all of his later poems will. The thrall experienced by both the knight-at-arms and Lycius, for example, will be disastrous because the coy muse of these early poems will have become the "maiden most unmeek, / . . . my demon Poesy" ("Ode on Indolence" 29–30). The female figure that represents the imagination will have forsaken both the earth and her borrowed sensuality, evincing a sexuality that entraps the male through his own desire for her. The desire causes his own impotence as well because, ironically, it will originate with the search for masculine identity.

In the present poem, however, all visions are those of the earth, and the earth is not the cold and diseased setting it will become in "Isabella," nor the mythical dying place of "Hyperion." Calidore's earth, like the poetics that inspire it, is luxuriously naive and superficially lush, with "green tufted islands casting their soft shades / Across the lake; sequester'd leafy glades" (46–47), and "long grass which hems / A little brook" (51–52). The setting suggests enclosure and distance and safety. In this lushness, Calidore is "burning / To hear of knightly deeds, and gallant spurning / Of all unworthiness" (142–44). It is a comfortably androcentric scenario, and while Calidore petitions the aid of heaven, unlike the later heroes, he never tries to reach it. The sublunary world that offers both "leafy" and "soft" luxuries is enough for the knight who has not been initiated into the complexities of the poetry to come.

Because they are mortal, the women of "Calidore" accommodate the natural setting rather than destroy it as la belle dame will do or transcend it as the females of the odes will: "The sweet-lipp'd ladies have already greeted / All the green leaves that round the window clamber, / To show their purple stars, and bells of amber" (135–37). The "green leaves" that "clamber" around the window show more activity than the ladies, and the "purple stars" and "bells of amber" seem the benign precursors to the "wreath'd trellis" with "buds, and bells, and stars without a name" of "Ode to Psyche" (60–61), and, a problem Keats would not have for long, the vegetation in this poem is far more interesting than the "sweet-lipp'd ladies." Their sweet lips foreshadow the sensuality and seductiveness that will inform Keats's greatest female figures and evoke the famous kisses of "slippery blisses" that Endymion will share with Cynthia. But here the sweet lips do little more for the women themselves than reinforce their virginal status because they "greet" the leaves that encircle the window rather than the male speaker, who wished to "greet the maid" (of poetry) in the epistle to Mathew. Both greetings involve a rudimentary attempt at fusing mortal with immortal in order to create— Keats with poetry and the female with the surrounding nature.

But fusion is more a benign entrapment in the early poetry. By virtue of their status as "other" to the male, both the female and her surrounding natural environment are enigmatic symbols of imprisonment, regardless of how "pretty" each may be. Both are cultivated and controlled to become symbols of adornment rather than symbols of power that each will eventu-

ally be, and the fusion of mortal with immortal that will domi-
nate the later poetry is premature here. The fusion will be
enacted through sex between the female figure and the male
in the poems to come, and neither is yet capable of sex because
neither has full identity in the poems of the earth.

Cultivation of the female continues in the epistle "To George
Felton Mathew." She remains a "fine-eyed maid" (35), but na-
ture is "some flowery spot, sequester'd, wild, romantic, / That
often must have seen a poet frantic" (37–38). The "leafy lux-
ury" is being overgrown, and for the first time, a forbidding
darkness accompanies the poetic process, a glimpse into the
contradictions to come: "There must be too a ruin dark, and
gloomy, / To say 'joy not too much in all that's bloomy' " (51–
52). While the female remains one-dimensional, nature begins
to take on a complexity that will grow more problematic in
future poems. The close association between nature and the
female in these poems is a sure indication that the female will
not for long remain innocuous, however. As her identity is
contingent on her environment, it is perhaps too frightening a
specter to Keats right now, who immediately dismisses the dark
lines as premature. "Yet this is vain," he tells Mathew (53), and
the foreboding lines are replaced with convivial images of the
poet and his muse who will "sit, and rhyme and think on
Chatterton" (56).

Despite the quick transition, this is the first indication by
Keats that the beauty of the earth may not be sufficient for him
to experience the highest splendors of the imagination. This
small crack in the poetic foundation will become almost irrepa-
rable later as the great odes, "Lamia," and "The Fall of Hyper-
ion" will destroy in order to recreate the idea of beauty as a
symbol of both disillusionment and empowerment.

In this epistle, for the second time in the volume, Keats uses
the word *thrall*:

> Too partial friend! fain would I follow thee
> Past each horizon of fine poesy;
> Fain would I echo back each pleasant note
> As o'er Sicilian seas, clear anthems float

'Mong the light skimming gondolas far parted,
Just when the sun his farewell beam has darted:
But 'tis impossible; far different cares
Beckon me sternly from soft 'Lydian airs,'
And hold my faculties so long in thrall,
That I am oft in doubt whether at all
I shall again see Phoebus in the morning:
Or flush'd Aurora in the roseate dawning!
                                                (11–22)

The thrall here, different from the gentle thrall of "Calidore,"
beckons the poet "sternly" and captures his "faculties" in much
the same way that the knight-at-arms will be held captive by the
"lady in the meads" ("La Belle Dame" 13), the most frightening
female to emerge from the relative obscurity of the "sweet-
lipp'd ladies" of this volume. The "Lydian airs," evoking pleas-
ing scenes of "Sicilian seas" and "light skimming gondolas,"
belong to the beauty of the natural world, the "leafy luxury"
that exists outside the "dark city" in which the poet now dwells.
Furthermore, they belong outside the realm of "a ruin dark,
and gloomy" that this poem acknowledges, if only fleetingly, as
necessary to the imagination. The gentle muse is beginning to
change into a strict taskmistress, and with this change, the poet
is "sternly" beckoned away from scenes of "leafy luxury," that
is, from "all that's bloomy."[8]
    Coinciding with the burgeoning hints here of the contradic-
tions to come are more frequent allusions to the god Apollo
who will eventually pose unreconcilable dilemmas to the poet,
as shown in the epistle "To My Brother George":

Full many a dreary hour have I past,
My brain bewilder'd, and my mind o'ercast
With heaviness; in seasons when I've thought
No spherey strains by me could e'er be caught
From the blue dome, though I to dimness gaze
On the far depth where sheeted lightning plays;
Or, on the wavy grass outstretch'd supinely
Pry 'mong the stars, to strive to think divinely:
That I should never hear Apollo's song,

> Though feathery clouds were floating all along
> The purple west, and, two bright streaks between,
> The golden lyre itself were dimly seen.
>   (1–12, my italics)

The relative serenity of "I stood tip-toe" is missing from these lines. As if in confidence to his brother, Keats expresses doubts over his ability to create. The previous poems' scenes of sublunary beauty, so crucial to the poetic imagination before, are now superseded by the introduction of heaven, as the poet will "pry 'mong the stars, to strive to think divinely," that is, to attempt imaginative powers that lie beyond the temporal beauty of the earth.

The fear of loss of creativity is assuaged again, in part, by the thought of "bard[s] of old" ("I stood tip-toe" 163), for this poem avers that "the Poet's eye can reach those golden halls" (35), the same reached by the poet's predecessors. The goal is the tradition of male creativity, seen like the Holy Grail here as the "golden lyre" of Apollo in the sky. Keats's poetic identity, which will emerge with his own initiation into the all-male lineage of worshippers of Apollo, is thus perceived not only as that of a poet, but of a fully evolved man, one who, like the seekers of the Holy Grail, has met and overcome all challenges to his own masculinity.

Marjorie Levinson notes that Keats "is not just a poet to us, he is a poetic career. . . . one watches him station himself where a great precursor had rested, discover the limitations of that position, step up to the next rung, and finally kick away the ladder altogether" (*Fragment* 174). It is the masculine tradition of besting one's opponent that will both haunt and inspire Keats's career, and, although the origins of his own final victory in the contest are obvious in these early poems, Keats's doubts over his place in the "golden halls" are not fully abated, as the following lines from the epistle to his brother testify:

> Ah, my dear friend and brother,
> Could I, at once, my mad ambition smother,
> For tasting joys like these, sure I should be

Happier, and dearer to society.
At times, 'tis true, I've felt relief from pain
When some bright thought has darted through my brain:
Through all that day I've felt a greater pleasure
Than if I'd brought to light a hidden treasure.

(109–16)

These lines are the beginning of the theme that will haunt
Keats throughout his career, the dilemma that will culminate
in Moneta's harsh words to the dreamer in "The Fall of Hy-
perion":

> Thou art a dreaming thing;
> A fever of thyself—think of the earth;
> What bliss even in hope is there for thee?
> What haven? Every creature has its home;
> Every sole man hath days of joy and pain,
> Whether his labours be sublime or low—
> The pain alone; the joy alone; distinct:
> *Only the dreamer venoms all his days,*
> *Bearing more woe than all his sins deserve.*
> (1.168–76, my italics)

The poet will be "happier, and dearer to society" only when
poetry becomes the healing agent that Keats (and Moneta)
wishes it to be. In the epistle to his brother, however, Keats
recognizes how far he is from this; the healing powers promised
in the previous poems are accused of being a sham, nothing
more than "mad ambition" offering only fleeting relief brought
on by "some bright thought" that has "darted" through the
poet's brain. Like his self-identification as a poet, the powers
are premature.

In "I stood tip-toe," the soul had been "lost in pleasant smoth-
erings" (132) when "moving on luxurious wings" (131); all
distractions were "smothered" by poetry, a word that indicates
the poet's continuing frantic attempts at poetic identity. In the
present poem, however, poetry itself has become the supreme
distraction. The serenity found in the earthbound pleasures of
the previous poems is diminishing. And the female of this poem

is a "lovely lass" (86) who, like Bertha of "The Eve of St. Mark"
to come, reads "a tale of hopes, and fears" (97). She is identified
by "innocent dimples" (101), however, making her, unlike Ber-
tha who will be characterized as a "poor cheated soul" ("St.
Mark" 69), simply another aspect of the ultimate embodiment
of naïveté, a mute prisoner of the leafy luxury of the earth, too
inexperienced to take on the burdens of the imagination.

Following this poem to his brother, though, Keats's allusions
to maidens become infrequent, giving way to an increasing
domination by goddesses rather than mortal females, a direc-
tion made evident by his growing infusion of mythological
figures into his poetry—a sure way to compete with his male
predecessors who first invoked the panoply of female deities.
Keats can no longer describe the imagination as a coy and
gentle muse, who is both obscured by and an extension of
nature, but he is not yet able to admit that his "demon poesy"
is slowly emerging.

The poem's ending is directed toward the west:

> Now I direct my eyes into the west,
> Which at this moment is in sunbeams drest:
> Why westward turn? 'Twas but to say adieu!
> 'Twas but to kiss my hand, dear George, to you!
> (139–42)

As Walter Evert points out, the west is where Keats will find
Apollo, the symbol of the masculine creativity he seeks. And
Evert contends that the act of turning westward into the sunset
ends the epistle with a rhetorical question "which one feels
certain was intended to introduce an exposition of the Apolli-
nian [*sic*] ideal" (53n). This intention is disappointingly aban-
doned, he asserts, with the last two lines. But while Keats is
certainly beginning to look in the direction of Apollo, he is not
yet ready to abandon the earth. Both Keats and his poetry, in
this volume of 1817, remain at a crucially tentative stage.

The epistle "To Charles Cowden Clarke" goes farther to-
ward establishing a direction for Keats's poetry, one that will
be characterized by an obsession with the ideal of permanence,

an ideal that cannot be found in the ephemeral and naive beauty of the earth. Comparing himself with a swan that strives "to take / Some diamond water drops" (8–9) from the "surface of the lake" (7), Keats tells Cowden Clarke:

> Just like that bird am I in loss of time,
> Whene'er I venture on the stream of rhyme;
> With shatter'd boat, oar snapt, and canvass rent,
> I slowly sail, *scarce knowing my intent.*
>   (15–18, my italics)

These lines give a first glimpse into the poetic ability "of being in uncertainties, Mysteries, doubts, without any irritable reaching after fact and reason," which Keats calls Negative Capability (*Letters* 1:193). As focus begins to shift from the earth to those pleasures that exist beyond temporal boundaries into a "loss of time" altogether through the use of myth, the focus will become diffused, ever more intangible to the creator. The heretofore serenity of the imagination that received its strength from the earth will surrender to the complexities of the "demon poesy" who dismisses the pleasures of the earth, and the poet will indeed "scarce [know his] intent." At the same time, the masculine ideal that is so apparent here, especially in Keats's epistles to the various men, will become more fluid and even androgynous with the new complexities.

To Keats, the attempt to dwell in the realm of timelessness is an attempt to find permanence for his art. In a very brief span of time chronologically, the attempt to escape time will become overwhelming, as will the imagination itself, forcing the abandonment of the benign maidens of these poems and replacing them with empowered female figures who are not content to be "a friend / . . . of man" ("Sleep and Poetry" 246–47).

The final poem of the volume of 1817, "Sleep and Poetry," contains the first instance of the internalization of the poetry of the earth in order to apotheosize it. Charles Rzepka observes that the poet "of 'no-self' " to which Keats now aspires, "approaches his subjects stealthily or imagines them or stumbles

on them, surprised at his find" (170). Thus the external scenes
will become the poet's own "visions":

> a bowery nook
> Will be elysium—an eternal book
> Whence I may copy many a lovely saying
> About the leaves, and flowers—about the playing
> Of nymphs in woods, and fountains.
>
> (63–67)

Sleep, the state that induces these visions and allows them to
become a part of the poetic self, now joins poetry as a healing
agent, but to a lesser degree:

> What is more gentle than a wind in summer?
> What is more soothing than the pretty hummer
> That stays one moment in an open flower,
> And buzzes cheerily from bower to bower?
> What is more tranquil than a musk-rose blowing
> In a green island, far from all men's knowing?
> More healthful than the leafiness of dales?
> More secret than a nest of nightingales?
> More serene than Cordelia's countenance?
> More full of visions than a high romance?
> What, but thee, Sleep? Soft closer of our eyes!
>
> (1–11)

As a state beyond waking consciousness, "more full of visions
than a high romance," sleep may be compared here with the
imaginative experience of "I stood tip-toe"—the poet is stand-
ing tip-toe, but has not left the earth; his feet still touch the
ground. The poet cannot leave the earth until the state that is
"higher beyond thought than" (19) sleep is reached:

> What is it? And to what shall I compare it?
> It has a glory, and nought else can share it:
> The thought thereof is awful, sweet, and holy,
> Chacing away all worldliness and folly.
>
> (23–26)

Poetry is alive with the visions produced by the deathlike state of sleep. Through the transforming power of imagination, poetry idealizes sleep because it internalizes the visions. Thus, while sleep is the catalyst, poetry is the chemical reaction produced, so to speak.

Mario D'Avanzo remarks that this poem "might well have been entitled 'Sleep as Poetry' . . . [because] the slumbering mind has the ability to create spontaneously and effortlessly, sleep is poetry" (61). Keats makes a rather significant distinction between the two, however, as noted above, and while one may successfully compare sleep with the beauty of the earth, as Keats does, "nought else can share" the glory of poetry, which is greater than sleep because it does not exist merely as a state of unconsciousness.

Another important distinction between sleep and poetry is that of gender. Poetry is always female to Keats, but sleep is male here, "quiet with his poppy coronet" (348). Sleep's masculine gender may be associated with the poet himself. While, like sleep, he is the catalyst or creator, the visions of the poetry, being female, are becoming increasingly independent of him. The conjunctive "and" in the title also reiterates the sexual union of sleep (male) and poetry (female) that serves as a metaphor for the creative process to Keats, which manifests elsewhere in this volume, but especially in "I stood tip-toe." The procreation that results from the union of sleep and poetry is too significant to allow their being identified as the same thing.

The luxury of "Sleep and Poetry" is not the "leafy luxury" of the earth. To support the sexual and procreative metaphor, it is the luxury of "dying into life," the theme of "Hyperion" to come:

> O Poesy! for thee I grasp my pen
> That am not yet a glorious denizen
> Of thy wide heaven; yet, to my ardent prayer,
> Yield from thy sanctuary some clear air,
> Smoothed for intoxication by the breath
> Of flowering bays, that I may die a death

Of luxury, and my young spirit follow
The morning sun-beams to the great Apollo
Like a fresh sacrifice.

(53–61)[9]

Reaching immortality by "dying into life" will be a frequent theme to Keats, but here, at the first mention of it, he seems unable to separate the poet as deity from his human environment. The poet wishes to be "like a fresh sacrifice" to the immortal Apollo, to internalize fully the god's direction, yet later, in the same paragraph, he asks only to be able to "write on [his] tablets all that was *permitted*, / All that was for *our human senses fitted*" (79–80, my italics). The "young spirit" that would "follow" Apollo seems inextricably bound to mortality and temporal limitations, still standing tip-toe.

Immediately following these lines, however, as though Keats himself had recognized an inconsistency, the spirit regains control and the strongest indication yet of the direction his poetry will take emerges to conclude the paragraph:

Then the events of this wide world I'd seize
Like a strong giant, and my spirit teaze
Till at its shoulders it should proudly see
Wings to find out an immortality.

(81–84)

As the poet "dies into life" his spirit finally gains wings, and we assume the flight will take him to Apollo's "morning sun-beams" (60). But something happens along the way, for the next lines find the poet once again clearly cognizant of time and mortality:

Stop and Consider! life is but a day;
A fragile dew-drop on its perilous way
From a tree's summit; a poor Indian's sleep
While his boat hastens to the monstrous steep
Of Montmorenci. Why so sad a moan?
Life is the rose's hope while yet unblown;
The reading of an ever-changing tale;
The light uplifting of a maiden's veil;

A pigeon tumbling in clear summer air;
A laughing school-boy, without grief or care,
Riding the springy branches of an elm.
                                        (85–95)

The juxtaposition of these lines cataloging and celebrating images of the earth with the lines that immediately precede asking for "visions," shows that the poet, even with "wings to find out an immortality," is hesitant to give up the earth. The "death of luxury," happily sought in order to effect the spirit's fusion with Apollo, is again temporarily abandoned here in favor of life, the "rose's hope" as well as the poet's. The denunciation of the earth is a crucial step made even more frightening by Keats's knowledge that he must forsake his predecessors' ideals to discover his own.

Thus, ironically, the same poet who told Charles Cowden Clarke that he becomes lost in time when writing poetry now sets up radical temporal dimensions to the life span of his imagination: "O for ten years, that I may overwhelm / Myself in poesy; so I may do the deed / That my own soul has to itself decreed" (96–98). In ten years' time the poet hopes to "overwhelm" himself in poetry, an act of personal deification that will lead him away from the temporal realm and into that of "Flora and old Pan" (102). Time and the earth here, as well as the mortal maidens absorbed therein, serve, like the little hill upon which the poet stood tip-toe, as a catapult to the imagination that wants to soar.

The theme of escape will become an obsession later, as epitomized in these lines to Charles Dilke three months before Tom Keats's death:

> [Tom's] identity presses upon me so all day that I am
> obliged to go out—and although I intended to have
> given some time to study alone I am obliged to write,
> and plunge into abstract images to ease myself of his
> countenance his voice and feebleness—so that I live
> now in a continual fever—it must be poisonous to life
> although I feel well. (*Letters* 1:369)

As his obsession with escape grows, Keats will repeatedly denote both sexuality and poetry as "feverous" as well, and they, too, will be considered "poisonous to life" at times. The need to free himself of the identities of others, as well as of the destructive sexuality that will delineate his later females, leads to Keats's idea of the "camelion poet," who "has as much delight in conceiving an Iago as an Imogen" (*Letters* 1:387). The poetic identity that Keats seeks here is one that ultimately dismisses the masculine tradition for a process that originates in a new and genderless ideal; the poet "has no identity—he is continually . . . filling some other Body—The Sun, the Moon, the Sea and Men and Women who are creatures of impulse are poetical and have about them an unchangeable attribute—the poet has none" (*Letters* 1:387).

The "camelion poet" is itself a form of escape, from both the masculine and the traditional. Its identity, like that of Keats's own imagination as female, is protean by nature and cannot be held accountable, as Keats asserts in a letter to Benjamin Bailey of July 18, 1818:

> I know my own disposition so well that I am certain of writing many times hereafter in the same strain to you—now you know how far to believe in them—*you must allow for imagination—I know I shall not be able to help it.* (*Letters* 1:340–41, my italics)

Rzepka writes that the "camelion poet" that Keats aspires to "feels his body to be a thing apart from but enclosing him," and Keats will begin "to project his own sense of bodily disengagement onto others. . . . Others are derealized" (168). Others "must allow" for his imagination, which will supplant the "pressing identities" that he attempts to escape through it.

Thus the "camelion poet," like Apollo's Delphic priestesses whom Keats will frequently include in his poems, is allowed to give responses that puzzle rather than clarify. And the identity that emerges with these first poems is a fledgling one with a clearly delineated option to follow—that of either escape from or confrontation of the pain, "the agonies, the strife / Of human hearts" ("Sleep and Poetry" 124–25). In works to come, the option will not seem so dichotomous, and it is then that Keats will discover his own identity as poet to mean having "as much delight in conceiving" a Moneta as a Madeline, for the compassion he will seek through the "human heart" will be achieved, by necessity, with the female, whose very nature is perceived as theoretically identical to the poet's own Negative Capability.

For now, however, the dilemma is polarized into an either/or proposition, and the poems of this early volume are set up in a way that clarifies the polarity by dramatizing it. Like the odes to come, these first poems show the poetic mind in conflict, one which vacillates between forthright, facile statements that exemplify but do not resolve the dilemma, and the "ruin dark, and gloomy" imagination that proclaims " 'joy not too much in all that's bloomy' " ("To George Felton Mathew" 51–52).

Finally a "sense of real things comes doubly strong" ("Sleep and Poetry" 157), and the visions are "fled" (155). The "real things," like the pressing identities of others, "would bear along / [the poet's] soul to nothingness" (158–59). All identity would thus be dissipated, the primary step to Keats's realizing his role as "camelion poet." The identity, rich in the androcentric tradition of Dante, Spenser, and Milton, that he will continue to enforce upon the imagination is an identity that apparently does not "press" negatively but is nonetheless questioned in this final poem of the volume of 1817. He ends the volume with lines that signal a belief in his own burgeoning creativity:

> And up I rose refresh'd, and glad, and gay,
> Resolving to begin that very day
> These lines; and howsoever they be done,
> I leave them as a father does his son.
>
> (401–4)

Positioned at the end of the volume as well as the end of the poem, these lines show an offering of poetry, "howsoever [it] be done," for the audience's approval, emitting the perfect response to the rhetorical question posed at the end of the first major poem of the collection, "Was there a Poet born?" ("I stood tip-toe" 241). The sexual metaphor is clear, and the inheritance the son receives from the father is, in this case, the lineage Keats still accepts and desires from his male predecessors in order to become their successor.

Thus the poems published in 1817 represent the solid foundation of works to follow, solid because they rest upon the earth and, for the most part, are restricted to it. The pursuit of the earth, unlike that of heaven that Keats will eventually attempt, produces poetry based on the tangible, on "things real," as Keats calls them—the "Sun Moon & Stars and passages of Shakspeare [*sic*]" (*Letters* 1:243). Here, like Wordsworth, Keats creates scenes of natural beauty that, when imbued with his own empathic imagination, become something much more than natural. The natural world depicted in this volume offers only glimpses into the contradictions and complexity that will emerge with the increasing power of the female in successive poems. Beauty will become secondary to and contingent upon knowledge, as the female will acquire power not from being an extension of nature, a "borrowed" power as here, but from her ability to transcend nature altogether.

Keats's control over the imagination in these early poems is nowhere better exemplified than in the way he depicts his female figure. She is docile and ineffectual and, like the imagination that concentrates only on the earth, deficient to Keats's search for immortality. He simply runs out of ways to portray sweet-lipped ladies and coy muses. The females that originate with the poet's identity of this early volume lack what Keats calls "intensity," the capability "of making all disagreeables evaporate, from their being in close relationship with Beauty & Truth" (*Letters* 1:192). They lack, in fact, another "close relationship," one with the poet himself, as evidenced by Keats's own facile control and dismissal of them. The docile maidens of these first poems are the product of a mind that has not yet undergone, in earnest, the tragic experience of a "ruin dark, and gloomy." As the experience that Keats attempts to escape in these poems becomes instead the focus of later poems, making the disagreeables more readily apparent, the female will become, by necessity, more powerful. As symbol and product of the imaginative mind, the female cannot remain, as the poet himself wishes to be, merely an observer. While she will continue for awhile, like nature here, to be objectified by her delineation as end rather than means, by Keats's continuing androcentric acknowledgment of his desire for her but not his need, she can never be "derealized" (Rzepka 168), as Keats does both his own and others' identities. She will no longer be the goddess who slept in Keats's "boyish imagination" (*Letters* 1:341), but Keats is no longer a boy, and the imagination, by degrees, will shed its puerile fantasies.

The relationship between poet and imagination will begin in earnest with the next major poem, *Endymion*, in which both the imagination and the female will undergo changes that do not yet "evaporate" the "disagreeables," but at least go a long way toward identifying them.

2

Endymion
"He awoke and found it truth"

To follow the work of sleep and the visions of dreams that create poetry, Keats's next poem is taken from the myths of Endymion, a shepherd who, in the original stories about him, sleeps forever, oblivious to the passion bestowed upon him by the goddess of the moon. However, Keats makes rather significant changes in the myth in order to convey the sensuality with which he imbues the goddess Cynthia. Endymion is allowed consciousness throughout most of the poem, asleep long enough only to have a dream of the goddess that he will impart to his sister Peona; both Peona and another female figure important to Keats's version, the Indian maiden, are introduced into the myth. The brother and sister theme may have originated from the fact that Cynthia is the sister of Apollo. But Peona is much more than a sister to Endymion—she serves as guide, friend, and when the occasion demands, gentle admonisher to Endymion, a benign precursor to the powerful Moneta.

When Endymion relates to Peona the dream he has had of Cynthia that perplexes him, Peona responds:

> how light
> Must dreams themselves be; seeing they're more slight
> Than the mere nothing that engenders them!
> Then wherefore sully the entrusted gem
> Of high and noble life with thoughts so sick?
> Why pierce high-fronted honour to the quick
> For nothing but a dream?
>
> (1.754–60)[1]

The speaker of these words is close in poetic stature to the unnamed maidens of the early poems, as she is called Endymion's "sweet sister."[2] And Endymion's dream is, like the visions that derive from sleep in the earlier "Sleep and Poetry," a vehicle of escape from and transcendence of the earth. Dreaming has not yet become the source of emasculation it will be in the later poems, but the advice from his sister to the shepherd who would be a god is tellingly similar to the advice from the later Moneta to the dreamer who would be a poet. Not yet Moneta, Peona nonetheless has a wisdom that removes her from the maidens of the volume of 1817, as they were so closely associated with the earth that they became mere objectification of it, with neither advice to give nor voice to speak it. Peona is the first of Keats's early female figures to break away from the dependence and sanctuary of the earth, but not yet autonomous, she remains an extension of her brother—a type of "guardian angel" who peers over his shoulder, offering direction. Although the earth itself in this poem, a lush setting of mythical growth and ripeness, does not smother and entomb Peona as it did the previous maidens, it remains, aside from her brother, Peona's only connection. Unlike the entrapment within nature that the earlier maidens suffered, Peona and the earth seem interdependent.

Dickstein notes that, in fact, Peona leads Endymion "to the bower of the 1817 *Poems,* a world of soothing nature and refreshing sleep, which provide antidotes for excessive reflection and under whose influence he is 'calm'd to life again' "(76). Peona is thus a visitor to the natural world, like the poet himself, rather than a prisoner of it. She is a vehicle to more than beauty, as her predecessors were not; she is the channel to Endymion's own knowledge and immortality.

True feminine wisdom, Keats's poetry contends, can come only from a female whose power is complete within itself, autonomous from nature as well as from the male. As overtly an extension of her brother, Peona is not yet that power, but she is ultimately an interesting sleight of hand by Keats. It is obvious from her introduction that she is not simply a "sweet sister" like the earlier "sweet-lipp'd ladies" who remained beautiful and mute:

Who whispers him so pantingly and close?
Peona, his sweet sister: of all those,
His friends, the dearest. Hushing signs she made,
And breath'd a sister's sorrow to persuade
A yielding up, a cradling on her care.
Her eloquence did breathe away the curse:
She led him, like some midnight spirit nurse
Of happy changes in emphatic dreams,
Along a path between two little streams,—
Guarding his forehead, with her round elbow,
From low-grown branches, and his footsteps slow
From stumbling over stumps and hillocks small;
Until they came to where these streamlets fall,
With mingled bubblings and a gentle rush,
Into a river, clear, brimful, and flush
With crystal mocking of the trees and sky.
A little shallop, floating there hard by,
Pointed its beak over the fringed bank;
And soon it lightly dipt, and rose, and sank,
And dipt again, with the young couple's weight,—
Peona guiding, through the water straight,
Towards a bowery island opposite.

(1.407–28)

Peona comforts, guides, and protects her brother, even from the nature that surrounds them and obscures their way, finally leading him, as Dickstein says, to the "bowery island." Like poetry itself, Peona "heals" Endymion ("breathe[s] away the curse") by leading him away from his sorrow to the bower of imagination, where he will relate his dream, Peona becoming the channel through which he relates it. Like the previous poems, these lines are an example of what Ross calls "bower poetry," which "derives its pleasure from its status as an illusive, protective, self-containing, self-restraining space of pure beauty within a larger world of woe." As all creativity in these early poems must occur within such protective bowers, such poetry uses a type of language that allows temporary disregard of "patrilineal rituals" but that finally gives "ultimate value and power to the dominant reality that it seeks to escape"

("Fragmented Word" 120). As a secluded place away from the reality of the world that Keats's poetry will eventually confront, the "bowery island" is the means of escape for Endymion, and his "sweet sister," whose power comes from the new female "eloquence" she derives from her current relationship with the setting, is enough to enact the illusion.

Peona is not Apollo, for the sun god is not needed in poetry that seeks escape from the "patrilineal rituals." But if Peona's role here sounds similar to that of Apollo in "Sleep and Poetry," it is surely more than coincidental, for the name Peona, as Lemprière points out, derives from the Greek word *paean,* a hymn of thanksgiving directed to Apollo (473). The connection suggests that Peona is more than a sister to Endymion; like Apollo to the poet of "Sleep and Poetry," she is the liaison between her brother and immortality because, through her ability to lead him away from reality and to the "bowery island," at least temporarily, she is his imagination, the channel through which his dream becomes reality. While Peona is able momentarily to "heal" Endymion's sorrow, she cannot, as Moneta will later, effect a reconciliation between the two separate realms in which Endymion unhappily exists through his mortal love for an immortal—heaven and earth. She can only offer escape through dreams, the same escape that Moneta will eventually denounce, but one that Keats (and Endymion) now seeks. There will be no bowers through which escape is possible in the later poetry. They, like the nameless and voiceless females, are a part of the young Keats's naïveté, a belief that the imagination (and the metaphorical female who induces it) can only be found where "all is bloomy," as here. Thus Peona's powers are benign because Keats's own imaginative powers are immature, not yet capable of rendering la belle dame, the figure in whom all escape will be irretrievably lost.

Endymion falls asleep beside Peona in the bower, and his sleep produces the dream that will eventually become the transformative reality of all of Keats's bower poetry:

> O magic sleep! O comfortable bird,
> That broodest o'er the troubled sea of the mind

> Till it is hush'd and smooth! O unconfin'd
> Restraint! imprisoned liberty! great key
> To golden palaces, strange minstrelsy,
> Fountains grotesque, new trees, bespangled caves,
> Echoing grottos, full of tumbling waves
> And moonlight; aye, to all the mazy world
> Of silvery enchantment!—who, upfurl'd
> Beneath thy drowsy wing a triple hour,
> But renovates and lives?—Thus, in the bower,
> Endymion was calm'd to life again.
>
> (1.453–64)

As in "Sleep and Poetry," sleep here precedes visions, and the visions are again cataloged into a list of places and things that could only be found in the bower of imagination. It is a "mazy world / Of silvery enchantment" that exists at the heart of the escapist poetry, and Keats must ultimately discover the way out of the maze in order to become the poet he desires to be.

But here the maze is where the imagination happily lingers, and Endymion, through Peona and their place in the bower, is "calm'd to life" by the salutary powers of sleep. Peona's role here is a precursor to Mnemosyne's at the birth of Apollo in "Hyperion," as Endymion regains consciousness from his sleep, "opening his eyelids with a healthier brain" (1.465), through his sister's ministering. The complexities of the later poem, at the darker stage of Keats's development, will now allow such a facile transformation, however. The agonies that Endymion escapes here in the bower poetry will surface during the process of Apollo's "dying into life" in "Hyperion," when the female figure becomes visionary rather than a vision. As the female grows in wisdom and autonomy, the male's search for identity becomes increasingly difficult because it is obscured by the more fascinating transformation of the female herself. Here, though, in a poem that develops its theme of restoration from the facile creative process of "Sleep and Poetry," the imagination, as channeled by Peona, is controllable and salutary. Guidance rather than the admonition that will come with the later females characterizes Peona's primary relationship to her brother. Peona is the only type of imagination in Keats's grasp at this point in his career—gentle, healing, and inspirational, she represents the imagination that must be a "friend" to man—in this case, Endymion's dearest friend.

Through her connection with the healing powers of poetry at this inexperienced and untested stage of Keats's career, Peona has become a muse to Endymion, who, in turn, has taken on all the attributes of Keats's idea of a poet through the tale he tells, the visions he attempts to internalize, and the "mortal bars" he will try to burst. Peona is a present ideal to Keats as well as to Endymion, representing the burgeoning imagination that strives to reach the state of permanence, to change Endymion's dream into reality.

The ideal of the poems of 1817, before the move toward mythology as a vehicle, existed primarily in the visions of nature, whether illusory or real. In *Endymion*, however, the visions of the earth reach their highest idealized state in the actualized female—as mortal and as goddess. Peona, Cynthia, and the earthly Indian maiden are transformative agents, and, like Adam, who "awoke and found [his dream of Eve] truth" (*Letters* 1.185), Endymion will seek to transform his dream of Cynthia into Cynthia herself, a transformation that will occur through the females themselves rather than Endymion. For the first time in the poetry, the object will become the subject. Endymion pleads to Cynthia:

> "Let me entwine thee surer, surer—now
> How can we part? Elysium! who art thou?
> Who, that thou canst not be for ever here?
> Or lift me with thee to some starry sphere?
> Enchantress! tell me by this soft embrace,
> By the most soft completion of thy face,
> Those lips, O slippery blisses, twinkling eyes,
> And by these tenderest, milky sovereignties—
> These tenderest, and by the nectar-wine,
> The passion."
>
> (2.752–61)

Like Calidore before him, Endymion loses sight of the earth for the "elysium" of a "soft embrace." But the passion he seeks does not end there. In bower poetry, the female must be as sensuous and evocative as nature itself, even more so, if she is to lure the male away from the seclusion of the bower. In the same type of cataloging previously reserved for the beauties of the earth, Endymion lists the appealing physical qualities of the goddess. The "slippery blisses," kisses he has shared with the goddess, cannot be compared to anything he has experienced in the bower, however, and the introduction of the present female evokes a word from the male in his response to her that will be highly descriptive of the poetry from now on: "The passion." Like wisdom, passion can be attributed to a female only when she is no longer an extension of nature, and the passion that the poetry's males will increasingly feel for the female will take her farther and farther away from the nature that once defined her. The high degree of sensuality that is a hallmark of Keats's poetry begins to take shape in this poem, and the passion that overcomes Endymion when musing on Cynthia is the same that will consistently accompany Keats when writing poetry—with this poem, the imagination and its symbol begin to merge.

Camille Paglia writes that Keats restores to nature "the sensuality and eroticism that Wordsworth removed" (381). But, with the exception of the final "To Autumn," such restoration is found primarily in the early poems because it is in these poems that the female herself is so closely associated with nature. Once the female figure reaches her later visionary (and sexual) state, the eroticism of nature will be secondary to her own. Even here nature cannot completely accommodate Endymion's need for passion; overwhelmed by a passion that cannot be contained within earthly boundaries, the shepherd asks Cynthia to lift him "to some starry sphere," the same heavenly domain that Keats seeks through his imagination.

"O bliss! O pain!" Cynthia cries in response to Endymion's request, however, a cry of contradictory emotions that could equally be attributed to Endymion in this poem that focuses on earthly bowers rather than the heaven of immortality, because Cynthia cannot do what he asks of her, a failure of imagination that will occur in the odes as well:

"O bliss! O pain!
I love thee, youth, more than I can conceive;
And so long absence from thee doth bereave
My soul of any rest: yet must I hence:
Yet, can I not to starry eminence
Uplift thee; nor for very shame can own
Myself to thee."

(2.773–79)

Leon Waldoff writes that "usually when Keats begins a line or stanza with 'O' he gives voice to a sense of melancholy that derives its intensity and meaning from a pained consciousness of something felt to be absent or lost" (106). He is referring here to the odes of 1819, so the melancholy is one experienced by the poet himself, the only speaker of the odes. The melancholy in the above lines, though, is Cynthia's, and the loss is just as great. Cynthia's inability to transport the sleeping Endymion into the realm of immortality foreshadows the same inherent limitations that will compel the speaker of "Ode on a Grecian Urn" to call the urn in which he has found disappointment "cold Pastoral" (45). Endymion cannot, at this point, share Cynthia's immortality any more than the ode's mortal speaker can share the urn's, but it is only the urn and Cynthia, the two female figures, who realize the ramifications and extent of the dilemma. The female will have become a symbol of untenable immortality in the odes, which will dramatize Keats's perceived failure of her powers of salvation in which he believes so unreservedly now, because along with her inability to save the poet will come a wisdom that she cannot share with him either, unlike Cynthia's here.

The original myths of Endymion made no attempt to surmount the difficulties posed by Cynthia's immortality—as the shepherd remained asleep, he was unconscious of the goddess's visits to him. Keats's version recognizes the difficulties but goes on to solve them by a facile resolution that characterizes all of the bower poetry—the dream becomes reality through an "unlook'd for change" by which Endymion becomes "spiritualiz'd" (4.992–93). The resolution occurs as unconsciously as does the dream itself.

The relative ease with which Endymion achieves immortality, even though he consistently recognizes it as an agonizing impossibility, is one of the basic differences between Keats's early and late poetry. The speaker of the odes struggles with the dilemma posed between the attempts at permanence and the reality of mortality and finds no facile resolution, only hard-won acceptance. Interestingly, the melancholy derived, as Waldoff says, from "a pained consciousness of something felt to be absent or lost" in the speaker of the odes, reaches its most intense point in this poem when articulated by Cynthia, an immortal. In her divine wisdom, she apparently sees beyond the poem's ending.[3]

In a passage that follows Cynthia's sorrow over her recognition of the dilemma, "bliss" in the form of sexual union occurs, symbolic of the highest state of imaginative activity in Keats's poetry, because it is a way to restore loss through creativity. Cynthia entreats the sleeping Endymion, "O let me melt into thee; let the sounds / Of our close voices marry at their birth; / Let us entwine hoveringly" (2.815–17). Language that attempts to effect the desired fusion precedes the sexual act in these lines, as Cynthia asks to "melt into" Endymion, to let their voices "marry", and to "entwine hoveringly." When sexuality is an ideal rather than a means of destruction, it is expressed throughout the poetry in terms of fluidity that connote not only the sexual act itself but the outcome that Keats desires—that of the dissolving and blending of two distinct entities into one— whether earth and heaven or poet and imagination. Only when the barrier between mortal and immortal is eliminated through the metaphor of sex will Endymion be granted his immortality.

Cynthia initiates and leads Endymion into sex in the same way that Peona led her brother into sleep in the "bowery island"—both are representative of a means of transformation, but only the former is capable of the permanence both the poet and the shepherd seek. The transformation here illustrates the desired fusion, at least momentarily, but it is ultimately as elusive as Cynthia herself at this untested stage of poetry, and, following the goddess's departure, Endymion awakens to the pain of lost vision.[4]

Like the poet of "Sleep and Poetry," Endymion discovers
that "the visions all are fled . . . and in their stead / A sense of
real things comes doubly strong" ("Sleep and Poetry" 155–57):

> "And now" thought he,
> "How long must I remain in jeopardy
> Of blank amazements that amaze no more?
> Now I have tasted her sweet soul to the core
> All other depths are shallow: essences,
> Once spiritual, are like muddy lees,
> Meant but to fertilize my earthly root,
> And make my branches lift a golden fruit
> Into the bloom of heaven: other light,
> Though it be quick and sharp enough to blight
> The Olympian eagle's vision, is dark,
> Dark as the parentage of chaos."
>
> (2.901–12)

Some critics have objected to the fourth line of this passage
because Endymion's loss here is one of physical rather than
spiritual dimensions, via sex. Cynthia's "sweet soul," that is,
does not seem pertinent. But Keats regards the sexual encoun-
ter between Endymion and Cynthia as a step toward the ulti-
mate fusion of mortal with immortal and nothing less. And, as
Christopher Ricks writes, there is a "primacy of eating" in
Keats's poetry: "the luxury of food is connected with, and in a
sense gives place to the luxury of sexuality" (120, 123). Both
oral and sexual pleasure merge as the primary metaphor in
Endymion's and Cynthia's meeting, as he has "tasted her sweet
soul to the core." There is no better way to internalize the
metaphor of sexuality and its creative powers than to make it
the delicious sustenance of Endymion himself.

Significantly Cynthia's plea to Endymion before she
"melt(ed) into" his dream contains the words "marry" and
"birth," reminiscent of the question that emerged at their first
meeting in "I stood tip-toe": "Was there a Poet born?" (241).
As the highest state of imaginative activity to Keats, sexual love
is more than erotic—it is supremely poetic, and will reappear

even in a poem for which the soul is very pertinent, "Ode to Psyche."

Because it means a loss of both imagination and sexual identity, the return to consciousness for Endymion is as sorrowful as it will be for the poet of the nightingale ode, who is tolled back from his vision to his "sole self" (72). A loss of light accompanies the return to consciousness of mortality in both poems, light characterized here as Cynthia and as the power of imagination in the ode. In both poems, it is a relationship that is lost—sexual here, imaginative later, but in Keats's mind, as stated, the distinctions between the two are blurred, for they are both creative, and, to Keats, they are both identified with the female. It is this blurring of distinctions that causes Keats to describe the power of the moon/Cynthia over Endymion in the same way that he explains the power that poetry has over him. In an address to the moon, Endymion laments:

> O what a wild and harmonized tune
> My spirit struck from all the beautiful!
> On some bright essence could I lean, and lull
> Myself to immortality.
>
> (3.170–73)

In the following passage from the letters, the "immortality" that Endymion seeks becomes Keats's "eternal poetry":

> I find that I cannot exist without poetry—without eternal poetry—half the day will not do—the whole of it—I began with a little, but habit has made me a Leviathan. (*Letters* 1:133)

Neither Keats nor his shepherd can escape the increasing desire for immortality that both singlemindedly pursue through the female.

Endymion is the prototype of the speaker who will emerge in Keats's later poetry, especially in the odes where the dream becomes an obstacle rather than a channel to immortality. But the difference in the outcome between the two stages of poetry lies in the fact that the female as imagination is a "friend" to

the poet here, the ideal put forth in "Sleep and Poetry." The
female as adversary, so prevalent later, is given a secondary role
here, in the story of Glaucus, Circe, and Scylla—a triumvirate of
terror who obviously contrasts with Endymion, Peona, and
Cynthia and foreshadows things to come for Keats.

Glaucus enters the poem by relating his own tale to En-
dymion:

> "My soul stands
> Now past the midway from mortality,
> And so I can prepare without a sigh
> To tell thee briefly all my joy and pain."
>
> (3.314–17)

These few lines make Glaucus's story similar, so far, to Endymi-
on's. Endymion's tale, too, is one punctuated with a "soul"
that appears to exist "past the midway from mortality," and
Endymion has had his share of "joy and pain" as well, the
dichotomy that will define the later poetry. But although Glau-
cus has a tale to tell, he is not a poet, and, even though he is
immortal, he does not aspire to the imaginative heights that
Endymion does. Thus the immortality that Endymion wishes
to "lull" himself into is perverted in the story of Glaucus, and
sleep becomes a "wretched thrall," a "long captivity," similar to
that of the knight-at-arms to come, who is "lulled" into his own
perverted state by la belle dame. Glaucus continues:

> "Aye, thus it was one thousand years ago.
> One thousand years!—Is it then possible
> To look so plainly through them? to dispel
> A thousand years with backward glance sublime?
> To breathe away as 'twere all scummy slime
> From off a crystal pool, to see its deep,
> And one's own image from the bottom peep?
> Yes: now I am no longer wretched thrall,
> My long captivity and moanings all
> Are but a slime, a thin pervading scum,
> The which I breathe away, and thronging come
> Like things of yesterday my youthful pleasures."
>
> (3.326–37)

Glaucus will not find elysium as Endymion will. Rather, Glaucus will merely survive, perhaps an elysium of sorts to a figure who must utter the words "slime" and "scum" repeatedly in order to describe the state of his existence. He has lost identity through the female, and, although the words he uses are shockingly unfamiliar to Keats's vocabulary, especially in the early bower poetry, they clearly denote the very lowest earthly state possible, and so opposed to the heavenly realm of immortality that it has become analogous with layers of impurities that cover rather than cultivate the beauties of the earth. "Slime" and "scum" represent to Keats, and to Glaucus, a deathly stagnation and perversion of nature caused by Glaucus's loss of masculine identity, a loss that will grow increasingly fearful to Keats as well.

Glaucus's immortality has become a curse, and the perpetrator of the curse, Circe, is a "cruel enchantress" (3.413), an ironically similar epithet to Endymion's portrayal of Cynthia as simply "enchantress" (2.756).

The idea (or ideal) of woman as enchantress is a positive one until an adjective such as "cruel" precedes it. Merlin's Vivien, for example, was clearly an enchantress, and he enjoyed her power; when she entombed him in the hollow of a tree, however, she became a "cruel enchantress"—while her capabilities remained the same, the direction of her powers changed. Any woman identified as an enchantress by a man has the potential of becoming cruel. From the male perspective, it is the cruelty that is the perversion, not the powers themselves, powers often seen as inherent to the female. The perversion that constitutes the cruel enchantress is similar to the perversion of nature that Glaucus emphasizes with the words "slime" and "scum." The female's power, bifurcated and polarized in this poem into two individual women, will eventually reside in a single figure, whom Keats will call his "demon Poesy," the oxymoronic "maiden most unmeek" ("Ode on Indolence" 30, 29). Like the figures of the later poetry, Circe's role and her power are adversarial to the male. She is the first female of the poetry to dissociate herself from nature completely, assuring autonomy, and the results are disastrous to the male. Her progeny will include la belle dame, adrift in a barren environment that has become natureless, whose prey will be the descendent of Glaucus, the woebegone knight-at-arms. Like Glaucus, he will encounter earthly stagnation—in the withered sedge and the birds who do not sing. He, too, will give himself up to a female whom he believes to be an enchantress, only to discover that she is a cruel one as well. Female cruelty to the male can only be perpetrated through powers that he can neither understand nor control, and because the evolution of the poetry's males will lag far behind that of its females, the cruel enchantress will take on many shapes in the poems to come, while the male will remain the unwitting prey.

Stuart Sperry comments that Glaucus's "infatuation with Circe and its end in powerlessness and withered age represents a caricature of the whole notion of the romantic quest which inevitably raises certain questions concerning Endymion's own pursuit" (108). It is certainly an "infatuation" that the males of the early poetry find in the women they pursue. Until the "Ode to Psyche," in fact, the encounters between men and women that the poetry defines as "love" are immature and egocentric on the part of the men. There is no poem in Keats's canon, with the possible exception of "Isabella," who loses both Lorenzo and his severed head, however, that pursues an actual love relationship between a man and a woman in which the man is not seeking an enchantress.[5] With the odes that follow "To Psyche," infatuation is abandoned but love does not take its place. Rather, the male becomes an intrusive observer and questioner of the female and the encounters produce solipsism instead of relationships. The romantic quest, like the quest of the knight-at-arms before his turned into an empty "sojourn," will produce a "better self" for the participant, and Sperry is correct in his assessment of Glaucus's own pursuit of the ideal as a "caricature." But Glaucus himself is a caricature of Endymion because the nature of their individual quests also contains differences inherent to the characters' personalities, and therein lies the difference to Keats. As previously mentioned, Glaucus is not a poet. He "touch'd no lute, . . . sang not, trod no measures" (3.338); Endymion, because of his relationship with

Peona as imagination and with Cynthia as the product of that imagination, can certainly be considered a poet figure. The point at which each quest begins, therefore, is profoundly different from one another. What Glaucus has that Endymion does not is immortality—the state of permanence that is the goal of the romantic quest in general, and of Endymion specifically. So what is it that Glaucus seeks?

In the original myth of Glaucus, he seeks Circe's help in winning Scylla and repels the powerful goddess's advances toward him. Keats, however, changes his version in order to parallel more closely Glaucus's story with Endymion's. Glaucus is unable to resist Circe. He becomes her "tranced vassal" (3.460) and would not "have mov'd even though Amphion's harp had woo'd / (him) back to Scylla o'er the billows rude" (3.461–62). A "tranced vassal" is similar to what Endymion has become to Cynthia at this point, but the differences lie in the place of origin of Endymion's quest. The shepherd begins his quest from the bower, from the mortal earth, unlike the immortal, and thus heavenly, Glaucus. The bower's pleasures derive from illusions that cannot remain because they are temporal; permanence, the majority of Keats's poems purport, exists only within immortality, the goal of Endymion and the original state of Glaucus.

In his search for immortality, Endymion will be led "by desire to some arbitrarily happy conclusion, instead of, as in patrilineal narrative, forever claiming the need to lead and shape every object into a predetermined objective" (Ross, "Fragmented Word" 118). This is the ultimate difference between Endymion and Glaucus and the primary reason that Glaucus serves as caricature to Endymion. Endymion is a shepherd who seeks to attain immortality completely through the Negative Capability of the female—to replace the earthly ideal of feminine nature with the immortality of the ideal feminine persona. His quest, unlike that of Glaucus, is delineated by the quest for the ultimate salutary female—what Keats deems poetry. Glaucus, however, was not content with the salutary figure of Scylla and, like the discontented male speakers of the odes to come, needed to "lead and shape every object into a predetermined objective," rather than accept the arbitrary magic that characterizes Endymion's wanderings.

The fact of Glaucus's immortality is all but forgotten by Keats. We are reminded of it only by the sea god's impending death, a doom that has taken a thousand years to materialize. It was before his capture by Circe that Glaucus had become discontented, understandable when one is earthbound as both Keats and Endymion are, but not when one is immortal. When a god becomes discontent with immortality, the quest for change can lead only in the opposite direction—to mortality, or, in Glaucus's case, to death in life for a millennium. The longings that precipitated Glaucus's quest are obviously different from those of Endymion, for they are "distemper'd." Glaucus says to Endymion:

> "Why was I not contented? Wherefore reach
> At things which, but for thee, O Latmian!
> Had been my dreary death? Fool! I began
> To feel distemper'd longings: to desire
> The utmost privilege that ocean's sire
> Could grant in benediction: to be free
> Of all his kingdom. Long in misery
> I wasted, ere in one extremest fit
> I plung'd for life or death. To interknit
> One's senses with so dense a breathing stuff
> Might seem a work of pain; so not enough
> Can I admire how crystal-smooth it felt,
> And buoyant round my limbs. At first I dwelt
> Whole days and days in sheer astonishment;
> Forgetful utterly of self-intent."
>
> (3.372–86)

Glaucus exhibits human characteristics here rather than Endymion's of godlike quality. He is not content to be "forgetful utterly of self-intent," the state of Negative Capability in which Endymion exists. Thus he will surrender his immortality for a specious heaven rather than for the elysium that Endymion will attain. Glaucus's quest is an indictment of those who do not participate in the attainment of an ideal. It is, in short, perversion rather than parody, just as Circe herself is a perversion of Cynthia, and Glaucus will find himself in a "net" at the end, woven by the false "tears, and smiles, and honey-words" of Circe (3.427, 426), an appropriate means of imprisonment for the god who was once a fisher.

The sea nymph, Scylla, whom Glaucus abandoned for Circe, is also destroyed in Keats's narrative. Thus all instances of immortality are lost, to be regained only through Endymion, the poet figure, through labors whose meanings rival the riddles of the Delphic oracle:

> "Who can devise
> A total opposition? No one. So
> One million times ocean must ebb and flow,
> And he oppressed. Yet he shall not die,
> These things accomplish'd:—If he utterly
> Scans all the depths of magic, and expounds
> The meanings of all motions, shapes, and sounds;
> If he explores all forms and substances
> Straight homeward to their symbol-essences."
>
> (3.692–700)

Fairy-tale dimensions enter the poem at this point, to recur frequently until the end. Appropriately, the fairy tale evoked seems to be that of Princess Aurora, named, like the god of poetry, after the sun, and better known as "Sleeping Beauty." She, too, awoke to find her dream truth, a fitting example of the power of dreams in the early poetry. When Aurora is condemned to death by a witchlike character similar to Circe, the spell cannot be broken. No one, that is, "can devise / A total opposition." But it can be modified, and Aurora is instead condemned to sleep for one hundred years, to be awakened by a youth, also by "heavenly power lov'd and led" (3.708), as Endymion is. Glaucus, too, will be "awakened," but first he must scan "all the depths of magic, . . . [expound] / The meanings of all motions, shapes, and sounds." In other words, he must give up all patriarchal predeterminacy that has no place in this poem of arbitrary and feminine magic, and restore his own lost ideals of magic and beauty by deobjectifying all objects, unraveling them to their fluid "forms and substances / Straight homeward to their symbol-essences"—that is, he must become like a poet. While the dreamer in "The Fall of Hyperion" will be admonished by Moneta to "think of the earth," Glaucus is being told here to think of heaven, for it is in that direction that Keats's early imagination pursues the magic of poetry.

The second stage of Glaucus's labors elucidates the contrary nature of the task that awaits him:

> "Moreover, and in chief,
> He must pursue this task of joy and grief
> Most piously;—all lovers tempest-tost,
> And in the savage overwhelming lost,
> He shall deposit side by side, until
> Time's creeping shall the dreary space fulfil."
>   (3.701–6)

Glaucus must not only restore the magic and beauty of poetry, but, as these lines indicate, he must also pursue, through the "joy and grief" that poetry inheres, its "great end," its healing powers. When that occurs, the "lovers tempest-tost" will be brought back to life. The imagination will once again be "a friend / To sooth the cares, and lift the thoughts of man" ("Sleep and Poetry" 246–47)—salvation to Glaucus and a further step in Endymion's own quest. In effect, the lines that delineate his tasks describe Glaucus's own "gradations of Happiness" that correspond with Endymion's famous lines to Peona in Book 1 where "at the tip-top,"

> There hangs by unseen film, an orbed drop
> Of light, and that is love: its influence,
> Thrown in our eyes, genders a novel sense,
> At which we start and fret; till in the end,
> Melting into its radiance, we blend,
> Mingle, and so become a part of it,—
> Nor with aught else can our souls interknit
> So wingedly.
>   (1.805–13)

Glaucus must become fluid, like the sea that once defined him, in order to blend and mingle and thus become a part of the "orbed drop / Of light . . . that is love." He must give up the rigid masculinity that he is trying to retrieve following his experience with Circe in order to discover the "symbol-essences" that originate with Endymion's lines above, where the "souls interknit" with the "radiance" of the light. In Glaucus's "distemper'd longings" speech, it is the "senses" that "interknit," a rendition of William Blake's "mind-forg'd manacles" ("To London" 8), and further evidence of Glaucus's own misdirected bond with mortality. Thus, in order to find salvation, Glaucus must internalize what Endymion already knows. He must discover the passion that reveals itself through visions of the imagination rather than through the carnality of the senses.

For this reason, I do not see this section of the poem as a "warning" to Endymion, as some critics do, primarily because Endymion is so obviously the only means of salvation for Glaucus. I see the reason for the episode as being closer to Waldoff's observation that the story of Glaucus "reveals the way Keats's imagination tends to divide women into fair maids and 'femmes fatales.' Cynthia and Circe are obvious contrasts, each representing the possibility of a metamorphosis but of radically different kinds, one promising a spiritualization, the other a dehumanization" (54).[6] The only problem with this observation is one of emphasis. Keats is certainly using the Glaucus story to portray a contrast, but the contrast between the women is the outcome rather than the source of the portrayal. The two myths show how Keats "tends to divide" the imagination into opposing forces: the "fair maids" and what some would call "femmes fatales" personify this division, but the power of metamorphosis lies within the imagination itself. Cynthia and Circe are the first in a succession of women to wield this dual power and are the only separate figures of its representation in a single poem. Both sides of the imagination's power will eventually cohere in single female figures in poems to come.

The woman who follows Circe is yet another side of the protean female—the Indian maiden. Her voice appears when

Endymion "to heaven's airy dome / Was offering up a hecatomb of vows,"

> Whereupon he bows
> His head through thorny-green entanglement
> Of underwood, and to the sound is bent,
> Anxious as hind towards her hidden fawn.
>
> (4.38–43)

Images of earth and nature return with the Indian maiden's appearance.[7] Seemingly an inhabitant of the earth, she interrupts Endymion's vows to heaven, compelling him to bow his head instead to the "thorny-green entanglement," which may threaten its own type of "enthrallment" because his quest undergoes a significant change in direction here.

The narrator warns Endymion to "vanish into air" at the sight of the maiden: "See not her charms? Is Phoebe passionless?" (4.56), two obviously rhetorical questions, setting up a possible repetition of the Glaucus and Circe episode. Endymion recognizes the situation but, like Glaucus, is powerless to resist, and the fear of losing his already vulnerable identity overtakes him:

> Upon a bough
> He leant, wretched. He surely cannot now
> Thirst for another love: O impious,
> That he can even dream upon it thus!—
> Thought he, "Why am I not as are the dead,
> Since to a woe like this I have been led
> Through the dark earth, and through the wondrous sea?
> Goddess! I love thee not the less: From thee
> By Juno's smile I turn not—no, no, no—
> While the great waters are at ebb and flow.—
> I have a triple soul! O fond pretence—
> For both, for both my love is so immense,
> I feel my heart is cut for them in twain."
>
> (4.85–97)

Endymion's heart, like Keats's imagination, is cut "in twain," divided equally between the poem's female symbols of heaven and earth—Cynthia and the Indian maiden. He would rather die than have to make such a choice between them ("Why am I not as are the dead?"). And in the line that follows the above recognition of the dilemma, he "groan'd, as one by beauty slain" (4.98), reminiscent of the "groans of torture-pilgrimage" (3.524) that Glaucus heard from the men who had become Circe's captives. Glaucus, too, experiences a "slain spirit, over-wrought with fright" (3.559) at the realization of his situation. Beauty is inextricably bound with death in the story of Glaucus, and Endymion now surrenders to what he believes to be his own similar fate:

> Dear maid, sith
> Thou art my executioner, and I feel
> Loving and hatred, misery and weal,
> Will in a few short hours be nothing to me,
> And all my story that much passion slew me;
> Do smile upon the evening of my days:
> And, for my tortur'd brain begins to craze,
> Be thou my nurse; and let me understand
> How dying I shall kiss that lily hand.—
> (4.110–18)

Being "slain" by beauty will be particularly apt in the "Ode on Melancholy," in which the speaker warns other men against becoming one of the goddess Melancholy's "cloudy trophies" (30). Praz writes that "to such an extent were Beauty and Death looked upon as sisters by the Romantics that they became fused into a sort of two-faced herm, filled with corruption and melancholy and fatal in its beauty—a beauty of which, the more bitter the taste, the more abundant the enjoyment" (31). Such close connection between beauty and death will make pleasure turn to "poison while the bee-mouth sips" ("Melancholy" 24), another Keatsian example of internalization through eating. Melancholy, like Circe, is a Fatal Woman, and her practice, the same that Endymion fears from the Indian maiden, is what Praz calls "sexual cannibalism," whose key elements are a youthful, obscure male lover who "maintains a passive attitude, . . . inferior either in condition or in physical exuberance to the woman, who stands in the same relation to him as do the female spider, the praying mantis, &c., to their respective males" (205). To be "slain" by beauty, the male must be vulnerable and unsure of or discontented with his own identity, certainly an appropriate way to describe Endymion at present and Glaucus before him.

But, in this poem of arbitrary magic, something happens to transform both the shepherd and his quest for identity. When Endymion asks the Indian maiden to smile for him "upon the evening of [his] days," she weeps instead ("Dost weep for me?" [4.119]). Her tears elucidate the difference between life and death for Endymion, between the "specious" heaven that Glaucus found in Circe's false tears and a real one. The Indian maiden's empathy becomes a song of sorrow that leads into a hymn to Bacchus," 'Great God of breathless cups and chirping mirth!' " (4.236).

As the god of the grapes of the earth and the only major deity whose parents are not both immortal (a splendidly Keatsian attribute), Bacchus is also the tragic and suffering god. Lemprière writes that he "assisted the gods in their wars against the giants, and was cut to pieces" (109), to suffer the split between life and death forever. Thus, Bacchus is associated with the earth rather than with heaven, and the Indian maiden's song is the only major allusion to him in Keats's panorama of deities in the poem. Her clearly recognizable sorrow—"the agonies, the strife / Of human hearts" ("Sleep and Poetry" 124–25)— compels Endymion to love her, and therein lies the difference between Endymion's and Glaucus's fates. Rather than death, the shepherd will find restoration:

> "Poor lady, how thus long
> Have I been able to endure that voice?
> Fair Melody! kind Syren! I've no choice;
> I must be thy sad servant evermore:
> I cannot choose but kneel here and adore."
>   (4.298–302)

As the Indian maiden's "sad servant" Endymion seems danger-ously close to Glaucus's self-description as Circe's "tranced vassal," but the Indian maiden is an oxymoronic "kind Syren," which makes her, like Cynthia, simply an enchantress rather than a cruel one, and there is no evidence of Endymion being entranced by her. In fact, there is no indication that Endymion's choice of the maiden is anything but a conscious one—the word *thrall,* for example, that Glaucus used in his description of Circe's entrapment of him, is never mentioned. Nonetheless, like Bacchus, Endymion will continue to suffer "tearings apart" produced by his own guilt, indecision, and finally, by a true loss of identity—the first of Keats's males to suffer the dual loss of identity and salvation, but the only one to regain them so easily. It is, in fact, the only time both loss and restoration will occur in the same poem.

The identity of the Indian maiden is never in doubt, how-ever—thus Endymion's guilt. She is described as "the stranger of dark tresses" (4.462) as opposed to Cynthia's "golden" hair (4.451). While all women are alien to the male perspective, the darkness that characterizes the maiden, as well as her apparent desire to supplant Cynthia, removes her even further from the masculine vision of things familiar and she becomes, unlike the golden Cynthia, a "stranger" to Endymion, causing his previously known surroundings to become strange to him as well.

Implicit in this contrast of heaven and earth is the opposition of life with death. Even with the Indian maiden in residence, the earth no longer offers "life" for Endymion, a term which now must include in its definition the elements of permanence to Keats. The burden of trying to choose between the two females proves to be too much for the shepherd and even his newly acquired "triple soul" is not enough to sustain identity:

> What is this soul then? Whence
> Came it? It does not seem my own, and I
> Have no self-passion or identity.
> Some fearful end must be: where, where is it?
> (4.475–78)

Having "no self-passion or identity" and unable to make a decisive choice between Cynthia and the Indian maiden, Endymion reaches the nadir of solitude, the state of Keats's own "no-self" in which others' identities claustrophobically press against his own:

> Despair! Despair!
> He saw her body fading gaunt and spare
> In the cold moonshine. Straight he seiz'd her wrist;
> It melted from his grasp: her hand he kiss'd,
> And, horror! kiss'd his own—he was alone.
> (4.506–10)

The Keatsian "melted" is not used here as a means of fusion as it usually is in the poetry, especially when it involves the female. Instead, it is a means of dissolving in order to separate the female from the male. The Indian maiden's wrist "melted from [Endymion's] grasp" and he kisses his own hand, an act that depicts the same solipsism that the knight-at-arms will suffer when his elusive female disappears. It is a profound loss not only because it delineates the absence of the female but, in both poems, it makes clear the extremes of the androcentrism of masculine identity and its dependence for survival upon her— here the kiss is perverted, and in "La Belle Dame sans Merci," the knightly quest will be reduced to an aimless "sojourn" (45).

Jack Stillinger has pointed out that one of *Endymion's* major themes is the conflict of self and solitude with love and humanitarian activities: "in his quest for union with Cynthia, Endymion renounces the world and worldly activities; in much of the poem he is a 'solitary.' " (*Hoodwinking* 18). Unlike Wordsworth's solitaries, however, Endymion's state of separateness is not one that apotheosizes the characteristics of common mortality until they become sublimely uncommon. There is too much at risk here—not the "egotistical sublime" that Keats terms Wordsworth's poetry (*Letters* 1:387)—but the fragile masculine identity that both he and his male creations share. To be completely alone and cut off from the female is, as Endymion calls it, "despair," the nadir of passion. Thus Endymion's solitude is oppressive, as oppressive as the various identities from which Keats's "camelion poet" tries to escape, and it causes a split between the surroundings and his own identity that hinders rather than enhances spirituality. Endymion's indecision, brought about by his lack of identity, causes him to lose all connection with the earth and the bower of imagination; his kissing of his own hand rather than the Indian maiden's perverts the act of love and the fusion of sexuality into a condition that recognizes only the self. A return to empathy for the maiden's suffering is the only way Endymion will be brought out of his destructive preoccupation with self and lost masculinity and into renewed concern for, and association with, humanity.

Endymion's return to reality after the Indian maiden disappears is, like all of Keats's descents of the imagination, one of deathly disenchantment:

> His first touch of the earth went nigh to kill.
> "Alas!" said he, "were I but always borne
> Through dangerous winds, had but my footsteps worn
> A path in hell, for ever would I bless
> Horrors which nourish an uneasiness
> For my own sullen conquering: to him
> Who lives beyond earth's boundary, grief is dim,
> Sorrow is but a shadow: now I see
> The grass; I feel the solid ground."
>
> (4.614–22)

Endymion's plea here is different, however. He asks not for his lost elysium, but for "dangerous winds," "a path in hell" worn by his footsteps, because he "lives beyond the earth's boundary," and thus all "grief is dim." These rather strange images of comfort most likely refer to the canto of Dante's *Inferno* that would become Keats's favorite—the fifth, in which Francesca and Paolo are eternally buffeted by strong winds as punishment for their own illicit passion, a fitting punishment for Endymion who has been "illicitly passionate" with both the Indian maiden and, in her wake, his own separated self.

In a letter to George and Georgiana Keats, the poet discusses his attraction to the canto:

> The fifth canto of Dante pleases me more and more—
> it is that one in which he meets with Paulo and
> Franc[h]esca—I had passed many days in rather a low
> state of mind and in the midst of them I dreamt of be-
> ing in that region of Hell. The dream was one of the
> most delightful enjoyments I ever had in my life—I
> floated about the whirling atmosphere as it is de-
> scribed with a beautiful figure to whose lips mine were
> joined at it seem'd for an age—and in the midst of all
> this cold and darkness I was warm. (*Letters* 2:91)

This letter was not written until April 16, 1819, but Keats was obviously familiar with Dante long before this date, as many of his earlier letters reveal. Thus Endymion's strange speech that seems to indicate some sort of plea for self-flagellation in order to achieve atonement is in truth a plea for the restoration of passion, even that which is forbidden. Endymion is willing to undergo anything besides the earth where, because of the dark stranger who precipitates his own lack of power and identity, "blank amazements . . . amaze no more" (2.903). On the earth, he is alone, cut off from others, trapped in a darkness exempli-fied by both the appearance and suddenly the disappearance of the Indian maiden.

Endymion quickly rediscovers the maiden, however, and just as quickly forgets his plea for passion, his love for Cynthia, and his major problem of indecisiveness:

> I have clung
> To nothing, lov'd a nothing, nothing seen
> Or felt but a great dream! O I have been
> Presumptuous against love, against the sky,
> Against all elements, against the tie
> Of mortals each to each, against the blooms
> Of flowers, rush of rivers, and the tombs
> Of heroes gone! Against his proper glory
> Has my own soul conspired: so my story
> Will I to children utter, and repent.

> There never liv'd a mortal man, who bent
> His appetite beyond his natural sphere,
> But starv'd and died.
>
> (4.636–48)

In words very similar to Peona's in response to her brother's dream, Endymion denounces his dream of Cynthia as a "nothing." It is the only time such belittlement will occur in the poetry until the nightingale ode, in which the dreaming state will be summarily eliminated as a channel to the imagination. Like the speaker of the poetry of 1817, Endymion catalogs the beauties of the earth, in a frantic attempt to return to the familiarity of them, but further admits his own "presumptuous" state against reality; then the shepherd becomes similar to Coleridge's Ancient Mariner, another tragic figure of masculine presumptuousness against nature, and will tell his story to children "and repent." Endymion's indecisiveness up to this point is clearly Keats's as well, and he, too, will repent in order to find salvation when he realizes, later in his career, that he has clung to nothing "but a great dream."

But here, in the reality of the bower, following Endymion's act of atonement, Peona reenters the story after a long absence. Peona's task is to save her brother from the mortality he is about to accept. It is a role similar to that of Cynthia; the female's well-known dual role of savior and destroyer to the male continues to take shape in this poem. Peona comforts her brother and again becomes the channel through which he finds Cynthia. Behind "Dian's temple" (4.914), an appropriate setting for the dream to become reality, Endymion beholds "his passion" (4.987).

The passion that Endymion feels for the Indian maiden is a supremely carnal one, and it threatens to overwhelm the "spiritualization" that must take place in order for the shepherd to become immortal. But both passion and spirit become fused by "some unlook'd for change" (4.992), a fusion that has obviously not encountered the dilemma of the later poetry, and the Indian maiden magically transforms from the darkness that characterizes her as both a mortal and a stranger to the golden and thus immortal Cynthia.

The poem ends appropriately with Peona. As the agent of imagination by which Endymion finds Cynthia, and through whom Keats writes the story, she is the last character to exit. The dream and the poem, both brought to reality through her presence, now end with her disappearance into the "gloomy wood" (4.1003).

While *Endymion* is not the great poem Keats wanted it to be, primarily because all resolutions come about through unexplained and mechanistic supernatural devices, it does differ significantly from the 1817 poems in its portrayal of the relationship between Keats and his female figures—a relationship that will, in fact, continue until the end of his career. The maidens of the earth of 1817 have become goddesses who, like Keats, shun the earth for the new realm of timelessness. The figure in *Endymion* most like the earlier females is Scylla—docile, mute, and, most of the time, dead. Scylla's death, or long sleep, is neither transcendent nor visionary. Like the somnambulant maidens of 1817, Scylla is more of an afterthought than an integral part of the poetic process. As a mutable corollary to the demythicizing of nature that Keats's poetry will undergo next, Scylla serves as reminder of the impotence of both nature and woman when each is objectified into a "tranced vassal" of the other. The passionless condition of both the earlier maidens and Scylla—the ultimate "maiden," attendant on and subjugated by the conscious male—will be explored further before it is altogether abandoned. The relationship between women and death and its effect on male creativity will be a major factor in the next works—"Isabella," "The Eve of St. Agnes," and "The Eve of St. Mark"—the only poems to focus exclusively on the mortal rather than immortal female as a subject.

The Mortal Females
Isabella, Madeline, and Bertha

In *Endymion*, the Indian maiden, as a figure of mortality who represents the end to the shepherd's dream, appears to Endymion as his "executioner" (4.111). Her sorrow, like his, derives from her mortal state but ultimately dissipates through her ability to transcend mortality, and therefore death, by becoming one with the immortal Cynthia. Death has no impact in *Endymion* because, at this early stage of Keats's career, mortality can be, in effect, simply wished away by "some unlook'd for change" (4.992). Aileen Ward comments that when Endymion "finally realizes that to renounce the maid is to deny life itself, he is rewarded by the maid's transformation into a goddess" (143). To the Keats of *Endymion*, accepting the real is the ideal; the transformation, or "reward," manifests itself, however, as a complete denial of the real—of death and the mortal state altogether—a denial that Keats's poetry after *Endymion* will no longer be able to pursue in so facile a way.

This chapter will focus on the three poems that follow *Endymion*, which not only do not deny death but which clearly pursue its consequences, especially for women.

Autonomous despite their mortality, Isabella, Madeline, and Bertha have significantly evolved from the mute maidens of 1817, but Keats will demand more change, in that the females who inhabit his poetry must have the power to transcend the woes of the world, an impossibility when they are mortal. Human tragedy is exacerbated, the poems of this chapter contend, when it is a woman who shuns life, or worse, when life offers her no ideal to embrace, as in "The Eve of St. Mark." For it is women who represent, from the male perspective, life at its most passionate—as mother, lover, and, to Keats, as imagination itself. Attainment of the male's identity necessitates control of and participation in the extremes of feminine passion, while at the same time distancing himself from them by virtue of his gender. Identity cannot be "motherless" nor, as made clear in *Endymion*, can it be acquired solipsistically. In an attempt to find the maternal source as well as the lover, Keats turns now to the mortal female—to accept the real as the ideal. The female must be able to create her own identity before she can grant it to the male, though, and, with the exception of Madeline, whose quest parallels too closely Endymion's own easy "spiritualization," mortality conveys in these poems a condition that is lifeless and drained of the passion both the hero and the poet seek. Like the "dead" Scylla and the ineffectual maidens before her, two of the mortal females, Isabella and Bertha, cannot participate in the dream state that has become the apex of passion and the vehicle of imagination to Keats. And when women can neither nurture nor sustain the passion men perceive them to embody, life and the act of creation become a sham.

In June 1818, Keats wrote to Bailey, "were it in my choice I would reject a petrarchal coronation—on accou[n]t of my dying day, and because women have Cancers" (*Letters* 1:292).[1] Mortality evinces a suffering, explored in both the poetry of 1817 and *Endymion*, that is neither transcendent nor visionary. No "pleasant pain" ("Psyche" 52) is evoked, and thus feminine passion—the ultimate salve to the young Keats—is lost by the male. Praz writes that romantic literature is largely defined by the "inseparability of pleasure and pain" as well as a search for "themes of tormented, contaminated beauty" (28). It is this search that leads Keats to explore the subject of mortality when visited upon the female.

"Isabella," "The Eve of St. Agnes," and the fragmentary "Eve of St. Mark" all portray females who continue to be depicted in the shadow of their predecessors of 1817. Although they are treated as subjects rather than objectified as their predecessors were, they remain characteristically and primarily docile, maidenly, and most importantly, mortal. Isabella and Bertha are extensions not of Cynthia, Circe, or even Peona (whose ability to articulate gave her the power to create), but because of their inability to control or transcend their scenarios of human suffering, they are closely linked with the chaste, "sweet lipp'd" maidens of the first poems. After *Endymion*, Keats once again seeks control through a facile imagination, and it is while writing "Isabella" that he tells John Hamilton Reynolds the

> Imagination brought
> Beyond its proper bound, yet still confined,—
> ....
> . . . Cannot refer to any standard law
> Of either earth or heaven.
> > ("Dear Reynolds, as last night I lay in bed"
> > 78–82)

Like his desultory shepherd, Keats finds his imagination, which will identify him as a poet, lost between the realms of earth and heaven with no clear direction in sight. He will "take refuge" (112) from what he calls his "detested moods" in the "new romance" (111) of "Isabella." His need for poetic control as well as the passion of creating tales of the "human heart" demand a thematic return to mortality rather than the imaginative flight experienced so tentatively in *Endymion*. Thus, the present poems explore the mortal female's often desperate attempts to remain autonomous in the presence of death, with no bower in which to escape and without the reward of transcendence through any unprecipitated spiritualization.

I

In the first poem, "Isabella," written primarily in April 1818, love and death are resolutely bound and are the powerful catalysts to Isabella's own "unlook'd for change"—not a transformation into immortality, but a change characterized by a loss of innocence resulting from the death of her lover, Lorenzo, and manifested by Isabella's metamorphosis from her role as his shy lover to the desperate maternal role she acquires in order to care for his severed head. The passion that should define the lovers' relationship is perverted into something akin to a mother's mourning for her lost child. Death rather than the passion of love becomes the determining factor to Isabella's identity, as Lorenzo's death compels her to acknowledge mortality as an end to happiness and her own lover's anticipation.

In *Endymion*, such acknowledgment is accompanied by tears of human sorrow from the Indian maiden. Isabella's tears express more than the recognition of mortality, however, as she "hung over her sweet basil evermore, / And moisten'd it with tears unto the core" (423–24). The basil holds Lorenzo's head, and so her tears serve not only to delineate her new maternal identity, procured through the transformation of her lover into the macabre object of a "child," but they also represent an ideal new to Keats's poetry. Because Isabella's tears nurture both the severed head and the basil plant itself, "whence thick, and green, and beautiful it grew" (426), they become the sustenance not only of the plant, but of the memory of Lorenzo as well, thereby offering the only type of transcendence that can be derived from the mortal state—that of memory, a tenet that will become especially critical to the near-mortal race of the Titans in "Hyperion."

Isabella's perverse maternal identity that eventually dominates the poem appears briefly in the early stanzas, when she is still lover to the living Lorenzo. Her

> untouch'd cheek
> Fell sick within the rose's just domain,
> Fell thin as a young mother's, who doth seek
> By every lull to cool her infant's pain.
> (33–36)

It is an image of passionate anticipation, and Lorenzo responds to it by silently promising to "drink her tears" (39), an infantile act of internalizing Isabella's love that he wishes for in life, but can achieve only in death. Because of his frequent inability to articulate his desire for Isabella while alive, Lorenzo is nearly as mute as the early maidens, and his death is seen poetically as merely a vehicle to Isabella's transformation from lover to mother. The male will often be no more than a vehicle to the evolution of the female in the poetry, but here the transformation of Isabella and Lorenzo's inherent role as vehicle are seen to begin to occur while both lovers are alive, for Lorenzo is certainly a "man/child" in his relationship with Isabella, and his unrealized problems with identity, shown through his inability to speak in masculine discourse to Isabella, makes death the only option available to him.

Death, in effect, forms the identities of both Isabella and Lorenzo. Through death, he becomes a symbol of the child he wished to be in life, able finally to drink her tears, and, through her tears, she becomes a caricature of the nurturing mother. As Isabella moistens the severed head with her tears, she

> forgot the stars, the moon, and sun,
> And she forgot the blue above the trees,
> And she forgot the dells where waters run,
> And she forgot the chilly autumn breeze;
> She had no knowledge when the day was done,
> And the new morn she saw not.
>
> (417–22)

The nature that once identified and entombed the female is forgotten by Isabella. She is the first female to emerge completely from her natural surroundings, but she has no wings of immortality to allow her full escape, and, while her initial emergence is an important step in the process of evolution of the female, her identity as a deobjectified female is premature and will be ultimately aborted.

In the lines above, a desperate attempt to defy death, through the memory of Lorenzo, insists on a Lethean obliviousness to everything else. The attempt to forget the nature that defines her mortality will cause the perversion of the maternal in this poem, however, and will prove to be disastrous to Isabella.

Barbara Schapiro writes that

> the relationship with the woman which [romantic] poetry either expresses or implies is rooted psychologically in the relationship with the first woman of all our lives, the mother. Not only does this relationship oc-

cupy a central position in the imagery of every major
Romantic poet, but it also bears directly on the particu-
lar style and general thematic preoccupations of each.
For the psychological dimensions underlying the im-
ages of women inform the poetry at its deepest, most
fundamental level. (1x)

While Keats's "preoccupation" with the female as mother is
more "antitypal" than archetypal, as will be discussed later, the
burgeoning concept of female identity, both physiological and
psychological, is clearly fundamental to "Isabella." The hero-
ine, like Endymion before her, finds her identity splintered
into conflicting parts throughout the poem. As she rapidly
progresses from lover to perverse mother to finally a woman
gone mad from separation from Lorenzo's head, the difference
in her ultimate identity, unlike Endymion's, lies in the differ-
ence between mortality as a donnée and an immortality that
cannot be reached. Her identity as a female will simply not
allow easy transition from one state to the other as that of the
male, dependent on the female, can. While the male, as both
hero and creator, draws creative power from the female as a
source of salvation, the female must be both means and end of
her own very tenuous salvation. Thus, while madness threatens
Endymion ("he fled / Into the fearful deep, to hide his head /
From the clear moon, the trees, and the coming madness"
[2.216–18]), he will be saved through the female; madness
becomes reality to the ever-mortal Isabella, however, unable to
save either Lorenzo or herself, and although the poem opens
and closes with her as subject, the persona is dramatically trans-
formed, as the opening line portends: "Fair Isabel, poor simple
Isabel!"

An actual relationship between the lovers while Lorenzo is
alive is almost nonexistent, to be carried out primarily after his
death. Communication between them exists almost exclusively
within their imagination. At the beginning of the poem, their
relationship is so fraught with obstacles, in fact, that the lovers'
activities can only be described through a series of negations:

> They could not in the self-same mansion dwell
>   Without some stir of heart, some malady,
> They could not sit at meals but feel how well
>   It soothed each to be the other by;
> They could not, sure, beneath the same roof sleep
> But to each other dream, and nightly weep.
>
>   (3–8)

The poem continues to depict a lack of immediate and articulated communication between them:

> "To-morrow will I bow to my delight,
>   To-morrow will I ask my lady's boon."—
> "O may I never see another night,
>   Lorenzo, if thy lips breathe not love's tune."—
> So spake they to their pillows; but, alas,
> Honeyless days and days did he let pass.
>
>   (27–32)

The narrator makes clear that it is Lorenzo who will not verbalize his love, and thereby create his masculine identity. Isabella can find no identity as a lover because Lorenzo has no voice to tell her of his love. Because of Lorenzo's reticence, Isabella's identity as a female will be formed not by love, but by death, two states that traditionally mingle in Keats's life as well. He will tell Fanny Brawne: "I have two luxuries to brood over in my walks, your Loveliness and the hour of my death. O that I could have possession of them both in the same minute" (*Letters* 2:133). To Isabella, the "luxury" is less than ideal, however; as female, she embodies the passion that Keats seeks in his plea to Fanny Brawne, and with Lorenzo's death instead of her own the passion becomes errant and smothering.

Isabella's maternal identity emerges from the fusion of love and death, clearly an unnatural one, as Keats shows in the morbid scene at Lorenzo's gravesite:

> Soon she turn'd up a soiled glove, whereon
>   Her silk had play'd in purple phantasies,

She kiss'd it with a lip more chill than stone,
  And put it in her bosom, where it dries
And freezes utterly unto the bone
  Those dainties made to still an infant's cries.
                                        (369–74)

A lover's passion ("purple phantasies") uncomfortably serves as prelude to the image of mother and child, as if Keats were unwilling to abandon completely the female as lover, even in such strained circumstances. It is an image so foreign to both Keats and Isabella that the word *breast* is not even used, but is awkwardly replaced by degendered "dainties," a term usually used for food in the poetry, such as the "spiced dainties" of "The Eve of St. Agnes" (269). Coldness and emptiness permeate the lines—the "slippery blisses" of Endymion have become a kiss "with a lip more chill than stone." All life, including the nurturance of the "dainties" that are "made to still an infant's cries," is frozen, making even the mother and dead child relationship between Isabella and Lorenzo a tentative one. The soiled glove is now forever devoid of life and the possibility of being further soiled, and it is the discovery of Lorenzo's lifeless body that begins the process of Isabella's transformation.

Isabella is accompanied in this transition from lover to perverse mother, which begins at the gravesite, by her nurse, a figure who appears only in this scene. The nurse's role is traditionally a parental one, and she at first offers motherly remonstrations ("What feverous hectic flame / Burns in thee, child?— What good can thee betide, / That thou should'st smile again?" [348–50]), but finally aids in the exhumation of Lorenzo's body, the rite of passage that will change Isabella from child to woman:[2]

That old nurse stood beside her wondering,
  Until her heart felt pity to the core
At sight of such a dismal labouring,
  And so she kneeled, with her locks all hoar,
And put her lean hands to the horrid thing:
  Three hours they labour'd at this travail sore.
                                        (377–82)

Lorenzo's head becomes Isabella's "prize," her own reward, but, unlike Endymion's reward, the prize will not ensure immortality, and as she carries it off with her from the gravesite, the transformation from lover to mother is complete, and the nurse, no longer necessary to Isabella's identity because Isabella is no longer a child, disappears from the poem:

> In anxious secrecy they took it home,
>   And then the prize was all for Isabel:
> She calm'd its wild hair with a golden comb,
>   And all around each eye's sepulchral cell
> Pointed each fringed lash.
>
> (401–5)

Lorenzo's "wild hair" connotes an image of madness and foreshadows Isabella's own condition at the poem's end. While he has been saved from his lack of masculine identity by death, it is Isabella who will suffer the consequences. To the romantic poets, madness is itself a form of escape, and is an especially romantic trope when it occurs in the female, as she seems naturally to overflow with already acute emotion.[3] But madness is a condition that is uncontrollable by the female as well as the male, and, as it is a state of exacerbated emotion, it is, in the female, both terrifying and sensual to the male.

In his "Ode to the West Wind," Shelley writes of "the bright hair uplifted from the head / Of some fierce Maenad" (20–21), a "frenzied woman," who, as follower of Dionysus, went mad and often murdered for the god. In his "Dear Reynolds, as last night I lay in bed," Keats speaks of "a beauteous woman's large blue eyes / Gone mad through olden songs and poesies" (53–54). A woman's madness symbolizes an intensification of the passion that women already ideally possess, and separates her even further from the male. Like an aberration of nature, a woman's madness is both beautiful and terrifying. Isabella's irrational behavior that begins with the acquisition of the severed head changes the cold gravesite image into one that again depicts this passionate ideal:

With duller steel than the Perséan sword
  They cut away no formless monster's head,
But one, whose gentleness did well accord
  With death, as life. The ancient harps have said,
Love never dies, but lives, immortal Lord:
  If Love impersonate was ever dead,
Pale Isabella kiss'd it, and low moan'd.
'Twas love; cold,—dead indeed, but not dethroned.
                                                    (393–400)

Isabella kisses the head and breathes back into it not life, as both fairy tales and Keats's previous poetry would recount it, but love—"dead indeed, but not dethroned." Because this is a poem about the mortal rather than immortal state, Isabella's kisses do not have the same effect on the masculine as Cynthia's did for Endymion. The fairy-tale imagery and the happy ending of *Endymion* have no place in "Isabella." While she cannot bring back life, though, Isabella can, through her memory of the live Lorenzo, reanimate love.

Even before Lorenzo's death, however, Isabella's existence is not a happy one, a fact that is continuously reiterated. Ward points out that a "string of images of medicine and disease run through the poem like a dark vein through marble" (174). Early stanzas characterize both lovers as experiencing, through their passion for one another, "some malady" (4), a "sick longing" (23), and a "sad plight" (25)—language that not only describes the futility of their love, when one desires infancy and the other the complete transference of herself as mother, but also prefigures events to come when both get what they seek. There is no "divine" pain when love is shared by mortals; nor is there a comforting present—all comfort must be achieved, as Isabella so willingly does, through memory of the past.

Sickness and death characterize Isabella's identity in much the same way as they do Keats's. Lorenzo's death changes Isabella from lover to mother to madwoman; Keats's mother's illness and early death changed the young boy to an unhappy nurse and a desperate orphan. In a letter to Bailey, Keats attributes his intolerance and suspicions of women to his having

been "disappointed since Boyhood" (*Letters* 1:341). Waldoff
sees this attitude as one directly related to Keats's mother:

> Because this comment about a disappointment felt
> since boyhood is made in the context of a passage con-
> cerning his attitude toward women, it would be diffi-
> cult not to think that it refers in some way to his
> mother. . . . We do not know . . . whether the sense of
> disappointment first arose as part of his earliest, pre-
> oedipal relationship with his mother, or out of later oe-
> dipal and sibling rivalry, or because of her remarriage
> soon after his father's death . . . or because of her
> seeming abandonment of him and the other children
> when the second marriage failed, or because of her
> death, or, indeed, because of some combination of all
> of these. (29)

Despite all that Waldoff admits we do not know, we do know
that somehow, perhaps from what Keats saw lacking in his own
mother, a maternal ideal was formed in his poetry, an ideal
from the antitype that became prototype to the poetry's fe-
males, elucidated most poignantly in the later works that re-
nounce the mortal female for the invulnerable goddesses of
the two "Hyperions." There will be no effective mortal mothers
in Keats's poetry. All maternal love and guidance will originate
with the goddesses. Perhaps because of his childhood "disap-
pointment," Keats's poetry would find no deserved intensity
and passion toward the mortal maternal figure. While Isabella's
maternity remains a perversion, the goddesses (already begun
with Cynthia) will demand and receive full maternal power to
the male. In "Isabella," however, there is simply "nothing to be
intense upon" (*Letters* 1:192). Both passion and the masculine
identity, equally lost almost from the beginning of the poem,
have surrendered to a female who derives life from memories
rather than from sexuality. Eroticism becomes perversion, as a
maternal ideal is reached without the prerequisite sexual activ-
ity, and all female passion is bestowed on a lifeless head that
becomes a deviant child/object.

For whatever reason, Keats did not like "Isabella." Several

months after writing it, he called it a " 'weak-sided Poem' with
an amusing sober-sadness about it" (*Letters* 2:174). In truth,
however, there is nothing "amusing" about the poem. Rather,
there are a starkness and overplayed sense of doom in its
language regarding death's intervention between lovers that
seem to betray Keats's own intense feelings about the equal
desperation produced by both love and death. The poem is the
first of two to evoke a solitary, solipsistic female, a role generally
held in reserve for the abandoned male hero.[4]

In one of his own poignant letters to Fanny Brawne, Keats
quotes from "Isabella" in order to express his own desperation
at being in love:

> In my present state of Health I feel too much sepa-
> rated from you and could almost speak to you in the
> words of Lorenzo's ghost to Isabella
>
>> Your beauty grows upon me and I feel
>> A greater love through all my essence steal.
>
> My greatest torment since I have known you has
> been the fear of you being a little inclined to the Cres-
> sid; but that suspicion I dismiss utterly and remain
> happy in the surety of your Love, which I assure you
> is as much a wonder to me as a delight. (*Letters* 2:256)

Chaucer's Cressida, whose betrayal of Troilus ultimately causes
his death, may be the archetypal female in Keats's private life,
as his own childlike dependence on Fanny Brawne illustrates,
but the women of his poetry, with a few notable exceptions,
such as the mysterious la belle dame sans merci, deny this
image of feminine betrayal. His works seek to enforce the male-
derived pleasures of the passionate female in her dual role as
lover and mother with as little of the accompanying pain as
possible.

And in the present poem, even after Lorenzo's death, Isa-
bella does not betray him. Instead, she literally gives up her life
for him, becoming for Lorenzo what Keats believed he never
had himself—the consummate mother: caring, protective, and

passionate to the point of madness, best delineated by an image
of the mother bird:

> For seldom did she go to chapel-shrift,
>   And seldom felt she any hunger-pain;
> And when she left, she hurried back, as swift
>   As bird on wing to breast its eggs again;
> And, patient as a hen-bird, sat her there
> Beside her basil, weeping through her hair.
>   (467–72)

The ghost of Lorenzo that Keats speaks of to Fanny Brawne
and with which he feels empathy because of his "present state
of Health," is the one indication of life beyond mortality in the
poem. Lorenzo, who could not become animated while alive, is
given another chance through his appearance to Isabella as a
vision:

> In the drowsy gloom,
>   The dull of midnight, at her couch's foot
> Lorenzo stood, and wept: the forest tomb
>   Had marr'd his glossy hair which once could shoot
> Lustre into the sun, and put cold doom
>   Upon his lips, and taken the soft lute
> From his lorn voice, and past his loamed ears
> Had made a miry channel for his tears.
>   (273–80)

Lorenzo speaks directly to Isabella, but it is a ghost that articu-
lates the words: "Go, shed one tear upon my heather bloom, /
And it shall comfort me within the tomb" (303–4). The ghost
of the dead Lorenzo asks for the same tears that the living
Lorenzo vowed to drink, and the reader recognizes an uncom-
fortable pairing of mortal with immortal, similar in type to the
unions that will dominate most of Keats's later poetry. The
difference here, though, is the female represents the mortal
half of the pair rather than the male. It is she, therefore, who
is vulnerable and will be ultimately abandoned and destroyed.
Keats is not yet able to depict the presiding female as invulnera-

ble, which the later females, through their immortality, will become.[5]

Dorothy Van Ghent refers to Isabella (and Madeline to come) as representatives of the "pure, chaste, and maidenly image of ideal love" that exists in all the early poetry (56). Certainly this is true of Isabella at the poem's beginning and end, but not here, at the appearance of Lorenzo's ghost. The power of this episode lies more in what Jeffrey Baker calls the "vividly expressed interrelationship between the beauty and the horror" (15). The meeting between Isabella and the ghost of her lover does indeed mingle beauty with horror, and is, as Praz calls it, a theme of "tormented, contaminated beauty," an inseparability that is "one of the chief exponents of Romantic sensibility" (28). The poem tries to rid Isabella of her maidenly status through the introduction of the unsettling sight and voice of Lorenzo's ghost, and it is Isabella's protean ability to abandon her identity as maiden that, temporarily at least, saves her. At the poem's end, though, Isabella is once again vulnerable and thus maidenly because her strength of transformation, along with her sanity, has deserted her.

Unlike Endymion, Isabella cannot wish away death (or mortality), but she can overcome some of the inevitable suffering by invoking a portion of the power of invulnerability through the change in her identity, a transformative feminine trait that is characteristically given an abundance of space in literature written by men. Most of the time the transformation at least increases the odds for the woman's survival; in Isabella's case, though, mortality has already eliminated all chances for survival, and her ability to transform to accommodate her present surroundings simply forestalls the inevitable.

Lorenzo's ghost says to Isabella, "thou art distant in humanity" (312), a statement that is ultimately not true. Because of Isabella's abandonment of her identity as the shy maiden, she becomes the aggressor in their relationship after Lorenzo's death, a role Lorenzo was incapable of in life. So through death there is an intimacy between the lovers that had been absent in life, made evident by the words spoken between them during the ghost's appearance, possible now only because of Isabella's new identity as well as Lorenzo's. The intimacy is irretrievably shattered, however, when, in essence, Lorenzo dies a second time to Isabella when her brothers steal the head and she goes mad:

> Piteous she look'd on dead and senseless things,
>   Asking for her lost basil amorously;
> And with melodious chuckle in the strings
>   Of her lorn voice, she oftentimes would cry
> After the pilgrim in his wanderings,
>   To ask him where her basil was.
>
> (489–94)

Isabella's ruin is finally one that cannot be averted by the only option of comfort available to mortals—religion.[6] "The pilgrim in his wanderings" can offer no solace, nor can the "dead and senseless things" that Isabella attempts to substitute for her lost basil, and she dies "forlorn" (497), a word always associated in Keats's poetry with the acknowledged impotence of the mortal state, as in the later nightingale ode.

II

As in "Isabella," images of death permeate "The Eve of St. Agnes," written in January 1819.[7] Coldness recurs throughout the poem and its setting, ending only in the warmth of Madeline's bedchamber, where the moon casts "warm gules on Madeline's fair breast" (218). Warmth is an integral part of the female in this poem, and is in danger of being destroyed by the surrounding cold. The female's role as lover now dominates nature and her own environment, a major step in the process of her evolution since the early maidens were allowed only identities that, chameleonlike, changed with the surroundings in which they tangentially existed.

The primary contrast in "St. Agnes," a poem full of contrasts, is that of life and death, characterized by the opposition of the lovers' warmth with their surrounding coldness. "The sculptur'd dead [that] seem to freeze, / Emprison'd in black, purgatorial rails" (14–15) situated at the poem's opening represent the

ever-present agents of death that surround Madeline and the
maze that Porphyro must successfully pass through in order to
find her. Unlike "Isabella," though, "St. Agnes" contains very
few images of sickness; while the former poem opens with a
portrait of the living who suffer and then die, "St. Agnes"
begins in a world that is already dead, thus invoking the process
of creation for the poet:

> St. Agnes' Eve—Ah, bitter chill it was!
> The owl, for all his feathers, was a-cold;
> The hare limp'd trembling through the frozen grass,
> And silent was the flock in woolly fold:
> Numb were the Beadsman's fingers, while he told
> His rosary, and while his frosted breath,
> Like pious incense from a censer old,
> Seem'd taking flight for heaven, without a death,
> Past the sweet Virgin's picture, while his prayer he saith.
>   (1–9)

The coldness produced by this portrait of death-in-life is ac-
companied by the mute silence of a frozen, static nature, and,
except for Porphyro later, by a lack of vision as well, always a
harbinger of pain for Keats's characters. In order to fulfill the
ritual of St. Agnes' Eve whereby she may see her future hus-
band in a dream, Madeline must not see anything else, thus
setting the stage for the upcoming delusion.

The poem's deathly environment and the personae's ensuing
inability to see probably derive from the underlying myth itself,
from which the title comes, of Agnes's virginity and subsequent
execution. Condemned to be debauched before the execution,
her virginity (but not her life) was miraculously saved through
the intervention of heaven. Agnes's parents later saw her as a
vision of an angel with a white lamb by her side, proof of
her intact virginity beyond life—both an immortal ideal and a
sexual *memento mori*, as frequently exemplified in the works of
the cavalier poets of the seventeenth century.

On the eve of the day of her observance, January 20, young
women practice what may be termed trancelike rites to envision
images of their own future husbands. They become, like En-

dymion, "tranced vassal[s]" (*Endymion* 3.460), but the idea of
attempted rape leading to the love and affections of a husband
is a difficult connection to understand, and must have been for
Keats as well, precipitating the poem's ambiguities to come. As
sexual love is symbolic of the creative powers of the imagina-
tion, rape is perversion and thus stifling to those powers. There-
fore vision, as both precedent to and the result of the imagina-
tion, is absent in this poem, along with life itself in the opening.
Passion does not exist in Madeline's castle outside her bedroom,
and before there can be any vision, sexual passion itself must
be created from the dearth of life that surrounds and inhabits
the castle.

Like the ghostly and visionless Beadsman, Madeline must
neither "look behind, nor sideways, but require / Of heaven
with upward eyes" (53–54); a captive of the ritual, she "danc'd
along with vague, regardless eyes" (64). The eyes of the castle
guests are "muffled" as Porphyro enters (83), and the nurse
Angela leads Porphyro to Madeline's bedroom to hide him "in a
closet, of such privacy / That he might see her beauty unespied"
(165–66). Vision is uncommunicative and one-sided here be-
longing only to Porphyro, and so it cannot as of yet be creative;
it is instead voyeurism, in which Porphyro is an "observer . . .
posted by chance or choice at the perimeter of a voluptuous
sexual scene, to which he plays Peeping Tom" (Paglia 189).[8]
Because there is no shared vision involved here to elucidate
the process of creation, Porphyro's voyeurism from Madeline's
closet, is, like the story within the original myth, a form of
rape—it is intrusive and demands unconsciousness on the part
of the woman. While titillating and bawdy, it is not passionate.

To Keats, the ability to see is analogous to the ability to know,
and it is this knowledge that is in danger of being lost in "St.
Agnes." Porphyro must not only awaken Madeline to conscious-
ness, he must restore her passion and her own vision as well.
It is a strangely aberrant role for Keats's males, but, as the
only character to live outside the castle and, thus, outside the
religious ceremony that has caused the blindness, he is the only
one in the poem capable of such restoration. His role is similar
to that of Amor's to the sleeping Psyche, the female who awak-

ens to the passion of falling in love with Love. It is a peculiarly aggressive role for Keats's heroes to take on, especially since they will again be characterized as a series of "voyeurs" in the poems to follow, especially the odes. But Porphyro is not the nameless male who will become the observer in the odes. His name is a derivative of the Greek word for purple, "porphura," a color that always denotes either passion, wine, or sensuality in Keats's poetry. And, according to Lemprière, Porphyry, "a man of universal information," not only "applied himself to the study of magic," but, in his most famous work, argued against Christianity. For this, Lemprière says, "he has been universally called the greatest enemy which the Christian religion had" (556).[9] Thus Porphyro's identity combines the powerful elements of magic and passion, the only time in Keats's poetry that these attributes are part of the male rather than the female character, probably because of the strangely anti-erotic myth of intact virginity that the female is a part of here. Like Apuleius's Amor and Psyche, the lovers will create their own myth of discovered passion.

But first Porphyro, an obvious descendent of "the greatest enemy" of Christianity, must rid Madeline of the religious ceremony that threatens to overpower her. "The sculptur'd dead" decorate her castle. "Carved angels, ever eager-eyed" (34), "carven imag'ries" (209), "twilight saints, and dim emblazonings," and "A shielded scutcheon blush'd with blood of queens and kings" (215–16) surround her. All passion belongs to the castle's predecessors; all life is frozen in the past. She parallels the lifeless statuary herself as, in a "wakeful swoon,"

> perplex'd she lay,
> Until the poppied warmth of sleep oppress'd
> Her soothed limbs, and soul fatigued away;
> Flown, like a thought, until the morrow-day;
> Blissfully haven'd both from joy and pain;
> Clasp'd like a missal where swart Paynims pray;
> Blinded alike from sunshine and from rain,
> As though a rose should shut, and be a bud again.
>   (236–43)

The sleep of "Sleep and Poetry," which had been the source of more visions "than a high romance" (10), is gone, only to be replaced by sleep that "oppress[es]" with a "poppied warmth." It is a lack of consciousness that defines sleep in this poem, and Madeline's soul, the barometer of the imaginative state, is "fatigued away." All of her senses, like those of the "sculptur'd dead," are in danger of being lost. "Blinded," her sleep is a deathly trance rather than a catalyst to visions.

Porphyro, too, momentarily takes on the characteristics of the statuary as he sinks to his knees, "pale as smooth-sculptured stone" at Madeline's awakening (297). The voyeur is in danger of being caught, his singular vision being destroyed, and, in awe of both the possibility and the sight, cloaks himself in the protection of lifelessness. The danger represented here by the occasional death-in-life postures experienced within the castle is at any moment the castle could become a tomb to the lovers, just as it has already become to the Beadsman, who, without imagination, lives in a perpetual entranced state, blind to all that occurs around him, obfuscated by the religious rituals he performs. Like Endymion at the nadir of his search for identity, in which he kisses his own hand, the Beadsman, through a ritual that does not include passion for the living, is dangerously solipsistic. And eventually, just as the earth will become a tomb to Saturn and Thea in "Hyperion" to follow, the Titans "postured motionless, / Like natural sculpture" (1.85–86), the Beadsman, frozen into stasis by his participation in the ritual, will be "entombed" in the castle through his denial of the reality outside of it. The opening stanza, which introduces the Beadsman, contains more images of coldness than any other in the poem—the numbness that has settled within his fingers threatens, by virtue of its precedence, to spread into the rest of the poem as well.

Madeline and the Beadsman are essentially identical at the poem's opening in their zealous adherence to the religious ceremony that is at the center of the story. Madeline's name, rich in religious overtones, connotes an obsessive piety that is antithetical to life. Her spectral attitude as well as her virginity aligns her to the saint whose holiday she observes, but, as Keats

repeatedly emphasizes, Madeline is not a saint, she is simply a
mortal maiden "full of this whim" (55), and the castle, decorated
with relics of the past and the dead, could more appropriately
become her tomb rather than the shrine to marriage she hopes
it to be.

Porphyro's passion that counteracts the cold ceremony
comes "like a full-blown rose, / Flushing his brow, and in his
pained heart / Made purple riot" (136–38). His feminine char-
acteristics will empower Porphyro to overcome the sacred and
inviolable persons and events frozen in time, the lineage that
creates the barriers to Madeline. Like the barriers to Keats's
own poetic imagination, Porphyro must rid Madeline of the
"predecessors" that haunt her. He must awaken Madeline from
her sleep "in laps of legends old" (135) and replace her supersti-
tions with magic.

To do so, Porphyro appears at Madeline's bedside in a man-
ner reminiscent of Lorenzo's appearance to Isabella as a vision.
While Isabella's vision gave her courage and transformed her
identity, however, Madeline's is a source of fear:

> Her eyes were open, but she still beheld,
> Now wide awake, the vision of her sleep:
> *There was a painful change*, that nigh expell'd
> The blisses of her dream so pure and deep:
> At which fair Madeline began to weep,
> And moan forth witless words with many a sigh;
> While still her gaze on Porphyro would keep;
> Who knelt, with joined hands and piteous eye,
> Fearing to move or speak, she look'd so dreamingly.
> (298–306, my italics)

The "painful change" that Madeline experiences, unlike En-
dymion's "unlook'd for change" by which he becomes "spiritu-
aliz'd," threatens to expel the "blisses of her dream" rather than
turn them into the putatively desired reality. Like the speaker
of the nightingale ode to come, Madeline is afraid of being
"toll[ed] back" from her dream to her "sole self" ("Nightingale"
72), to mortality, by the appearance of Porphyro. Thus she

attempts to transform the very alive Porphyro standing before her into a spirit, not unlike the "sculptur'd dead" of the castle:

> "Ah, Porphyro!" said she, "but even now
> Thy voice was at sweet tremble in mine ear,
> Made tuneable with every sweetest vow;
> And those sad eyes were spiritual and clear:
> How chang'd thou art! how pallid, chill, and drear!
> Give me that voice again, my Porphyro,
> Those looks immortal, those complainings dear!"
>
> (307–13)

Believing in the power of her dream and being oblivious to anything outside of it, Madeline refuses to accept Porphyro's presence as anything more than a vision she created through religious ritual, whose looks are "immortal," and whose eyes, like her own, are "spiritual and clear." The lines that follow hers emphatically denounce this spiritualized description of Porphyro, however:

> Beyond a mortal man impassion'd far
> At these voluptuous accents, he arose,
> Ethereal, flush'd, and like a throbbing star
> Seen mid the sapphire heaven's deep repose;
> Into her dream he melted.
>
> (316–20)

Carnal terms such as "impassion'd," "voluptuous," and "flush'd" replace Madeline's deific adjectives. Porphyro melts into her dream, always sexually connotative to Keats, but not as Madeline had hoped. Rather, his very mortal passion causes the dream to dissipate. But gone, too, are the superstitions and legends that had haunted her, blinded her to the life around her, finally forcing her to become little more than a ghost herself, as she believes Porphyro to be. Her dreams involve no passion, only cold ritual.[10] Thus Madeline's sleep, like the sleep of the poetry to come, is one that oppresses rather than transcends, and her dreams, the product of superstition rather than of imagination, offer no comfort.[11]

The very real Porphyro is not a conjured vision, though, and thus the sexual act is more akin to rape than to the visionary experience both Keats and Madeline seek. The gender roles of the lovers are curiously reversed in this poem, as noted in Porphyro's passionate identity. But beyond his emotional association with the female, reversal occurs in that virtually every other major poem in which sex takes place portrays the female as the seducer or pursuer of the male, whether the end result is favorable or not. It is the female's intractable passion that ensnares the male. Yet here sex is enforced rather than seductive because passion must be created by the male rather than the female in this poem of cold ceremony. In Madeline's idiom, the dream, originating in an "oppressive" sleep, becomes both obstacle to and grander than the passion itself. Like the archetypal prince of fairy tales, Porphyro will awaken the sleeping princess to her own undiscovered passion. Unlike the fairy tales, however, the process of awakening ends with more than a kiss.

Another myth underlies the poem—one that, like the myth of St. Agnes, is graphic in its delineation of sexual cruelty toward women. The story of Philomela, the virgin who was raped by Tereus, king of Thrace, exists within the fringes of the poem's events—in the various mention of birds and, most specifically, in the "tongueless nightingale" that Philomela became.[12] The metaphor is iterated in the description of Madeline, whose "heart was voluble" (204), as she prepares for bed under Porphyro's espial:

> Paining with eloquence her balmy side;
> As though a tongueless nightingale should swell
> Her throat in vain, and die, heart-stifled, in her dell.
> (205–7)

The nightingale's plaintive song, to be given life in the great ode, can find no voice here. She is, like the early maidens, mute and defenseless. The rape of Philomela, like that of Madeline, threatens to destroy the passion that should be inherent in the act of sex, and only the creation of myth can restore it. Likewise,

"music's golden tongue" (20) beckons the Beadsman early in
the poem, but he heeds it not, for his passion has long ago been
spent and the "joys of all his life were said and sung" (23).

The "eloquence" and passion struggling to emerge in Made-
line, as elucidated in the desperately mute images of Philomela,
will finally occur not through sex, but through its oral analogy,
food—the Keatsian luxury that sometimes "gives place to the
luxury of sex" (Ricks 123). The "luxury" of sexuality is obvi-
ously lacking in this poem, despite the use of "melted" to de-
scribe the sexual act. How to make what is clearly rape, even to
the sensibilities of the nineteenth-century male, sensual instead
is Keats's problem, so true sensuality occurs before and after the
sexual encounter—in the form of a table spread with delicacies.

Paglia comments that "the most brilliantly written part of the
poem is when the male reverses sexual convention and feeds
the female. Keats's language suddenly intensifies into a sensual
cascade of ripe nouns and adjectives. The poem turns cornuco-
pia" (383):

> [Porphyro] from forth the closet brought a heap
> Of candied apple, quince, and plum, and gourd;
> With jellies soother than the creamy curd,
> And lucent syrops, tinct with cinnamon;
> Manna and dates, in argosy transferr'd
> From Fez; and spiced dainties, every one,
> From silken Samarcand to cedar'd Lebanon.
>   (264–70)

The passive voyeur becomes an active seducer in these lines, as
Porphyro brings the food from the closet where he has hidden.
Although the food is never consumed, it is the prelude to the
myth that occurs at the poem's end, and the oral gratification
of which it is capable makes Madeline's enforced initiation into
sex, from the male perspective, somewhat less terrorizing. The
table overflows with sensual delights for the mouth making the
actual sex that follows of secondary importance. Levinson says
of Porphyro's supper as initiation into sex (that the dream itself
is supposed to be): "As a dramatic representation, the scene [of

the food] not only postpones the union of hero and heroine, it absorbs much of the interest and energy which properly attends that union" (*Allegory* 149). It is certainly desirable to Keats that interest in the "union," when it is an enforced one, be diverted.

Much debate has focused on the poem's ending—is it a "happy" one? Does Keats approve of the lovers' actions, or does the ambiguity that envelops them in the final stanzas cast doubt on their survival?

It is clear to me that the only means of survival for Madeline and Porphyro lie outside the castle through the myth that is developed at the end.[13] Nothing will prevent the lovers from escaping because in the castle "was heard no human sound" (356). Silence pervades, and no human agency either helps or hinders the fleeing lovers. They are now beyond the need or control of the human because, in fleeing the castle, they have become elements of the imagination—ethereal, immortal, and beyond temporal boundaries.

At the poem's end, the power of the supernatural inter-venes—an intervention that strongly suggests Keats consciously introduces the idea of magic in order to oppose it to the sinister specter of superstition that permeates much of the poem. Magic is genuinely spiritual and transcendent because it is the product of imagination, found in the "charm'd magic casements" of the nightingale ode (69), a realm that will not admit mortality. And the lovers "glide, like phantoms, into the wide hall; / Like phantoms, to the iron porch, they glide" (361–62). Twice Keats calls them "phantoms," twice they "glide" to the freedom of myth that exists outside the castle. And Porphyro will transport Madeline to his home "o'er the southern moors" (351), a geo-graphic direction that connotes warmth, and thereby life.

It is an escape into a higher knowledge that Madeline and Porphyro experience when they flee the castle. Like them, Keats is at the threshold of such knowledge. The lovers have gone "ages long ago" (370). The imaginative realm in which they will now exist, invulnerable to human sorrow, is the same world of the nightingale, but in this early poem it allows entry to the mortal. At this point in his career, in fact, such entry was not only possible to Keats, it was necessary.

After the starkness and brutality of "Isabella," Keats will not allow another female to suffer such unrequited passion. With "St. Agnes," he distances himself not only from "Isabella," but from all poems of unmitigated mortality. While both "Isabella" and "The Eve of St. Agnes" portray females who, by virtue of their mortality, are "cheated"—Isabella by Lorenzo's death, Madeline by her self-imposed deathlike state—only Madeline is saved. It is becoming increasingly difficult for Keats to write poems that portray the female as mortal, as shown in the next, and last, poem about a maiden of vulnerable mortality.

III

"The Eve of St. Mark" depicts yet another "poor cheated soul" (69), Bertha, in a poem that fully incorporates and extends the coldness and silence of the two previous works of mortality.

Critics have collectively ignored this fragment. Evert calls it an " 'occasional' poem, resulting from a mood, either immediate or induced. When the mood passed, or its materials were used up, composition stopped; hence, the question of purpose or significance hardly enters in" (302). The unfinished poem's significance to this study, however, is indeed a direct result of a "mood," but that mood is anything but trivial. Keats was in the same mood when he produced "Isabella" and "The Eve of St. Agnes," and although the mood did eventually pass, it left in its wake the only three major poems to portray a mortal female as the central figure and subject.

Although Keats himself refers to the poem as "a little thing" (*Letters* 2:62), it is more than coincidental that Bertha, willingly shut up in her small room, cut off from the life of the small town outside, bears a striking resemblance to her immediate predecessor, Madeline, before the arrival of Porphyro. Keats's "mood" here is one that again, as in "Isabella" and "St. Agnes," starkly questions the wisdom of attempting to control the imagination through romantic narratives that require the female, the representative of the poetic imagination and thus personification of an often overwhelming passion, to be mortal.

Written between February 13 and 17, 1819, immediately

following "St. Agnes," the poem's completion was always in
doubt to Keats, as he says to his brother and sister-in-law:

> Some time since I began a Poem call'd ["]the Eve of
> St. Mark["] quite in the spirit of Town quietude. I
> th[i]nk it will give you the sensation of walking about
> an old county Town in a coolish evening. I know not
> yet whether I shall ever finish it—I will give it far as I
> have gone. (*Letters* 2:201)

It may have been a "detested mood" that precipitated the
writing of "St. Mark," like that of "Isabella" ("Dear Reynolds"
111), but whatever his attitude at the time, even Keats believed
that the mood might not last long enough to finish the poem,
as the above lines show.

The fragment depicts "a maiden fair" (39) whose only activity
is reading, an act akin in its solitude to Madeline's obsessive
praying. Again, as in both *Endymion* and "St. Agnes," the solitary
state is accentuated until it becomes solipsistic:

> A curious volume, patch'd and torn,
> That all day long, from earliest morn,
> Had taken captive her two eyes
> Among its golden broideries;
> Perplex'd her with a thousand things—
> The stars of heaven, and angels' wings,
> Martyrs in a fiery blaze,
> Azure saints mid silver rays,
> Aaron's breastplate, and the seven
> Candlesticks John saw in heaven,
> The winged Lion of St. Mark,
> And the Covenantal Ark,
> With its many mysteries,
> Cherubim and golden mice.
>
>   (25–38)

Like the walls and windows of Madeline's castle, the images in
Bertha's book threaten to overtake her. Representing people
and things that no longer or never did exist, the images lead
Bertha to a "perplex'd" state because they can no more replace

life than Madeline's icons could. As in "St. Agnes," vision is
conspicuously absent in this poem. Bertha's eyes have been
"taken captive" by the curious book. Bertha is finally "dazed
with saintly imageries" (27, 56), just as Madeline had been
dazed by the ritual. Like her predecessor, Bertha is "hood-
wink'd with faery fancy" ("St. Agnes" 70).

Bertha, too, has a "vision" of sorts, like both Isabella and
Madeline—her own shadow, as it "in uneasy guise / Hover'd
about, a giant size" (73–74). Just as Keats sees the products of
the imagination as distinct from the mind, Bertha's shadow
becomes an entity distinct from her body:

> Untired she read; her shadow still
> Glower'd about as it would fill
> The room with wildest forms and shades,
> As though some ghostly queens of spades
> Had come to mock behind her back,
> And dance, and ruffle their garments black.
>   (83–88)

The shadow is "some ghostly queens of spades" to Bertha,
and Bertha is, in effect, haunted by herself, as the shadow
adopts all the attributes of a ghost. The apparent absence of
passion from her life makes it impossible for Bertha to see a
vision of a dead lover, as Isabella did, or of one very much
alive, as Madeline's. Bertha's ghostly shadow would possibly
have been a precursor to the spirits reportedly seen to leave
the church on St. Mark's Eve had Keats finished the poem, but
as it is, the shadow, in its "giant size," serves only to envelop all
of Bertha's room as a settling fog, or, more appropriately, a
shroud:

> On ceiling beam and old oak chair,
> The parrot's cage and pannel square,
> And the warm angled winter screen,
> On which were many monsters seen,
> Call'd doves of Siam, Lima mice,
> And legless birds of paradise,

Macaw, and tender av'davat,
And silken furr'd Angora cat.
(75–82)

The cataloging here is not like the cataloging that occurred in the early bower poetry, of the pleasures of nature; rather, the lists contained in the poems in which mortality is the subject are of legends and superstitions and domesticated nature objectified and enclosed in dark rooms. Bertha's shadow threatens to overtake her and all within her room in the same way that her vision has been seductively overpowered by the fantasies of her book. As in "St. Agnes," the female who is both repository and an embodiment of masculine identity and desire has shut herself off from the passion and life that create them.

Again Keats portrays a solitary female made even more so by her abject willingness to separate herself from the world. At the poem's center, Death takes the form of "saintly imageries" and "martyrs in a fiery blaze," and Bertha's room, twice described as "silent" and full of "gloom," is like a tomb where she seems buried alive.

At this point, it would be easy to contend, as some critics have, that, closed up in her room, Bertha's turning her back on the life around her is an undesirable act of negation, punishable by the threat of imminent death, as it had been for Madeline. A closer look at the setting reveals this not to be the case, however. As similar as they may at first appear to be thematically, an important difference exists between "The Eve of St. Mark" and the previous two poems, one that is especially obvious between this and "St. Agnes," for not only is Bertha's room, like Madeline's castle, reminiscent of a tomb, but, in "St. Mark" life is profoundly absent outside the room as well. Bertha lives in the Minster Square, whose name derives from the Latin monastery and is used today to denote a monastery church. Thus while Madeline only slept in the "lap of legends" (135), Bertha literally lives at the very center of religious ritual. And her window offers no escape, no "southern moors" toward which to flee—but simply other inhabitants of the square who, like Bertha, are immersed in their own silent rituals:

> Twice holy was the Sabbath bell:
> The silent streets were crowded well
> With staid and pious companies,
> Warm from their fireside orat'ries,
> And moving with demurest air
> To even song and vesper prayer.
> Each arched porch and entry low
> Was fill'd with patient folk and slow,
> With whispers hush and shuffling feet,
> While play'd the organs loud and sweet.
>   (13–22)

The rituals of religion are "moral torture" here, "inflicted in imagination upon the believer" (Praz 107). All creativity is absent, as the square's citizens form "staid and pious companies," and the Beadsman's "pious incense" of "St. Agnes" is personified through them. The silence that permeated Madeline's castle now characterizes both Minster Square and life itself, with the female at the center of the silence.

The view from Bertha's fireside (the single image of warmth in the poem) provides only "rich antiquity, / Far as the bishop's garden wall" (42–43) and crows, the feathered representatives of death, "gone to rest, / Each in its ancient belfry nest" (63–64). Levinson writes that the irresolution of fragmentary poetry "signifies the rejection of a mean, mechanical success. . . . [It] originates in the author's determination to realize an objective and . . . terminates with that realization" (*Fragment* 210). What Keats ultimately intended to do with the poem will never be known, but the existing fragment clearly depicts not simply another young woman who has become a willing participant in lifeless ritual, but a whole town that has. The "objective" is realized, but, like the creation of Apollo at the end of "Hyperion," there is simply no way the poet can take such a scenario any further.

Stillinger comments on what he sees as a "romantic remoteness from the everyday reality outside Bertha's room" (*Hoodwinking* 96). Indeed the remoteness is reality in itself to Bertha, and the only romance she is capable of enjoying in Minster Square is found in her "curious volume," the book of death and martyrs, and in the fantasy therein that functions as both her captor and her only means of escape from her surroundings:

> At length her constant eyelids come
> Upon the fervent martyrdom;
> Then lastly to his holy shrine,
> Exalt amid the tapers' shine
> At Venice.
>
> (115–19)

The only magic found in the poem is what Bertha's own imagination provides, through her reading. Finally transported by her imagination away from her room and the town, "her constant eyelids" arrive at the shrine of St. Mark, "exalt amid the tapers' shine / At Venice." What we may discern regarding Bertha's sense of romance is only that she cannot accept the reality that exists outside her room, one that offers only specious escape. Bertha is thus "cheated" not only by her romantic illusions, but also by her reality. So a fragment of only 119 lines that begins in a small town's streets ends "at Venice," Bertha's own "southern moors" ("St. Agnes" 351).

Various reasons have been suggested by critics for the unfinished condition of the poem, the most common being Walter Jackson Bate's contention that Keats simply was no longer interested in legends (456). Yet one of his most famous (and controversial) poems to come, "La Belle Dame sans Merci," will be based on legend, and virtually every major poem after "St. Mark" will come from the legends of mythology. Thus this argument cannot be considered reason enough for Keats's abandonment of the poem, an abandonment that he himself predicted in the previously noted letter to George and Georgiana.

Rather, the poet's lack of interest in Bertha and her "old county Town" probably has much to do with the direction that Keats's imagination will now take—away from female figures of mortality and toward those of immortality exclusively, capable of the transcendence and resistance to mutability that Keats sought for his work. This is the last poem to concentrate on a mortal female. The sonnet "Bright star, would I were stedfast as thou art," probably written after "St. Mark," introduces Keats's thematic concerns to come, that of a mortal male who seeks immortality through his lover, "still stedfast, still unchangeable" (9) like the star itself, a theme reminiscent of *Endymion*, but, unlike the early rendition, not so easily attainable in the works to come:

> Pillow'd upon my fair love's ripening breast,
> To feel for ever its soft swell and fall,
>   Awake for ever in a sweet unrest,
> Still, still to hear her tender-taken breath,
> And so live ever—or else swoon to death.
>
> ("Bright Star" 10–14)

These lines give a more plausible reason for Keats's failed interest in finishing "St. Mark." The doomed state of mortality threatens to destroy not only the female but the male, who, through her passion that can only be a part of her immortality, wishes to "live ever—or else swoon to death." The female must be strong enough to invest the male with his own identity. And in the poems to follow, Keats will pursue the immortality that allows women such strength, culminating in Moneta's "wan face / Not pin'd by human sorrows" (1.256–57). The "human sorrows" of the present poems will not be wholly obliterated, however, but will be transferred from the female to the male personae, associated with the poet himself who seeks the salvation offered by the female. By shifting the burden of mortality onto the male, the poetry will become what Keats now demands it to be—a means by which the poet may find both identity and immutability. The only poem that does not adhere to this new pattern completely, "Lamia," will allow the female a "borrowed" mortality, and will end in disaster for the male. But with the poems of the next chapter—"Hyperion" and "La Belle Dame sans Merci"—the quest by the male for the permanence he can find through the female is frighteningly advanced.

4

"Ripe Progress" and "Horrid Warning"
The Goddesses of "Hyperion" and "La Belle Dame sans Merci"

I

With little flourish, the mortals of the previous chapter, the females who could not offer transcendence to the male poet, are abandoned and replaced with the deities of "Hyperion" who acquire, as Waldoff calls it, "statuesque poses of mourning" (203).[1] With "Hyperion," mourning becomes part of the process of change. The sorrow that led to Isabella's destruction in the most mortal of Keats's poems leads here to a new era of cyclical permanence with the introduction of Mnemosyne and the new order of female personae, figures who will eventually become, at the end of the process, the subject of "To Autumn," who celebrates rather than mourns the earth.

While Isabella's suffering for the dead Lorenzo produced neither change nor transcendence but only allowed a glimpse of the past, the Titans' imminent extinction and subsequent suffering provide glimpses of the future—the new golden era of the Olympians that, allegedly, will eliminate all suffering because it will eliminate death.

The "sculptur'd dead" of "The Eve of St. Agnes" become the grieving Titans, "postured motionless, / Like natural sculpture in cathedral cavern" (1.85–86), magnificently frozen in their inability to transcend their situation. They are Keats's last poetic gasp of mortality before the odes move toward denying it completely. A new era is about to supersede the outdated Titans just as a new era of poetry lies in wait for Keats—one which, like the Olympians themselves, abandons the realm of mortality for permanence through immortality. While the Titans are themselves deities, their permanence, like that of Glaucus in *Endymion,* is threatened, making them more similar to mortals than immortals, and change is imminent.

As commonly noted by critics, "Hyperion" is a poem that seeks and questions identity. In September 1818, shortly before he began the poem, Keats wrote the letter previously noted about his ailing brother, Tom: "His identity presses upon me so all day . . . that I live now in a continual fever" (*Letters* 1:369). Like Keats, the Titans suffer from their own "pressing" identities, heavy with the weight of imminent annihilation, and seek identities removed from mortality and death. But they are not the Olympians, and transcendence is futilely sought in the midst of their own fall, a descent not into mortality, however, for they already possess what Van Ghent calls the "angst of mortality, . . . enduring the contradictions of fear and hope, dreams of serenity and dignity and fruitful function, and realities of bitter agony, impotence, and death" (218). Saturn is aged and gray-haired at the poem's opening; eternity is not being displaced by the transience of mortality, as in the Fall of Genesis. Rather, age is being superseded by youth, darkness by light, death by a life that involves no "contradictions."[2]

Keats now turns to the "abstractions" of "Hyperion," as he defines the first of his new order of poetry (*Letters* 1:370), a term that indicates a less assured, more probing imagination than that which informed the poems that precede this one. The death that haunted Isabella, Madeline, and Bertha will now, with mythopoeic gesture, be eliminated by a group of youthful gods led by Apollo, whose "white soft temples," "golden tresses" (3.122, 131), and in a canceled line, his "hue more roseate than sweet-pain," sharply contrast to the "gray-hair'd Saturn, quiet as a stone" (1.4).[3] In a bleak portrait that makes him as ineffectual as the early dormant maidens, Saturn is uncharacteristically mute.

"But cannot I create?" asks the doomed Saturn. "Cannot I form? Cannot I fashion forth / Another world, another universe, / To overbear and crumble this to nought?" (1.141–44). Saturn's anxiety is Keats's, and the litany of questions, as Saturn

faces the approaching death of his giant race and Keats faces
the approaching death of Tom, attempts to evoke the identity
both the character and the poet seek. Saturn struggles against
loss of his own identity just as Keats struggles to lose the "press-
ing" identity of the dying Tom, in order to achieve what Keats
will call the "poetical Character," the "no-self" that will define
his poetry. The masculine identity that Keats's heroes seek is
distinct from the "poetical Character" that the poet seeks. While
masculinity is comforting because it is so dissimilar to the fe-
male, it is not creative. All creativity will come from the andro-
gyne of the "no-self," the "camelion poet," who neither seeks
nor accepts masculinity.

Because he laments the loss of masculine power, the answer
to Saturn's plea is negative. He has "gone / Away from [his]
own bosom" and has left "[his] strong identity, [his] *real self*"
(1.112–14, my italics). The poet, who for Keats is capable of
fashioning "another universe" (as the character Saturn wishes
to do), has no "real self" to leave but is instead always "filling
some other Body" (*Letters* 1:387). Thus the only character in
"Hyperion" who is truly "poetical," in Keats's dictum, is not the
anxiety-ridden Saturn, but Mnemosyne, the one figure within
the poem to accommodate her own identity to that of the new
order of Olympians.

Mnemosyne's traditional role as mother of the Muses creates
an intriguing link in Keats's search for a new female and poetic
identity, for hers is a maternal as well as a lover's role, and both
create the identities of others. Thus the female continues to
serve as lover but, at the same time, acquires a new and second-
ary maternal role as well. This dual identity allows Mnemosyne
to oversee the "loveliness new born" of Apollo's godhood while
remaining the source of the apotheosis. Mnemosyne is not
bound to the earth as Keats's mortal females were, despite the
extinction of her Titan race that hovers in the background of
this poem, and therefore she embodies the contrary states Keats
sees as necessary to the creative mind. Beth Lau points out that
the goddess's role here, as the goddess of memory, "signifies a
poetry based on experience of life and knowledge of human
history" (328) that Keats will now pursue. With Mnemosyne,

Keats comes the closest yet to finding the poetry that explores the "human heart" that his poems of 1817 deemed necessary. It is a program of humanity that finds no solace yet in the human, however.

Ross contends that the completed narrative poems all concern the quest for love, while the narrative fragments, including "Hyperion" (but excluding "St. Mark," which is too much a fragment to define), focus on the quest for power. This distinction, Ross suggests, helps show "the way in which patriarchal culture always attempts to heal a fissure that it necessarily inflicts within itself" ("Fragmented Word" 114). The fragmented patriarchal culture that is the setting of "Hyperion" cannot be made whole by the masculine figure. Trapped in his Lear-like stubbornness and pride that inform his masculinity, Saturn has lost the ability to create because he has lost (or has never had) the Negative Capability inherent in the capacity for change that the females do.[4] But Mnemosyne, as figure of the "camelion poet," has "forsaken old and sacred thrones / For prophecies of [Apollo], and for the sake / Of loveliness new born" (3.77–79), and thus assumes creative power. In her maternal, procreative capabilities, she represents evolution; in her ability to create new identity, she represents revolution and the cyclic change that informs the whole poem. Thus Mnemosyne is the "poetical Character" precisely as Keats defines it—protean, chameleon, "every thing and nothing" (*Letters* 1:386–87).

Mnemosyne appears in "Hyperion" for the first time in the midst of images of old age and death. As one who imbues others with identity rather than receiving it, she seems to rise like a vapor, oblivious to her surroundings or to the presence of other figures or objects:

> Mnemosyne was straying in the world;
> Far from her moon had Phoebe wandered;
> And many else were free to roam abroad,
> But for the main, here found they covert drear.
> Scarce images of life, one here, one there,
> Lay vast and edgeways; like a dismal cirque
> Of Druid stones, upon a forlorn moor,

When the chill rain begins at shut of eve,
In dull November, and their chancel vault,
The heaven itself, is blinded throughout night.
                                    (2.29–38)

Images of life are "scarce" at Mnemosyne's arrival; even heaven
is compared to a "chancel vault." Loss of identity in the Titans'
world is loss of direction—Mnemosyne seems as forlorn as
Saturn at this point. The earth, too, poses an unnatural specter
in these lines—Phoebe has wandered from her moon, leaving
heaven "blinded." The Titans' own lost identity is replicated
within nature itself, chaos threatens, and Mnemosyne, the only
Titan capable of change, must restore the grandeur. At the
center of both the grandeur and the destruction is, according
to Ross, the "conflict between the demand for patrilineal per-
formance of language and the desire for a liberated use of
language that frustrates Keats" ("Fragmented Word" 121).

Restoration can occur only through the feminine, through
Mnemosyne as memory, for "remember" can effectively be
termed the opposite of "*dis*member," and the Titans' fragmen-
tation, in their attempt to hold onto their "patrilineage" results
in their own inevitable "dismemberment." From memory
spring the healing muses, the source of all poetic identity. Like
Wordsworth, Keats will increasingly discover salvation through
memory, tentatively but disappointingly begun in "Isabella."

Apollo reads "names, deeds, gray legends, dire events, rebel-
lions, / Majesties, sovran voices, agonies, / Creations and destroy-
ings" (3.114–16) in Mnemosyne's "silent face." The god who su-
persedes the Titans will know and begin to internalize their
history through the figure destined to give him life and identity.
Keats is creating a symbol here, through the embryonic begin-
nings of Apollo's godhood, but "the making of emblems and the
selection of parts to stand for the whole involves the forgetting
of that whole" (Simpson 75). Thus all knowledge will be a part of
Apollo rather than of the giant race who inspire it.

Just as Bertha found knowledge through the imaginative
process of her "curious volume" ("St. Mark" 25), Apollo finds
a "wondrous lesson" (3.112) in the face of the goddess. While

Bertha's legends are reduced to superstitions, however, Apollo's are those that poetry is made of—"creations and destroyings"—the knowledge that deifies rather than merely "perplexes." But the legends of both Bertha and Apollo seek the same end—to escape reality, to "die into life."

As Levinson writes, though, "Hyperion" ultimately "dissolves into a preliminary study, meaningful only in relation to the achieved work [of 'The Fall of Hyperion']" (*Fragment* 169). Mnemosyne's undeveloped identity, in the dangerous presence of the "patrilineage" of both Titans and Olympians that threatens to subvert her fluidity and compels her to remain mute for much of her appearance in the poem, is one of the reasons, I believe, that Keats left "Hyperion" unfinished. The "achieved work" that will ensue is not only "The Fall," but the supreme figure of Moneta. No longer created from the depths of Keats's obsessive search for masculine identity, Moneta will be not only the "finished" Mnemosyne, but the origin of the androgynous figure of "To Autumn." Mnemosyne cannot solve Apollo's dilemma, nor even offer advice, as Moneta will to the dreamer. In this fragmentary portrait of her the feminine power of the goddess figure is not yet fully realized. She can only give Apollo mute scenes of the past, the "names, deeds, gray legends," that are passively stored within her. Ross comments that the "narrative aborts itself because it has nowhere else to go. It has reached the limits of discourse as we have 'fathered' it, and as it reaches for that new knowledge just beyond the old, it trails off into muteness" ("Fragmented Word" 128).

Keats depicts Mnemosyne's power as a passive one, despite her immortality, because of his growing uncertainty toward the imagination and the new creative role, beyond the "limits of discourse," that it plays in his poetry. The goddess seems less powerful than, as the first immortal since the very effectual Cynthia, she has reason to be. Her relative silence extends to the end of the poem, however, when, in the scene of Apollo's deification, she "upheld / Her arms as one who prophesied" (3.133–34), but it is Apollo, not she, who "shriek'd" (135). Mnemosyne's power as creator here may be compared to that of Mother Nature who, as Margaret Homans says, "is hardly

powerless, but, enormous as her powers are, they are not the
ones that her daughters want if they are to become poets . . .
because [they stem] from what she is, not from what she does"
(16).[5] While Keats does not yet know what to do with Mnemo-
syne's parthenogenetic power, it is essential to his own search
for a new, less androcentric language. The problem here is that
the goddess's muteness aligns her more with the early maidens
rather than with the goddesses to come; it is indeed intrinsic to
"what she is" rather than "what she does," and the god of
masculine endeavors, Apollo, is childlike in his own mute de-
pendence on her, and thus from his birth, is ultimately as
passive as she.

The relative passivity of Mnemosyne and Apollo throughout
most of Book 3 is essential to the poem's meaning in two ways.
The first is their obvious contrast to the Titans. Static and
unable to transcend, the Titans are suffering a living death,
but are not at all passive. Frightened by the coming usurpation,
they rage against it—a rage that is impotent from the start,
however, for the same reason that the passivity of Mnemosyne
and Apollo is so very powerful; that is, while the Titans rage
hopelessly against the inevitability of death, the new Olympian
order reverses the cycle and, from death, effortlessly creates
life. As the first major poem to succeed those concentrating on
mortality, the emphasis of "Hyperion" remains focused on the
struggle, within a dying world, to achieve permanence rather
than on its actual achievement. The poem depicts a painful
cycle of death and birth but not the life to follow. Its completion
will be enacted in the poems to come, but will no longer focus
on the burgeoning Apollo or on the power of passivity in the
midst of impotent rage. Passivity will no longer be a part of the
female, but will be transferred to the mortal male, and will
define his vulnerability to her.

Apollo's deification is his own escape from the nightmare
that traps the Titans as well as its source, and Mnemosyne's
traditional dual nature as mother and lover allows her to be
both creator and facilitator of the apotheosis because "that
which is creative must create itself" (*Letters* 1:374), a uroboric
axiom that aligns the creation of identity with the inherently

female role of procreation, and one that will find ultimate verification in "To Autumn."[6] Such circularity corresponds not only with the protean nature of Mnemosyne, but with the structure of the entire poem. The fallen Saturn cannot create—not only because he does not have the procreative powers of the goddess, but primarily because the new order of Olympians represent "an unaccustomed set of values by which Saturn feels threatened, because he lacks the negative capability which would allow him to absorb them" (Hirst 93). Mnemosyne, on the other hand, represents the poetical character itself, more passive at this stage in Keats's career than it will be, and adapts because she creates rather than possesses identity. The "creations and destroyings" that Apollo reads in her face provide not only his deification, but the cyclical purpose to the structure of the poem, as the new order destroys in order to create.

The poem opens "deep in the shady sadness of a vale / Far sunken from the healthy breath of morn" (1.1–2), an archetypally female image far from the masculine heaven of Apollo. Saturn sits in darkness, "far from the fiery noon" (3), and death is the only intrusion:

> No stir of air was there,
> Not so much life as on a summer's day
> Robs not one light seed from the feather'd grass,
> But where the dead leaf fell, there did it rest.
> A stream went voiceless by, still deadened more
> By reason of his fallen divinity
> Spreading a shade.
>   (1.7–13)

"The dead leaf fell, there did it rest"—stark presentiment of the Titans' own unmitigated death. The vale's "shady sadness" of the opening line becomes, at the end of the passage, Saturn's own "shade." The healing feminine earth of the poems of 1817 has become a burial ground, absorbing the grief of the Titans and life is, as Helen Vendler calls it, "a 'posthumous' existence" (198).[7] Death is placed at the center of change and becomes a perverse catalyst to a dreaded revolution rather than the finality.

The poem seemingly travels away from this scene of death, however, in a linear ascension to the final word, "celestial," in Book 3 (136). Apollo's "dying into life" reverses the traditional process of death, and the feminine earth that has become a "pathetic fallacy" to the Titans is replaced by Apollo's masculine heaven, free of the limiting emotions of mortality. This linear movement from earth to heaven, death to life, is more apparent than real, though, for movement within the poem is not one that ascends, but rather, elliptically, turns with the implicit promise of return, as Oceanus makes clear to the Titans: "as thou wast not the first of powers, / So art thou not the last; it cannot be: / Thou art not the beginning nor the end" (2.188–90). The god invokes the power of mourning as a persistent part of the cycle of change, a cycle that will ultimately defeat the new order as well:

> 'Tis the eternal law
> That first in beauty should be first in might:
> Yea, by that law, another race may drive
> Our conquerors to mourn as we do now.
> (2.228–31)

The cycle within "Hyperion" is one of "ripe progress" (1.125), a fitting way to describe the "ripening" of Keats's poetics as well. The fall of one order to the other is as natural as what will occur in "To Autumn" because it elucidates a part of the cycle that, in turn, creates immortality, thereby "creating itself." The poem presents a "gradual progress of consciousness" that will become less gradual in the odes (Dickstein 200). And Keats's predecessor, Spenser, from whom he derives inclusion in the "patrilineage," and to whom Keats himself turned, puts the "progress of consciousness" this way: "still moving, yet unmoved," he writes, in his own work of ripe progress, the "Mutability Cantos": "all things [turn] to themselves at length againe" (7.7.6). Thus the primary action of "Hyperion" is not merely creation, but, more precisely, procreation—the feminine ability to recreate oneself, to become "every thing and nothing" through the poetical character. Mnemosyne is both mother and midwife to Apollo's birth into godhood:

> During the pain Mnemosyne upheld
> Her arms as one who prophesied.—At length
> Apollo shriek'd;—and lo! from all his limbs
> Celestial.
>
> (3.133–36)

"Hyperion" must end with the female because it began with her—the earth, the vestige of all the mortal females of the previous poems. Like the "southern moors" that replaced Madeline's cold castle at the end of "St. Agnes" and the vision of Venice that emerged from Bertha's passionless room in "St. Mark," the female has ascended to new meaning here, and the "shady sadness" of the earth, at the poem's beginning, becomes, at its end, "celestial." Although heaven is traditionally a masculine metaphor, the "ripe progress" of "Hyperion" redefines the image to refer to the passive and puerile Apollo Keats has created, dependent on the fluid female for life. Paglia calls Keats's sun god "a Hellenistic Apollo melting into Aphrodite" (386). The androgyny that characterizes Apollo is the first step in the direction of change from the old order and the most obvious recognition in the poetry thus far of the identity that can only be achieved through the female.

With the introduction of Mnemosyne, all female figures will characterize an imagination that apotheosizes the ideal of permanence but, at the same time, virtually disregards the birth of Apollo. Now Keats will invoke single females who consistently embody the polarities between which the imagination travels. Mnemosyne will eventually become Moneta, fierce rather than benign in her wisdom, but many figures will appear before then. The next poem, "La Belle Dame sans Merci," contains the most frightening figure of all, and a profoundly bizarre denouement to the fragmentary "Hyperion."

II

Drafted in a letter to George and Georgiana Keats on April 21, 1819, near the time of "Hyperion's" abandonment, "La Belle Dame sans Merci" again forces the question of masculine identity to a point of solipsism and rigidity, the same state of negation that had preceded Endymion's deification, but presents this time a female who, unlike Cynthia, deprives rather than creates. The theme of lost identity of the fragmentary yet lengthy "Hyperion," which could offer no life after Apollo's birth, is locked into a miniature portrait of the life that emerges from such loss of masculine identity that is frighteningly complete in only forty-eight lines.

The unnamed maidens of the volume of 1817, the later females of ineffectual mortality, and the benign goddesses are displaced in this poem by another "new order"—the female who destroys by emasculation. The sexuality of love is reduced to base carnality in this new relationship between mortal and immortal, or, as Karen Chase defines such a reduction, "from a divinity to an instinct" (1). The transformation of the female, by virtue of the changing imagination, turns the dream icon, once a metaphor of escape, into a stagnant nightmare here—Keats's only ballad among his major poems. Perhaps Keats was attracted to this form because of the plaintiveness inherent in its lyrical simplicity. Whatever the reason for the choice, the poem is the most haunting and elusive of all in its stark and anti-imaginative simplicity, producing the most damning portrait of the female.

The knight-at-arms' dream, a familiar vehicle of transformation in Keats's poetry, is not the same here as Adam's, Endymion's, or even Madeline's—no "finer tone" of spiritual repetition is realized on awakening. Neither woman nor music—the two symbols of escape to Keats—appears as a result of the dream. In fact, no music exists at all within the poem, except for the "fairy's song" (24) that the lady sings, music that, like the ideal that now inspires it, will prove a sham. "And no birds sing," a statement of loss reiterated at the beginning and end of the poem (4, 48). The loss is of an ideal—Circe replaces Cynthia as symbol of the imagination, and heaven becomes as "specious" as Glaucus himself had discovered it to be. Winter is approaching, the "squirrel's granary is full, / And the harvest's done" (7–8). It is a pathetic scene of endings rather than creations, and loss is the poem's raison d'être.

The frigid landscape reflects the change in attitude now evinced toward the imagination for the "sedge has wither'd from the lake" (3), an immeasurable distance from the mythopoeic setting of *Endymion*. A profusion of life existed in the former poem that celebrated creation, but the landscape of "La Belle Dame," like the poem's language, is stark, compressed into one desolate image of loss. The setting is the final extension of that depicted in the opening of "Hyperion," where Saturn sat "far sunken from the healthy breath of morn" (2), and the "voiceless" stream was "still deadened more" (11). There is no need for voice in the present poem because the knight-at-arms can merely reiterate the events that have befallen him rather than change them. Voicelessness, in both the knight and the lady, subsumes the poem. The silence of "Hyperion" that awaits impending doom becomes the embodiment of its aftermath here.

Keats's most frightening and sexually barren language occurs in this first poem to concentrate on lust rather than strive for its ideal counterpart of love. The "pale" kings and princes, all predecessors and successors of each other and representative of the knight's own "patrilineage," are robbed of life and identity and gape with "starv'd lips" (41) and "horrid warning" (42). Sexual union, once transcendent, has become the ultimate destruction, leaving the male immolated by the female, deprived of a masculine past as well as a present.

Just as Keats seeks to control the imagination, the knight seeks in vain to control the lady when she first appears. In purely erotic terms, the knight's experience actualizes Keats's own expressed fear of loss of control in the earlier epistle to Reynolds, but it is the knight himself rather than the imagination who becomes "lost in a sort of purgatory blind" ("Dear Reynolds" 80) through his attempts at control and ownership of her:

> I made a garland for her head,
>   And bracelets too, and fragrant zone;
> She look'd at me as she did love,
>   And made sweet moan.

> I set her on my pacing steed,
>   And nothing else saw all day long,
> For sidelong would she bend and sing
>   A fairy's song.
>   ("La Belle Dame" 17–24)

With the garlands of flowers that he wraps around her head and wrists, the knight attempts to restrict the lady's movements, to keep her in his purview and thus dispel her mystery and delineate her as simply his lover, compelling her to concentrate physically only on him. The knight wants to make the lady a part of his own, very narrow identity. His actions are, in effect, Keats's attempts to join the benign females of 1817 with the new Apollonian ideal. But this unnamed female, the first since the unnamed maidens of 1817, is not of the earth, and all attempts at control by a mortal, even a knightly one, are doomed. The garland itself becomes an antitype to the crown of laurel that represents poetry, as it is a symbol of destruction rather than creation here, and the knight, instead of the lady, as he wishes her to do, loses identity. Like Saturn before him, he cannot cope with the loss.

The sense of loss is made even more acute in the text of the poem that appeared in *The Indicator*, May 10, 1820. In this version, as well as in a copy that John Jeffrey possessed, "apparently [one of] the first rough copies" (Keats, *Works* 441), the first and fifth lines introduce and reiterate not a knight-at-arms but a "wretched wight." Thus the knight's "wretchedness," the source of which unravels with his telling the tale, is clearly established at the opening, becoming the defining characteristic of his identity and thereby eliminating the irony of his being a knight-at-arms from the beginning. The wretched state of the knight is immediately discernible in the earlier version, giving the reader insight into the mysterious lady even before her story unfolds.[8] In that version wretchedness precedes and accompanies the knight's tale of infatuation and perverted love, thus framing the entire poem in human rather than the earthly desolation in which it is now framed. The present version, Karen Swann suggests, "de-centers" the lady because we do not immediately know the reason for the knight's malaise. Swann suggests that the lady's function in the present text is to be a " 'lure,' not simply for the knight, but for the reader" (84).

The closeness that the lady lures the knight into believing they possess is certainly a parody of the emotional and physical distance necessary to the ideal of courtly love that disallows actual sexual activity, the requisite ideal for not only the knight but for his predecessors, the "pale" kings and princes, too, since the putative era in which the poem is set is a medieval one. Love for a woman from afar, with no opportunity (or actual desire) either to possess or control her, seems to be the scenario that is perverted here. When the politic distance is removed, the inherent dangers to the male become clear.

But the knight has lost his vision as well as his health, and his description of the courtship, as recounted by Swann, "realizes a familiar plot whose main character is the Ideal Woman and whose dynamics are a happily asymmetrical reciprocity: his active capture of the fairy lady brings about her passive, reflective response of 'love' together with its domestic signs—meals, sexual favors, lullabies" (88). This is indeed a "familiar plot" to Keats's poetry—and the last time we encountered it was in Cynthia's relationship with Endymion. Both escape and male identity were easily achieved through the domesticated nature of the female then, but the Ideal Woman has become the Fatal Woman, and the distinction between them can only be blurred by the male's loss of vision.

Thus the autonomy acquired by Endymion through his love for Cynthia and eventual abandonment of the earth becomes a deadly and irreparable solipsism here, when the knight attempts the same through the woman he believes to be ideal. No gain follows the knight's loss, no new identity, because the female's own identity is suspect. All that is known to the knight about the lady is that she is "full beautiful, a fairy's child" he postulates (14), and that her hair "was long, her foot was light, / And her eyes were wild" (15–16).[9] Once he goes through the actual and recognizable physical realities of her beauty, long hair and light foot, he gives the lady attributes that are more identified with masculine fantasies than with reality: as a "fairy's

child," she has "wild" eyes. Because her identity remains un-
known and inaccessible to him, the knight embellishes, perhaps
to boost his own sense of patriarchal control over her. But
neither fantasy nor sexual union, both of which previously
guaranteed transcendence, can repair the destruction that is
the outcome of this relationship. While Keats believes he is
losing power over his ability to create, his heroes lose not only
their power over the female, but the ability to perceive her
correctly.

Although Endymion's initial physical union with Cynthia
also produced a loss, it was the loss of Cynthia only, a type of
felix culpa that became the catalyst to Endymion's quest to
achieve permanence. The knight's loss, however, is character-
ized by an irreparable schism between reality and himself, a
loss not only of vision, initially, but finally of himself. Unlike
the theme of earlier poems, no quest is produced by the loss
here—rather, the stasis of immobility supersedes all desire for
change.

Traditionally emblematic of knighthood, the quest becomes
a "sojourn," and the knight describes himself as "palely loiter-
ing" (46). Stuart Curran writes that Keats "knowingly creates
the impasse by juxtaposing a knight's duty to act against the
uncertainties of his fantasy life" (182). Such a dilemma would
certainly produce the unknightly "loitering," and it is the same
dilemma that faces the poet himself—his "duty" to create is at
an impasse with his own uncertainties over the imagination.
The resolution can only come about through denial of iden-
tity—that of both knight's and poet's. The chivalric ideals of the
early poems, exemplified in the other knightly figure, Calidore,
were concerned with earthly values and are supplanted here
by an ideal that forsakes rather than apotheosizes the earth.
The "leafy luxury" is no longer operating on any level in this
poem, whose setting, like the knight's identity, is barren.

Schapiro comments that "La Belle Dame sans Merci" evokes
"the experience of oral deprivation," for having fed the knight
on "sweets and relishes," feeding also his conception of the
Ideal Woman, the elusive lady leaves him as she has left others,
with "starv'd lips" (41), the same lips that had before "shut

[the lady's] wild wild eyes / With kisses four" (31–32).[10] Unlike Mnemosyne, whose maternal powers created a childlike Apollo, la belle dame makes men cognizant of the frightening future of mortality rather than the comfortable past, as they become the walking dead, bereft of any identity they possessed in life. La belle dame is not only a castrating lover, but a "withdrawing and denying mother" (33).

In the letter in which Keats introduces the poem, he describes the acquisition of identity in the same maternal terms:

> Not merely is the Heart a Hornbook, It is the Minds Bible, it is the Minds experience, *it is the teat from which the Mind or intelligence sucks its identity*—As various as the Lives of Men are—so various become their souls, and thus does God make individual beings, Souls, Identical Souls of the sparks of his own essence—This appears to me a faint sketch of a system of Salvation which does not affront our reason and humanity. (*Letters* 2:103, my italics)

As these lines show, the masculine identity received from the maternal process of creation is an integral part of Keats's own "system of Salvation," a system most profoundly experienced, thus far, in the relationship between Mnemosyne and Apollo. The oral deprivation that Schapiro correctly claims to exist at the center of "La Belle Dame sans Merci" is more than a loss of the maternal—it is, in Keats's idiom, a loss of salvation.

With no hope of salvation, love with la belle dame leads to a state of torpor, existing, like the lady herself, somewhere between life and death. The inscrutable belle dame will survive, but, like the Grecian urn to come, it is a survival contingent on the deaths of those around her. Devoid of the promise of salvation, these deaths offer no finality—only an eternal sickness similar to the "life-in-death" undergone by the Ancient Mariner (2.193), the ultimate romantic portrait of the loss of salvation, who is condemned to a life of reiteration rather than creation too by retelling the events that befell him to strangers, as the knight does here to the disembodied voice that opens the poem.[11] The questioner possesses the voice that the knight has lost to the mysterious lady, but his own proximity to the knight is threatening, so his appearance ends with his initial recognition of the knight's diseased condition. Thus, the knight seemingly recounts the events that have led to his destruction in a vacuum.

As in "Isabella," images of disease run through this poem, beginning with the knight's own "continual fever . . . poisonous to life" (*Letters* 1:369) that he, like Keats, must live through. The questioner notices the diseased state:

> I see a lily on thy brow
>   With anguish moist and fever dew,
> And on thy cheeks a fading rose
>   Fast withereth too.
>
>   (9–12)

The knight fitfully exists at the center of the dichotomy between la belle dame's appearance and her reality. She has infected him but, to his horror, he will survive. His survival will be that of a chronic invalid, however, the result of his trying to control the ethereal female through mortal and patriarchal means.

The images of sickness culminate in one that characterizes Keats's attitude toward the imagination now:

> I saw pale kings, and princes too,
>   Pale warriors, death pale were they all;
> They cried—"La belle dame sans merci
>   Hath thee in thrall!"
>
>   (37–40)

Swann characterizes this deathly male lineage as "accession to a community of poetic masters, . . . perhaps the 'shapes of epic greatness' that haunted" the young Keats's dreams as well (92). They, like Keats himself, have been taunted and teased and finally emasculated by the voracious muse. The "horrid warning" from their own "starv'd lips" will become Moneta's warning to the dreamer in "The Fall," but here it comes too late, so their own "anguish moist and fever dew" is passed on to the knight.

Levinson points out that "theirs is not a state of contradiction, like the knight's, but one of nullity: men of power, impotent, statesmen unstated. Possessing themselves so completely, they possess, in effect, nothing" (*Allegory* 75), Keats's own fear regarding his creativity. Despite his own barren condition, the knight continues to exist within a vortex of contradictions. Unlike his predecessors, the knight is not allowed a "nullity" but exists within a waking dream, and, like the Ancient Mariner, is condemned to be a *memento mori* to both the questioner and the poet, who both seem, by their inability to save him, to be one and the same.

The apparent dual and contradictory nature of the mysterious lady—her beauty that becomes specious with the recognition of her reality that comes too late for the knight—evokes a corresponding duality of emotions within the male lover. Both attracted to and repelled by her, a state of impotence devoid of any direction is produced, similar to that of the Titans and, most important to Keats, fatal to the act of creation. It is a state that corresponds with Keats's own growing uncertainties and projects his struggle to control, and yet abandon himself to, the poetic imagination.

"La Belle Dame sans Merci" is a crucial poem not only for the mystery it poses but, more important, for the discoveries it makes. Keats completely abandons the "leafy luxury" of the earth, and, from the depths of his uncertainties over the new direction pursued, uncovers a female (and an imagination) who shows no compassion for what she destroys. The poet who once committed himself to poetry whose "great end" is to "be a friend / To sooth the cares, and lift the thoughts of man" ("Sleep and Poetry" 245–47) cannot long endure such lack of sympathy. In the odes to follow, the uncertainties become the vehicle for change, as the plaintive ballad gives way to a form of dramatic poetry that seeks comfort beyond lamentation. The female becomes an integral part not only of the mystery but of the resolution, as the control over the imagination that Keats seeks will be progressively regained through female symbols who gradually become demonstratively less threatening than la belle dame. Never again will the female be a mute part of the earth, but, equally important to the evolution of the imagination, neither will she again reach the destructive nadir of "La Belle Dame sans Merci."

With the introduction of Psyche, in the first of the great odes, Keats abandons his own role as the male who vainly seeks control at the cost of destruction, and steps back to his former role as passive observer, wounded by the enthralling experience of la belle dame. In the odes, the poet-lover changes his demands into questions, and the finest poetry of all emerges from the new relationship.

5
The Odes and Keats's "Branched Thoughts"

Following the defeat of all attempts at permanence by la belle dame, who proved destructive to both the poet and his knight, Keats presents his greatest variation on the theme of feminine identity in the odes of 1819 and, consequently, introduces the most enigmatic group of females to date.[1] They exist not only as symbols of the reconciliatory yet immutable imagination toward which Keats aspires, but as symbols that repeatedly "fade" throughout the series of poems beyond the poet's grasp, they are emblematic of the essence of mutability as well, the very state that Keats wishes to escape through them. As "happy, happy dove" ("To Psyche"), "light-winged Dryad" ("Nightingale"), "cold Pastoral" ("Grecian Urn"), a "beauty that must die" ("Melancholy"), or the "maiden most unmeek" ("Indolence"), the female of the odes first beckons and then frustrates the poet, creating the greatest schism so far between his imagination and himself. Like la belle dame to the knight-at-arms, the females of the odes finally become the poet's own *memento mori*, compelling him both to recognize and accept the mutability that he attempts to flee.

Each ode signifies a new attempt at resolution, precipitated by the destruction caused by la belle dame. The odes are an attempt to dilute the mysterious female's power by modifying it into five separate symbols that, unlike their terrifying predecessor, do not totally abandon the earth. In the end, though, there is still no satisfactory resolution for Keats, and the poet becomes one of Melancholy's "cloudy trophies" (30), not unlike the woebegone knight-at-arms, who, held in thrall by la belle dame, became her own trophy as well.

The hold over the male that the female is capable of becomes by degrees the only relationship that the speaker of the odes is able to have with the female. Content to observe the goddess Psyche in the first ode, his vision restored, and by his "own eyes inspired" (43), he is eventually drawn into and held by the "peerless eyes" of the female (20) in the "Ode on Melancholy." In these crucial poems that delineate the relationship between desire and identity, the female becomes as elusive and irresolute as the imaginative dilemma posed. Because she "cannot cheat so well / As she is fam'd to do" ("Nightingale" 73–74), and as the poet continues to ask her, she compels the speaker to confront the dilemma, and becomes, in an ode of oxymoronic proportions, his "demon Poesy" ("Indolence" 30). In this series of desultory thoughts and fitful starts, the female inheres the speaker's doubt as a part of her own inconstancy. As object of the speaker's search for poetic identity through immortality in each poem she becomes, at the end of each, the personification of his failure. With the increasingly uncertain status of the female, the male's own status as poet becomes precariously undefined. As neither the maidens of "Calidore" nor la belle dame, the females of the odes embody neither the distinct pleasure nor absolute pain encountered by the male speakers of those poems, respectively. Each present female is, in her inability either to satisfy or destroy, a portrait of the male's frustration over direction.

As neither savior nor destroyer, the females of the odes cannot sustain or eradicate the poetic identity sought. As a group, they provide an experimental testing ground for the direction Keats now seeks for the imagination—one in which both the poet and his imagination could become mired in irresolution.

Despite the lack of resolution achieved, however, the odes constitute a crucial link between the previous poems that aspire to forsake the Dionysian imagination for the Apollonian, and those to come, beginning with "Lamia," which seek to fuse the two realms, again uncomfortably forcing both into a single female. But in the odes the Apollonian is tempered by the poet's consistent recognition of the earth, one that is not yet synonymous with complete acceptance, but is nonetheless unavoidable. The nightingale, for example, is not a true immortal, but a "dryad," a "semi-goddess," as Lemprière calls her, "whose life and power terminated with the existence of the tree over which [she was] supposed to reside" (242). It is a frustration of direction that informs the odes, a recognition of failure that is expressed in a single word in the nightingale ode—"Forlorn!"—an expression that, like Waldoff's interpretation of the Keatsian "O!," implies both a loss and the consciousness of that loss.

Because of the new and tentative attempts made toward resolution in each of the odes, the series must be discussed more in terms of the differences between them rather than the similarities.[2] Each is a discrete example of the openness Keats saw as necessary to the poetic mind, "a thoroughfare for all thoughts" (*Letters* 2:213), the masculine desire for the feminine quality of changeability. The various approaches of the odes are a bid to regain the poetic equilibrium lost when Keats took the imagination "beyond its proper bound" in the destructive figure of la belle dame, who would not change. The first ode will involve a successful attempt at poetically restoring a fallen deity (Psyche), an example of, temporarily at least, restoring the imagination's "proper bound."

I

With the "Ode to Psyche," the process of reparation through the act of remembering, begun with the mourning of the Titans, continues. The attempt in this ode is not only toward regaining a "faded hierarchy" (25), but specifically toward restoring the beneficent female that once populated the poetry.

Written almost simultaneously with "La Belle Dame sans Merci," in the latter part of April 1819, the ode seems to be a conscious attempt on Keats's part to repair the damage done by the "fairy's child," to recapture the knight's lost soul along with the ability to achieve identity through sexual union once again. Pain suffered at the hands of a female can only be relieved through another female, and through Psyche, the poet seeks to restore the relationship between the female and himself, thereby restoring identity.

It is also a restoration of myth that Keats seeks as well—the deliverance of the female from the barren landscape of la belle dame back to the bowers of the poetry of 1817 and *Endymion*. He is "reconsecrating mythology for poetry [through a] myth too late-born to seem central otherwise" (Hollander 68). If successful, the attempt will again define both poet and imagination as sacred. The poet seeks amelioration through the only goddess capable of restoring a lost soul—Psyche, a personification of the soul itself.

Perhaps this is the reason, despite the ode's obvious textual difficulties, for Keats's letter to George and Georgiana upon its completion denying its complexities:

> The following Poem—the last I have written is the
> first and the only one with which I have taken even
> moderate pains—I have for the most part dash'd of[f]
> my lines in a hurry—This I have done leisurely—I
> think it reads the more richly for it and will I hope en-
> courage me to write other thing[s] in even a more
> peaceable and healthy spirit. (*Letters* 2:105–6)

The poet of "La Belle Dame sans Merci" must discover a "more peaceable and healthy spirit." And to Keats, to whom the female is, alternately, salvation and damnation, the only way to regain such spirit is to restore her role as savior.[3] Thus the "Ode to Psyche" restores not only a fallen goddess, but goes a long way toward restoring the imagination as a healing power.

The relationship between the poet and Psyche is, through this restoration, a procreative one, like that of Mnemosyne and Apollo. Whereas only through memory could Apollo become a god, it is only through the resurrection of memory that the poet can effectively recreate Psyche.

Waldoff writes that Psyche is presented as a "fading or dying immortal, and the mutability to which even a goddess and a religion must submit becomes the real subject of the ode" (106). "Mutability" is certainly the immediate concern of the ode, but it is more specifically, as I have suggested, the mutability of the imagination itself, the perverse way in which it manifests itself as either salvation or damnation to the poet, which concerns Keats. And his task in "To Psyche" is to hold onto a symbol of the imagination that, "too late for antique vows" (36), has no temple, no "altar heap'd with flowers" (29). The goddess to whom the poet turns for his own identity, that is, has no identity of her own. Mythologically represented with the wings of a butterfly, Psyche is emblematic of the essence of mutability and thus the role she now plays in the poetry is a link between the old era and the new. She is indeed a "dying immortal," but, like the cycle of the butterfly, she dies to be reborn. Through the resurrective powers of memory, Psyche, like Apollo before her, will "die into life," into an identity that the poet himself hopes to achieve through the new relationship with the imagination, for he too, at this tenuous point in his career, can be termed a "dying immortal."

In order to achieve his own identity, the poet must reinstate Psyche's identity through "sweet enforcement and remembrance dear" (2). And the usual accompaniment of dreaming, once transcendent, but, with the knight's experience now shown to be destructive in its adversity to reality, is quickly dismissed in the ode's first stanza in order to rid the speaker of the same loss of vision that destroyed the knight: "Surely I dreamt to-day, or did I see / The winged Psyche with awaken'd eyes?" (5–6). Dreaming is dismissed as unimportant here, for there is no schism between appearance and reality as there had been with la belle dame; Psyche's identity will emerge not from a separate and false reality, but from an internalized "remembrance dear." The poet will not find Psyche wandering "in the meads" ("La Belle Dame" 13), but in "some untrodden region of [his] mind" (51), the mind that must be "a thoroughfare for all thoughts." Unlike the knight-at-arms, who remained a helpless outsider to the mysterious lady and thus could not dispel her mystery, the poet here will internalize Psyche and his identity will create her identity.

The creation will not be able to repair the schism that recurs in the odes to come, however. The speaker becomes Psyche's prophet, thereby giving her life, but he remains merely an observer to the events of the poem, a repository for the "branched thoughts" (52) that result at the end. The ode's true activity takes place not between Psyche and the speaker, but between Psyche and Amor, the figure of "warm Love" (67) who both personifies and supplants the speaker's sexual desire.

The awakening of consciousness traditionally inherent in their tale allows the speaker vision as a result of it ("I see, and sing, by my own eyes inspired" [43]), but, because of his surrender of his own identity to her, little else is gained through his status as prophet. The last poem in which the speaker himself was sexually involved with the female produced "starv'd lips" ("La Belle Dame" 41). Because of the resultant destruction in that relationship, the poet keeps his distance sexually in this ode, but the current noninvolvement produces "pale-mouth'd prophet dreaming" (49) rather than complete serenity. The lack of gratification for the speaker, though not so graphic as that of the speaker of "La Belle Dame," is nonetheless evident.

The poet as prophet will deliver the goddess from the life-lessness of neglect she endures. As well as having no shrine or altar, there is no "virgin-choir to make delicious moan" (30). The "delicious moan" may be compared with the "sweet moan" of la belle dame (20), indicating a sexual connection between the two females, but having converted the moan into that of the "virgin-choir," Keats attempts to rid this relationship of the sexuality that he now deems destructive rather than redemptive. The lack of passion between speaker and female that informs this poem underlines the paleness, not as a symptom of disease as had been true of the knight, but rather as a characteristic of the poet as prophet—an indication of the "otherworldliness" of the sacred rites that replace sexuality. Restoration can begin, this ode contends, only when passion does not threaten to destroy the male. But although the passion involved in the virgin-choir's "delicious moan" is associated more with the ascetic prophet rather than with the "sweet moan" of la belle dame's destructive sexuality, the occurrence of the word in both poems signifies a troubling connection not only between Psyche and her predecessor, but between all females, even those who make up the virgin-choir. The aspect of sexuality is a natural result of Amor and Psyche, a personification of love and the soul. Their relationship suggests not only the union of love and soul, moreover, but of "sex and mind [and] expression and structure" (Chase 2). Even when the male speaker chooses to be merely an observer in poetry that derives its life from female identity, sex is a troubling but inevitable occurrence.

Once again, the male finds himself as a voyeur, not in order to initiate sex, as Porphyro had, but to avoid it. The speaker sees the lovers:

> calm-breathing on the bedded grass;
> Their arms embraced, and their pinions too;
> Their lips touch'd not, but had not bade adieu,
> As if disjoined by soft-handed slumber.
>
> (15–18)

Because of the avoidance of sexuality sought with this ode, the passion between Psyche and Amor is hardly carnal. They are "calm-breathing" and their lips do not touch; the portrait is one that is more evocative of sleep than of sex. There will be no frightening "sweet moan" here; all true sexual activity will, in fact, begin at the close of the poem when Psyche will leave "a casement ope at night / To let the warm Love in" (66–67). Psyche's need for identity enables the speaker to acquire identity as a creator, but it is a role previously allowed only the females, and thus further complicates his own tenuous masculine identity that has been largely surrendered to that of the asexual prophet who can observe, but not participate in, the highly desired sexual activity.

But this is a poem that focuses on healing the mind. Curran comments that the pastoral, or the "leafy luxury" of the early poems, is transformed in the later poems into a "mental state" (115), as indicated by the "branched thoughts, new grown with pleasant pain" (52) of this ode. The early bowers become the "wreath'd trellis of a working brain" here (60), an enclosure that is significant in the limitations it now puts on the imagination. But even with the new limitations that turn the poet into the ascetic prophet and put the new focus on thoughts rather than sensations, sexuality remains mandatory in order to create.

Vendler goes even further by seeing the ode as one that presents a "complete, exclusive, and lasting annihilation of the senses in favor of the brain" (47). While I agree that the ode presents a first attempt at complete "annihilation," manifested in the textual movement away from the external vision of Psyche and Amor and toward their internalization in the poet's mind, I cannot agree that the annihilation is a *fait accompli*, because certainly the odes that follow prove it not to be "lasting." Even in the final stanza here, in fact, the senses reemerge, as "soft delight" (64), reminiscent of the "soft luxury" of "Calidore" (92), a poem in which all delights were sensual. Moreover, because they are "new grown," the thoughts remain "shadowy" (65). Psyche remains, therefore, a product of both sensation and thought because, while it is the "working brain" that, through memory, revives the dying goddess, it is the "warm Love" of Amor from which she sustains identity. Keats is simply not prepared to give up sensuality altogether, despite its known destructiveness. And because the speaker who serves as current midwife is an asexual observer rather than an active female, the birth will be less than a total success here.

But salvation is tenuously assured for the poet by a female whose identity is the result of the combination of thought and passion rather than of passion alone, described in Keats's "system of Salvation" quoted previously in the same letter to George and Georgiana, intriguingly juxtaposed between "La Belle Dame" and "Psyche," that is, between damnation and salvation: "Do you not see how necessary a World of Pains and troubles is to school an Intelligence and make it a soul? A Place where the heart must feel and suffer in a thousand diverse ways!" (*Letters* 2:102).

In the original myth of Psyche, the "world of Pains and troubles" in which she was forced by the jealous Venus to undergo increasingly difficult feats, preceded her own immortality, her acquisition of a soul. And in this ode, Keats makes overtures toward uniting the suffering Dionysian imagination that he believed to limit the early poems of the earth with the

Apollonian that now threatens to overpower future ones. The depiction of the lush earthly landscape, for example, dotted with "cool-rooted flowers, fragrant-eyed, / Blue, silver-white, and budded Tyrian" (13–14), has not surfaced in such profusion since *Endymion*. It is not, however, a landscape to be relinquished and exchanged for the ethereal, as it had been in that early poem. Rather it is, like Psyche herself, saved from extinction by being internalized by the poet, becoming a part of the "wreath'd trellis of a working brain, / With buds, and bells, and stars without a name" (60–61). The lack of specificity in Keats's delineation of the landscape is both reminiscent of the profusion of nature in the early poems as well as indicative of the present uncertainties over the imagination. Dickstein notes that the figure of Psyche herself "lacks concreteness" (197) and the entire ode lacks the "genuine dialectical movement of the later poems" (196). While the earth is not barren here, as it had been in "La Belle Dame," the unspecified growth of nameless "buds and bells," from the important union of heart and mind, indicates the union is, at best, tenuous. Dickstein suggests the ode sums up and refines an earlier vision, "making it a more serious view of life and, by subsuming it in a new poem, bidding it farewell" (197–98). The ode "bids farewell," at least temporarily, to the vision of the destructive female and, restored through the unity of heart and mind, Psyche is representative of the female who, having endured "a World of Pains and troubles," is able, Keats believes, to offer salvation to the male. In her "rosy sanctuary" (59) within the poet's "working brain," Psyche becomes the same female of Keats's "Boyish imagination," where, in a "soft nest" in his mind she "slept though she knew it not" (*Letters* 1:341). But while she serves as a tentative step in the direction Keats aspires, the new female as Psyche, who unwittingly deprives the speaker of both sexuality and passion, is too similar to the early maidens who were smothered in their own lush surroundings. It is enough here to resurrect a dying immortal, and thereby restore the elusive female to her former role as the boyish Keats's "pure Goddess" (*Letters* 1:341), but the fragile link between sensation and thought, which will culminate in the sublime combination of earth and heaven in "To Autumn," is not yet strong enough to be sustained and will shatter on the wings of a nightingale in the ode to follow.

II

"Ode to a Nightingale" is one of only two major poems to have as its controlling metaphor for the imagination a symbolic rather than actual female figure—the Grecian urn is the other. We understand that the nightingale is female because Keats calls her the "light-winged Dryad of the trees" (7). Like the nightingale, the dryad represents the elusive, ephemeral quality that now characterizes Keats's conception of the imagination. Thus, like Psyche, the nightingale is also a "dying immortal," one who dies with the trees. And, to demonstrate further the ephemerality of the nightingale, the word fade or a form of it, used liberally throughout all of the odes, occurs four times here, more than in any other.[4]

As in all of the odes, the poet attempts to capture the evanescent, to turn the tenuous into the permanent, through the female, who remains the very symbol of the tenuous to the male. The poet of the nightingale ode attempts to achieve this permanence, though, through forgetfulness rather than the "remembrance dear" of "Psyche," through dissolution of the experience rather than internalization of it. To fade is to forget, to leave behind the senses that accompany mortality, making the entire experience recorded in the ode as tenuous as the imagination that evokes it and potentially as disastrous as the imagination that produced la belle dame. The parabolic structure of this ode thematically parallels the engagement and disengagement that occurred previously between the knight and the mysterious lady, but at the apex of the dream in each poem when transcendence should occur, reality intercedes instead, and the imagination is discovered to be a "deceiving elf" (74), closely related to the "fairy's child" she was before.

The dryad, like the "sweet-lipp'd ladies" of the early poems, has not the power to guarantee permanence for, like theirs, her power is contingent on her natural surroundings—the tree she inhabits. Hers is a contingency that, in these poems Keats hopes will evince a resolution, he must break; but la belle dame, independent of and thus destructive to her natural surround- ings, serves as an object lesson, and the females of the odes are conspicuous deviations.

The speaker wishes for

> a beaker full of the warm South,
> Full of the true, the blushful Hippocrene,
> With beaded bubbles winking at the brim,
> And purple-stained mouth.
>
> (15–18)

He is desirous not of retrieving a "faded" hierarchy or fading goddess, but rather to fade himself and to "dissolve" (21) through the wine, to forget, to transfer all identity onto some- thing else—a supremely feminine trait to Keats. While the speaker surrendered his male identity for that of an asexual prophet in "To Psyche," he is here transmuting his masculinity into a part of the traditional female. He seeks a passivity that "numbs," a tenuousness that allows escape through absence, and, at the same time, the sensuality that the escape through wine can offer.

But escape can occur only through the ephemerality of the female in this poem, and thus the speaker will try on the wings of the dryad—"viewless wings" (33)—that allow escape through feminine invisibility.

The speaker now seeks, as Vendler said of "Psyche," "com- plete and lasting annihilation" (47), but of nothing less than the self, through his own transference onto the female. The ode contains no attempts at creation or procreation; the speaker does not wish to save the female, but to fade with her. He no longer wishes either to control or abandon himself to the imagination, but to fuse with it. It is the "inability of Romantic art to think of itself as other than a failed idealism" that precipi- tates the speaker's frantic movement in this ode toward fusion with the female (Rajan 164). And further, "the odes seem to recognize and consent to the disjunction between the real and the ideal" (164), a consent that neither Keats nor his speaker can endure.

The metamorphosis of male identity into female identity is
one that clings to, even intensifies, the need for the senses—
for passion. Such intensity disallows the "working brain" newly
discovered in "To Psyche." The vision that was regained in that
ode is once again lost to a deceptive female with whom the
speaker believes he is joined—"Already with thee! tender is the
night" (35)—but lack of vision is analogous to death of the
senses entirely here. In his escape with the nightingale he "can-
not see what flowers are at [his] feet, / Nor what soft incense
hangs upon the boughs, / But, in embalmed darkness, guess
each sweet" (41–43). How can the speaker escape the void
created by the absence of sensuality?

The progression is obvious to Keats. It leads from an absence
of the senses to a welcomed absence of life altogether:

> Darkling I listen; and, for many a time
>   I have been half in love with easeful Death,
> Call'd him soft names in many a mused rhyme,
>   To take into the air my quiet breath;
> Now more than ever seems it rich to die.
>
>   (51–55)

The poet who looks "upon fine Phrases like a Lover" and has
thus given female status to the imagination, even that which
has proven destructive, is now "half in love" with a male Death,
not at all like the male sleep of "Sleep and Poetry." And Death,
the final form of escape offered in this ode, is not only male,
but is "easeful." The poet who has slipped into the female
persona to fade with the nightingale now looks at Death as the
ultimate male persona, the true channel to invisibility. It is
not the life-in-death endured by the knight-at-arms nor the
suffering that becomes intrinsic to any of Keats's male figures
when confronted with the destructive female. Death here is the
only form of escape when the "viewless wings of Poesy" fail. It
is no longer only the antithesis to life, but the absence of all
sensuality and all passion, even that which destroys. It is the
only time in the poetry that such a painless (and pleasureless)
escape is offered, and the only time, too, that escape is desired
through a male figure.

But it is, as Curran points out, ultimately "too acute a sensibil-
ity" (199) rather than the actual sensual abandonment that the
poet had hoped for. The natural richness that surrounded the
early maidens and offered no transcendence is transferred to
the male Death here, which, in its degendering of the female,
becomes the ideal. In essence, the masculine Death becomes,
for a moment, the speaker's own identity, and being "half in
love" with the figure recreates the solipsism of both Endymion
and the knight-at-arms that frustrates the imaginative process.
But it is a necessary maneuver because the poet can experience
either salvation or destruction through the female but, precisely
because of her sensuality derived from her conflicting nature,
he cannot experience the cessation of both that he seeks in this
ode.

Like the "dull opiate" (3), the wine, and the "wings of Poesy"
(33) that the speaker has dismissed as means of escape, Death,
too, is quickly abandoned, and the female is again given domi-
nance, this time in the portrait of Ruth:

> Perhaps the self-same song that found a path
> Through the sad heart of Ruth, when, sick for home,
>   She stood in tears amid the alien corn;
>   The same that oft-times hath
> Charm'd magic casements, opening on the foam
> Of perilous seas, in faery lands forlorn.
>
> (65–70)

The biblical Ruth, a wanderer and stranger to her "alien" envi-
ronment, is swept into the act of remembering that now over-
takes the poet, and she becomes his prototype of human sorrow.
In this poem, earth holds no solace, however, and Ruth is as
alien to her surroundings as the poet is to his, and the inability
of nature to offer comfort is manifested in the "alien corn."
When the imagination becomes the "deceiving elf" (74) of this
ode and the poet is tolled back to his "sole self" (72), he is left
alone, like Ruth, with only his memories of the past, making
his own alienation more profound.

But it is not only Ruth's alienation that is significant here.

She has become a symbol of reparation to Keats. As Lau writes, his description of her, "standing amidst a golden wheat field," evokes the image of an earth goddess (133). And, although she is a goddess who has no earth in this poem of heavenly dimensions, the reader recognizes that she has been made immortal by the poet's memory and the voice of the nightingale. She is the first female to be associated with Keats's present idea of "forlorn" fairy lands, the precursor to the figure of Autumn "sitting careless on a granary floor" ("To Autumn" 14), in the later poem that celebrates both the earth and the human and has no need of fairy lands. But here there is a difference, measurable in Keats's changed attitude toward the imagination, between the sorrowful Ruth as stranger and wanderer and the introduction of her predecessor Mnemosyne, equally immortal through memory, in "Hyperion." The goddess also wandered in an alien environment but, because she would give it identity, unlike the "alien corn" from which Ruth's sorrow originates, her solitude was not only powerful but necessary.

As representative of the new and alien earth that intrudes on the poet's attempt to escape, Ruth's own power lies in her tears. Like the Indian maiden who compelled Endymion to accept the earth through her tears, Ruth's own sorrow is contrary to the nightingale's song and forces the poet to realize that her sorrow, like the "faery lands forlorn," does not allow entry to mortals who seek escape. She remains a solitary image, distant from the poet's present, separated from him by a sorrow he cannot share.

The speaker is ultimately abandoned by the ode's females— both the nightingale and Ruth. As his only defense against his solitary state at the end, he questions the reality of the experience, never reaching a conclusion: "Was it a vision, or a waking dream? / Fled is that music:—Do I wake or sleep?" (79–80). The ephemerality of both the female and the poet's own experience with her is naively scrutinized—it is ultimately a distinction to which the imagination (and the female) does not need to submit. The poet's attempt to distinguish and delineate an experience so he may arrogantly comprehend it manifests his continuing desire to control the female, as the knight had done before.

Because she will not submit, the recalcitrant imagination becomes the pejorative "fancy" to the poet, whose powers stem from chicanery rather than the genuine magic of creativity, and she "cannot cheat so well / As she is fam'd to do" (73–74). The poet belittles in order to control, as a defense against his own unrequited passion and against the "deceiving elf" who is blind to it. Both the Apollonian imagination and the Dionysian memory of Ruth are reduced to "elfin" stature because of their inability to give succor to the male.

Passion is also belittled in this ode and, in the next, "Ode on a Grecian Urn," the poet chooses a lifeless artifact as symbol of the imagination, a product of mortality rather than a "dying" or very much alive immortal. Like the experience of this ode, the urn's will also be scrutinized and questioned by the male. But the truly pertinent question now becomes what role the female, as symbol of passion, will play in a poem that deliberately attempts to avoid its effects by turning the "deceiving elf" into a silent urn.

III

An absence of passion occurs as early as the opening line of "Ode on a Grecian Urn," in the poet's address to the female as "thou still unravish'd bride of quietness." The word "still," denoting either "forever" or "yet," has a more tacit meaning especially relevant here—a lack of motion which, like death, is the antithesis to both life and passion, yet proves to be the essence of the permanence discovered in the ode, and thus this meaning implicity informs the entire poem—becoming the source of this female's power.

As an artifact, the urn has no contact with life. Removed from the realm of "breathing human passion" (28), it is a "foster-child" rather than a fairy's, and its foster parents are the asexual "silence and slow time" (2). The urn has no "natural" parents because the act of sex did not produce it. Yet, as Van Ghent has noted, "there is no avoiding" the urn's female shape:

The fertility orgy depicted on one side of the urn
bears a direct relationship with that aspect of urn-sym-
bolism which has to do with fecundity and birth; and
relationship also with the female earth of which pots
are made. . . . for such rites were held when the earth
was thought to need the human example of love-mak-
ing in order to become fruitful, its common fruits of
daily use to be stored again in the mothering urn. The
sacrifice depicted on the other side is the natural coun-
terpart of the scene of ritual love-making, and is re-
lated to that aspect of urn-symbolism which has to do
with death; together they express the ritual laws gov-
erning all things. (158)

Through the contraries depicted on her frieze, the urn ex-
presses "the ritual laws governing all things." But, as an unnatu-
ral, inanimate object, she cannot partake of the ritual, one that
includes, as so many of Keats's poems do, love and death. For,
despite her female appearance, the urn can offer no procre-
ative power. As an "unravish'd bride" she can only render the
past rather than create the future, for the latter, to Keats,
is still wholly dependent on the sexual metaphor. Like the
nightingale, the urn forces the narrator to remember and, as
"sylvan historian" (3), the emphasis once again shifts to memory
as an attempt at resolution, as it had been in "To Psyche."
    The difficulty encountered by this present attempt to restore
through memory, however, is that, while Psyche was a "dying
immortal," the urn, eternal though it may be, has never lived
to die. The female can only grant salvation to the male when
she can bestow life. And the difference between these two
female figures is nowhere better expressed than in the scenes
between lovers from the two odes, scenes of physical intimacy
that appear in almost all of Keats's poetry.
    In "Ode to Psyche," the speaker comes upon Amor and
Psyche in the midst of an embrace: "Their arms embraced, and
their pinions too; / Their lips touch'd not, but had not bade
adieu, / As if disjoined by soft-handed slumber" (16–18). As
previously noted, passion in this earlier ode is problematic
because it does not involve the speaker, but although the pas-

sion between the lovers is not at its height, their lovemaking is interrupted by something as sensuous as the missing passion itself, "soft-handed slumber." And although their lips "touch'd not," they had not "bade adieu," indicating the passion between them will eventually increase.

In "Ode on a Grecian Urn," the scene between lovers is much different, however, for how does one instill passion into a lifeless tableau? The poet begins his relationship with the urn by a series of dogmatic questions, the same type that ended the nightingale ode and that emerge from the masculine desire to know, to "ravish": "What men or gods are these? What maidens loth? / What mad pursuit? What struggle to escape: / What pipes and timbrels? What wild ecstasy?" (8–10). The questions reveal the speaker's inability to discover any human passion within the lifeless urn, and the "wild ecstasy" that he seeks is thus presumably not the same that he previously encountered with the nightingale—"While thou art pouring forth thy soul abroad / In such an ecstasy!" (57–58). The urn, which has never known such passion, can reveal only what one can "know on earth" (50), only what is already known, rather than what exists in the realm of the Apollonian imagination, so the scene between lovers contains neither the "ecstasy" of the nightingale nor the anticipatory passion of Amor and Psyche:

> Fair youth, beneath the trees, thou canst not leave
>   Thy song, nor ever can those trees be bare;
>   Bold lover, never, never canst thou kiss,
> Though winning near the goal—yet, do not grieve;
>   She cannot fade, though thou hast not thy bliss,
>   For ever wilt thou love, and she be fair!
>
> (15–20)

The arrested motion that first appeared in the opening line with the word "still" transforms the scene between lovers from "Ode to Psyche," in which passion is interrupted by sleep, to one that is devoid of both passion and sleep. The scene exists not in the realm of the procreative imagination but in a single fixed moment of the past, a past that cannot be provoked into life through memory because it has never lived. While Psyche's and Amor's lips "touch'd not, but had not bade adieu," the lovers here "never canst" kiss. They are, like the urn that they "haunt" (5), caught in stasis, and the word "fade" here, used in literally every other ode to signify the evanescence of the imagination, instead signifies a lack of life itself. "She cannot fade" because she does not live. It is a state of negation made even more compelling by the double use of "never" (17) and is similar to that of the masculine image of Death in the nightingale ode who offered death as a cessation "with no pain" (56). It is also a state that has never before originated with the female. The poet can only attempt to rectify the impotence of the female here by concentrating not on her lack of passion but on the absence of pain.

Thus in stanza three, following the scene between the lovers, the word "happy," a diminution of the passion he has given up, occurs six times:

> Ah, happy, happy boughs! that cannot shed
>   Your leaves, nor ever bid the spring adieu;
> And, happy melodist, unwearied,
>   For ever piping songs for ever new;
> More happy love! more happy, happy love!
>   For ever warm and still to be enjoy'd,
>   For ever panting, and for ever young;
> All breathing human passion far above,
>   That leaves a heart high-sorrowful and cloy'd,
>   A burning forehead, and a parching tongue.
>   (21–30)

Critics have consistently noted the strain that appears in these lines, produced by the redundant use of "happy" and "for ever," finding a defensive, almost desperate attempt to "lend conviction to what [Keats] knows is not true" (Waldoff 136). The line that seems most forced, and contains three of the six occurrences of "happy" in rapid succession, "More happy love! more happy, happy love!," may be the germinal point of Keats's confusion, for, in the lines that follow, the love is "for ever warm" and "for ever panting," even though it leaves behind the ability to breathe, the "breathing human passion" that, to Keats, is responsible for both imagination and identity.

As in the nightingale ode, the speaker again belittles passion by making it akin to the knight-at-arms' deathly disease. It does not transcend mortality here, but rather is symptomatic of mortal disease, for passion "leaves a heart high-sorrowful and cloy'd, / A burning forehead, and a parching tongue." But, as Bate has pointed out, " 'cloy'd' at least implies fulfillment" and a " 'heart high-sorrowful' " is necessary "to experience the mystery of sorrow for which Keats, in the revised 'Hyperion,' was soon to find an image in the countenance of Moneta" (514). Furthermore, the feverous state in the last line is the same that Keats records in the previously quoted letter to Reynolds, used explicitly to delineate the "relief of Poetry": "the feverous relief of Poetry seems a much less crime" (*Letters* 1:370).

It is an "artifice of evasion" that Keats practices here (Rajan 133), the same masculine defense practiced in the nightingale ode, because the feverous state, associated in the poet's mind with both poetry and love, is too significant for him to forsake for an imagination that can only reach the specious level of "happy," regardless of the consequences. Although the urn is able to dismiss human passion, it becomes increasingly clear in this poem that Keats cannot. To the poet to whom "embarrassment, erotic feeling, and poetic creativity fertilize each other" (Ricks 163), the cold terrain of the urn is becoming as frustrating as the overimpassioned imagination has been.

In his frustration, the speaker returns to questioning the urn, again seeking more than the symbol can provide, in a fervent attempt to penetrate its silence. This poem contains more questions, ten altogether, than any of Keats's poems of comparable length, a manifestation of the urn's continued inscrutability, and the questions themselves are more rhetorical than valid because "to know" has been replaced in the odes by the speaker's masculine desire "to control, to possess." But the declarative lines that end the stanzas of interrogation are finally ones of acceptance: "And, little town, thy streets for evermore / Will silent be; and not a soul to tell / Why thou art desolate, can e'er return" (38–40). "Not a soul to tell"—neither the poet nor the urn. The speaker must remain an outsider to the urn, just as he was to both the sorrow of Ruth and the "faery lands forlorn" in the nightingale ode, and the final stanza begins with an apostrophe of frustration similar to that ode's "Forlorn!"—knowledge is achieved, but escape is lost:

> O Attic shape! Fair attitude! with brede
>   Of marble men and maidens overwrought,
> With forest branches and the trodden weed;
>   Thou, silent form, dost tease us out of thought
> As doth eternity: Cold Pastoral!
>   When old age shall this generation waste,
>   Thou shalt remain, in the midst of other woe
>   Than ours, a friend to man, to whom thou say'st,
> "Beauty is truth, truth beauty,"—that is all
>   Ye know on earth, and all ye need to know.
>   (41–50)

Like the knight-at-arms, whose experience with the mysterious lady rendered him impotent but cognizant of his destruction, the speaker reaches a knowledge of the urn that circumvents and undermines masculine power. It is the Negative Capability of the "knowing of not knowing" that defines the urn's knowledge. The "sylvan historian" of the first stanza, whom the speaker thought promised a "flowery tale" (4) has become a "cold Pastoral" instead. Nature is not the lush scene of welcome to the male that it had been in the poetry of 1817. It is "forest branches," skeletal rather than leafy, and "trodden weed" rather than flowers. And the inhabitants are not Calidore and the "sweet-lipp'd ladies"; they are "marble men and maidens overwrought." The nature that is externalized by the urn reflects its interior that "contains the ashes of the dead, of a civilization that is past" (Rajan 133). Death informs both the urn's silence and power and, because of this, she is not the "deceiving elf" (74) that the female became in the previous ode because no relationship exists between speaker and object—not even one that ends in deceit. Because there is no passion involved, there has been, in effect, no "greeting of the Spirit" necessary to make the urn "wholly exist" (*Letters* 1:243).

Ironically, because of the lack of passion, the urn becomes "a friend to man" in the end, a phrase reminiscent of "the great end" of poetry (245) that Keats postulated in the early "Sleep and Poetry." Since that poem, however, Keats's ideas regarding the function of the poetic imagination and the female who symbolizes it have changed. It is no longer enough that poetry be a "friend," characterized by the meek maidens of the early poems, just as the "happy" existence that the speaker enforces upon the urn in this ode is inadequate. The "friend" must become a lover, no matter how brief the relationship, because there must be something "to be intense upon": "The excellence of every Art is its intensity, capable of making all disagreeables evaporate, from their being in close relationship with Beauty & Truth" (*Letters* 1:192). While beauty may be truth in this ode, it is not life.[5] M. A. Goldberg defines what Keats seeks in this way: "Things, no less than actions, lose their value with Keats unless their external qualities can somehow be integrated with the self. In the beginning—but also in the end—there must be a relationship" (25). Thus the "disagreeables" in this poem, rather than "evaporate," are exacerbated, for without the passion that emanates from life, the "breathing human passion" of the mortal state made divine by the immortal, there is no creative process. The urn's creator, long ago, gave it beauty but could not give it life. Through her lack of passion and procreative powers the female in this poem is a "buried presence" (Homans 25), buried through her own history of "silence and slow time" (2). The kind of female beauty that Keats now seeks, characterized by intensity, must derive from life, no matter how brief, as the final "Ode on Melancholy" will make clear. The female of the "Grecian Urn" exists in a dual state of ambiguity and negativity—a supremely "effeminate" (but not feminine) mood that Keats will call "indolence" in the ode to follow.

IV

In "Ode on Indolence" the marble figures of the urn, intriguingly, come to life:[6]

> One morn before me were three figures seen,
>   With bowed necks, and joined hands, side-faced;
> And one behind the other stepp'd serene,
>   In placid sandals, and in white robes graced:
> They pass'd, like figures on a marble urn,
>   When shifted round to see the other side.
>
>   (1–6)

The serenity evoked in these lines is foreign to the first instance of the appearance of the figures, in the "Grecian Urn." All frenetic questioning and frustration over the absence of response is replaced here by a Lethean willingness to observe, perhaps because of the fact that this ode takes the contemplative mood of the others to the brink of sleep: "The blissful cloud of summer-indolence / Benumb'd my eyes; my pulse grew less and less; / Pain had no sting, and pleasure's wreath no flower" (16–18). It is a state of negation that Keats calls "effeminacy" in a letter to George and Georgiana:

> This morning I am in a sort of temper indolent and
> supremely careless: I long after a stanza or two of
> Thompson's Castle of indolence—My passions are all
> asleep from my having slumbered till nearly eleven
> and weakened the animal fibre all over me to a de-
> lightful sensation about three degrees on this side of
> faintness. . . . In this state of effeminacy the fibres of
> the brain are relaxed in common with the rest of the
> body, and to such a happy degree that pleasure has no
> show of enticement and pain no unbearable frown.
> Neither Poetry, nor Ambition, nor Love have any alert-
> ness of countenance as they pass by me: they seem
> rather like three figures on a Greek vase—a Man and
> two women—whom no one but myself could distin-
> guish in their disguisement. This is the only happi-
> ness; and is a rare instance of advantage in the body
> overpowering the Mind. (*Letters* 2:78–79)

This letter gives an equally "rare instance" of a prosaic summary of the poem itself and adds to the theme of lethargy that informs the ode. The "effeminacy" in which the "fibres of the

brain are relaxed in common with the rest of the body" pro-
duces no new figures, but three who are familiar and recogniz-
able to the poet. Effeminacy is a state that belongs to neither
male nor female, but to the absence of energy and creativity,
pleasure and pain. It is an unnatural state of lassitude, which
allows the body to "overpower" the mind, and thus the mascu-
line identity that the poet has surrendered to it conjures up
only redundantly familiar figures, and, like Bertha who was
haunted by her own shadow, the poet is "haunted" by his own
creations, his own earlier ambitions:

> I knew the three:
> The first was a fair maid, and Love her name;
> The second was Ambition, pale of cheek,
> And ever watchful with fatigued eye;
> The last, whom I love more, the more of blame
> Is heap'd upon her, maiden most unmeek,—
> I knew to be my demon Poesy.
>
> (24–30)

The figure of Ambition, the ghostly figure who, most like the
knight-at-arms' appearance at his own failure to possess the
female, appears "pale of cheek" and with "fatigued eye." It is
this male image of failed ambition in the midst of indolence,
the male desire for power through creativity, that stands be-
tween the two females—representatives of the early and later
feminine figures, created by the sickly figure of Ambition, who
make up Keats's own "demon Poesy." The lethargic mood
brings on the haunting figures, but also helps dismiss them
through a unique indifference that creates the first "active"
lines of the poem:

> O folly! What is Love? and where is it?
> And for that poor Ambition—it springs
> From a man's little heart's short fever-fit;
> For Poesy!—no,—she has not a joy,—
> At least for me,—so sweet as drowsy noons,
> And evenings steep'd in honied indolence;
> O, for an age so shelter'd from annoy,

That I may never know how change the moons,
Or hear the voice of busy common-sense!
                                              (32–40)

The activity considered in these lines is, ironically, that of giving up poetry—of surrendering all creativity for the present "honied indolence," to give up the active masculine brain for the effeminate state of the body. In his poetry, lately and adversely become his "demon Poesy," the poet discovers a passivity in himself that he had previously attempted to find in the female. But there is a significant difference between the passivity of the females and of their creator—their own passivity that Keats hopes to find is one that will show his creative abilities in tempering the errant imagination. The females' passivity is the result of male control rather than of lethargy. When found in a male figure, passivity is a state of perverse obliviousness to everything else, including creativity. It is to be "shelter'd from annoy" as well as from its counterpart joy. It is thus an extremely uncreative, impotent even, condition in the male, especially in one who wishes to control the three figures who will not leave when asked, thereby giving the poem its only true activity. And to crystallize the indolent state, the speaker cites twice that the figures came by "a third time" (21, 41), even though they "faded" (23) from sight in between the two citations. Having overpowered his creative mind, the indolence seems to have further impaired his ability to count correctly.

The lethargy causes the speaker's pulse to grow "less and less" (17), making its characteristic in the male, who is used to seeking activity, analogous to death. The state represented in this ode does not express the same consciousness of alienation between speaker and object as the others do, probably because the mind is unnaturally "relaxed." But Keats's greatest poetry, Levinson reminds us, "*signifies*—indeed, fetishizes—its alienation from its representational objects and subjects, and, thus, from its audience. . . . [It is] a discourse of self-possession" (*Allegory* 28), recognizable by the poet's very conscious dismissal of it. In this ode, it is a consciousness of only a borrowed feminization that embarrassingly becomes in the male an "effeminacy," a disempowerment through deliberate degendering of self, for no particular reason, that the poet unnervingly clings to rather than dismisses, which finally leads him to argue against his being "dieted with praise, / A pet-lamb in a sentimental farce!" (53–54), another phrase found carelessly placed in a letter as well, that of the one to Sarah Jeffrey, in which Keats hopes he is "a little less of a versifying Pet-lamb" (*Letters* 2:116). The audience from which Keats's greatest poetry alienates itself through the speaker's "self-possession" is clearly part of the poem on indolence, making the ode less an evolution of the poet or the female than a mechanical repetition of "the voice of busy common-sense" (40) found in the letters. The female of this ode, alien to the strange effeminate mood of her creator, offers no new knowledge to the poet; he is too busy trying to dismiss her to learn any object lessons from her. It is a poem more about the displacement of self-possession rather than the possession of the female, as the male figure of Ambition clearly shows through his weak and sickly condition. And there is neither closure nor resolution to the "Ode on Indolence" as the phantoms that have appeared from the Grecian urn are sent back to lifelessness, told to vanish, from the poet's "idle spright, / Into the clouds, and never more return!" (59–60).

The figures will reappear, however, and the sickly male, once the knight-at-arms, will become the "cloudy trophy" of the goddess Melancholy, who majestically reinforces the necessary consciousness of alienation in the next ode.

V

In the "Ode on Melancholy," beauty and life are defined not in terms of truth but by virtue of the intensity that originates with their brevity. In this ode, the very nature of intensity, like that of indolence in the previous ode, is illuminated, but here it is through the beauty that the female "dwells with" (21). The female figure is one of transience here, like the "morning rose" (15), "the salt sand-wave" (16), and the "globed peonies" (17). She is once again a part of a catalog of beauty as she had been in the poetry of 1817, but, unlike that of her early counterpart, the female's presence here represents a beauty that offers knowledge rather than escape, an attempt at permanence through change rather than through the stasis of the life-lessness of the Grecian urn or the effeminacy of indolence.

The message of the opening line of *Endymion*, that a "thing of beauty is a joy for ever," becomes obsolete in this poem, where beauty affirms its power in the fact that it "must die" (21). The Keats of *Endymion*, youthful, healthy, and just beginning to explore the possibilities of the imagination, could easily define beauty as the antithesis of mortality, an antithesis represented by the female deity. Since *Endymion*, however, both Keats and the female have undergone several transformations, and the apex of this imaginative process is no better expressed than in this ode of thirty lines, the briefest of all.[7]

At its literal center, images of death, the only type of perma-nence to exist within "Ode on Melancholy," surrender to images that celebrate the intensity of life by focusing on its inherent moments of intransience:

> But when the melancholy fit shall fall
>   Sudden from heaven like a weeping cloud,
> That fosters the droop-headed flowers all,
>   And hides the green hill in an April shroud;
> Then glut thy sorrow on a morning rose,
>   Or on the rainbow of the salt sand-wave,
>   Or on the wealth of globed peonies;
> Or if thy mistress some rich anger shows,
>   Emprison her soft hand, and let her rave,
>   And feed deep, deep upon her peerless eyes.
>   (11–20)

As in "La Belle Dame sans Merci," oral imagery represents the means by which salvation is either affirmed or denied, and it is affirmed here (momentarily at least) by a nurturing female, for the listener is instructed to "glut" his sorrow and "feed deep, deep" upon his mistress's eyes. The oral imagery that continues with the "strenuous tongue / [That can] burst Joy's grape against his palate fine" (27–28) occurs only in the second half of the ode, as remedy to the "poisonous wine" (2), "nightshade" (4), and "rosary of yew-berries" (5) that culminate in the "April shroud" of Melancholy when she is not sought through the moments of intensity that define her. The oral images are first poisonous then salutary, and as Keats was enthralled with Robert Burton's *The Anatomy of Melancholy*, probably much of the connection between the state of melancholy and food as both cause and cure of it is derived from Burton, who advocates the avoidance of certain foods because they "breed gross melancholy blood" and the inclusion of others in a diet that will "free" one's soul from "perturbations" (137, 134).

Janice Sinson calls Keats's marginalia in his own copy of Burton's tome "the nearest he ever came to keeping a personal diary" (13), and persuasively argues that Keats began weaving Burton's ideas into his own poetry as early as "La Belle Dame." Much of "Ode on Melancholy," too, is derivative of Burton's own thesis regarding "A Dialogue between Pleasure and Pain," especially the section entitled "Love-Melancholy," which, like Keats's poetry, establishes male love for the female as the unambiguous symbol for both pleasure and pain:

> "It is worth the labour," saith Plotinus, "to consider well of love, whether it be a god or a devil, or passion of the mind, or partly god, partly devil, partly passion." (426)

Furthermore, Burton designates Keats's two symbols of poetry and escape—women and wine—as "plagues":

> I may not here omit those two main plagues, and common dotages of human kind, wine and women, which have infatuated and besotted myriads of people; they go commonly together. . . . To whom is sorrow, . . . to whom is woe, but to such a one as loves drink? It causeth torture, and bitterness of mind.
>
> That other madness is on women, *Apostatare facit cor*, saith the wise man, *Atque homini cerebrum minuit*. Pleasant at first she is, like Dioscorides Rhododaphne, that fair plant to the eye, but poison to the taste, the rest as bitter as wormwood in the end (Prov. v.4) and sharp as a two-edged sword. (181, 182)

While women and wine are the primary causes of melancholy in Burton's treatise, with a specious beauty that is "fair . . . to the eye" but "poison to the taste," they work jointly toward amelioration in Keats's ode, for even the "poisonous wine" has an antidote in "joy's grape."

Burton describes the relationship between lovers as, at best, one of inconstancy; at worst, a state contrary to life itself:

> She looks out at window still to see whether he come,
> and by resort Phillis went nine times to the sea-side
> that day, to see if her Demophoon were approaching,
> and Troilus to the city gates, to look for his Creisseid.
> She is ill at ease, and sick till she see him again, pee-
> vish in the meantime; discontent, heavy, sad, and why
> comes he not? where is he? why breaks his promise?
> . . . *so she raves, restless and impatient.*
>
> But the symptoms of the mind in lovers are almost
> infinite, and so diverse, that no art can comprehend
> them; though they be merry sometimes, and rapt be-
> yond themselves for joy; yet most part, love is a
> plague, a torture, a hell, a bitter sweet passion at last.
> (500, my italics)

Burton invokes the tragedies of Phyllis and Demophoon and Troilus and Cressida, both of which culminated in his definition of love as a "plague," and finally death. And while Keats would later accuse Fanny Brawne of "being a little inclined to the Cressid" (*Letters* 2:256), here, as the poet of "Melancholy," he turns the problem into the cure, and his own mistress who "raves," as did Burton's, becomes not a symbol of restlessness and impatience, nor a "torture" that sucks the life from her male lover, but rather a symbol of life itself from which her lover may feed upon her "peerless eyes," an act of oral gratification that the poetry's heroes have been seeking since Lorenzo found sustenance in Isabella's tears.

The eyes of the mistress are "peerless" (20), a double enten-dre here, not only because of the supreme beauty that eyes consistently have for Keats, but also because, while she raves, her eyes lose their focus and become like Moneta's to follow, "visionless entire" ("The Fall" 1.267). Thus the male lover, while he feeds "deep, deep" into them, discovers, through this moment of intransience precipitated by the mistress's "rich anger" (18), a state of permanence contrary to that of Burton's inconstancy. It is oral gratification that is promised to the lover and ensures his salvation, thereby reversing the fate of the knight-at-arms who was destroyed by its denial.

We may once again turn to Burton as analogue to the salvation that Keats believed lay in the eyes of the mistress. "All parts [of the mistress] are attractive," Burton writes, "but especially the eyes, . . . which are love's fowlers; . . . 'the Guides, touchstone, judges, that in a moment cure mad men, and make sound folks mad, the Watchmen of the body; what do they not? How vex they not? all this is true, and . . . they are the chief seats of love" (467).

The goddess Melancholy, like the bittersweet earth figure of "To Autumn" later, symbolizes the precise moment that hangs, suspended, above joy and despair, the moment of intransience between the "aching Pleasure" and the "poison" it becomes (23–24). It is a transience that moves in the direction of death, and the only symbols of constancy, for both Burton and Keats, are the "peerless eyes" of the mistress.

By virtue of her contradictory nature, the goddess Melancholy possesses the power of both salvation and destruction. While Mnemosyne gave life to the immortality of Apollo and la belle dame robbed the knight of his immortality, Melancholy, as first representative of the admixture of pleasure with pain, is the first female to embody the "creations and destroyings, all at once" ("Hyperion" 3.116) that precede immortality. She is the first of Keats's veiled goddesses as well, most likely an allusion to Spenser's own veiled goddess, Nature (which Vendler believes Moneta to be), the apotheosis of change, who "could not any creature well descry; / For, with a veile that wimpled every where, / Her head and face was hid, that mote to none appeare" ("Mutability Cantos" [7.5.7–9]). Like Moneta, whose visage progresses "deathwards . . . / To no death" ("The Fall" 1.260–61), Melancholy symbolizes the immortality that, paradoxically, "dwells with" death (21).

Melancholy derives her power and immortality from the moments of intransience that exist within the mortality over which she presides. The ode itself can best be characterized by the moment that will later be immortalized in the phrase "full-grown lambs" of "To Autumn" (30). It is the point at which growth and decay first meet, or, in the language of this ode, joy and despair, but have not yet blended into one—the crystallization of Keats's "intensity."

Waldoff suggests that the "She" of the first line of stanza three ("She dwells with Beauty—Beauty that must die") can equally pertain to both the mortal mistress and the goddess Melancholy because the ode's "ambiguity permits the interpretation that 'She' is both, as Cynthia and the Indian maiden are one. . . . they are all, in their sublime, re-creations of the essential beauty and melancholy of a subliminal figure" (152). While the line's ambiguity alone would certainly lend itself toward such an understanding, we must remember that the ode consistently directs the listener not to the dwelling place of the mortal mistress, who has long been dismissed by Keats as either an object or a subject in the poetry, but to the "sovran shrine" of Melancholy. It is no surprise to find the lover's mistress dwelling with a "beauty that must die," but in the context of Keats's own definition of the "essential beauty" that Waldoff mentions, the female deity alone serves as exemplar, and, therefore, her close proximity to a terminal beauty shows the metamorphosis of the female in this ode—for the first time in Keats's poetry her means of salvation is one that combines the immortality he seeks with the mortality he attempts to shun.[8]

Melancholy is, moreover, the divine personification of Keats's own tenacious belief in the duality of the female nature. She is the "indissoluble union of the beautiful and the sad" (Praz 31). With her advent, the single female acquires the ambivalent and contradictory nature of both Cynthia and Circe, and she becomes precursor to Lamia, Moneta, and the figure of Autumn who will equally possess the power simultaneously to "ruin" and "save." As feminine symbol of the "creations and destroyings, all at once" that facilitated Apollo's immortality, Melancholy emerges from the point of anticipated change between the two and represents the apotheosis of the paradoxical female power and the dichotomous directions that, with "Lamia," the imagination will now take. It is a movement toward an identity that, like Lamia herself, will "unperplex bliss from its neighbour pain" (1.192); it is an unweaving of the female's own ambiguity that is sought by the male, an "exorcism" of her destructive powers, of her self from herself.

With "Lamia," the unweaving begins with a female who abandons her "real self" for a "borrowed" one that she disastrously presents to the male.

🦜 6

Lamia
The "Rainbow-Sided" Female

The tentative resolutions Keats reaches in the odes are destroyed by the "rainbow-sided" Lamia, the serpent/woman whose very nature is the essence of contradictions and takes the intensity of Melancholy to a deathly conclusion for her lover, Lycius. In "Lamia," the female is characterized by the unrelenting ambivalence produced by the constant flux of an imagination in turmoil. She has evolved from the desultory mental processes that lay behind the creation of the odes. Miriam Allott writes that the poem's ambivalence lies in the fact that Keats "had laid bare a series of paradoxes which it is beyond his power to resolve" (62). The paradoxes here began with the odes, and Keats's determination to resolve them forced the unsubmissive females of the odes to become, collectively, a portrait of his own "demon poesy." Even in the "Ode on Melancholy," in which the contradictions are allowed to coexist rather than being forced into an untenable synthesis, the male, who is both creator of and victim to the contradictory female (thereby delineating his own paradoxical identity), becomes an emasculated "cloudy troph[y]" (30). Control of the female imagination can only be sustained, the odes finally contend, through elimination of her inherently conflicting nature by unraveling the "gordian complication of feelings" that she produces in the male (*Letters* 1:342). There can be no benign acceptance of what he does not understand, regardless of the difficulties involved in comprehending it. Keats has "laid bare" this knowledge, apotheosized in "Lamia," the only poem of 1819 in which the putative hero dies, victim of his own benign acceptance of the mysterious female.

Lamia exists not only as a goddess, elusive and impenetrable

144

as all of the females since "Hyperion" have been, but, in her
primal identity as serpent, she is the incarnation of evil itself.[1]
She is not Eve, beguiled by the serpent; rather, she is physically
the serpent itself, who will attempt subterfuge by taking on the
characteristics of the prelapsarian Eve, by becoming:

> A virgin purest lipp'd, yet in the lore
> Of love deep learned to the red heart's core:
> Not one hour old, yet of sciential brain
> To unperplex bliss from its neighbour pain.
>   (1.189–92)

In her transformation from serpent to woman, Lamia surpasses
in innocence even the "sweet-lipp'd ladies" of the early poems.
As a "virgin purest lipp'd," she is a portrait of hyperbolic inno-
cence, drawn to extreme in order to illuminate her "other
side"—that which focuses not on her lips, "pure" from the taint
of kisses, but on the love that can be "learned" and the "sciential
brain" that supplies the knowledge. Marilyn Butler writes that
the "description of Lamia's change from serpent to woman
allows for both possibilities—the ominousness of her ser-
penthood, the beauty and naturalness of it" (134).

During the writing and revising of "Lamia," Keats's letters
to Fanny Brawne, the lover who also allowed for possibilities
and whom Keats would suspect of being "a little inclined toward
the Cressid," become increasingly desperate with a plea first
for self-denial of her presence and finally for male possession
over her. I "strive not to think of you," Keats writes in August
1819, "but when I have succeeded in doing so all day and as
far as midnight, you return as soon as this artificial excitement
goes off more severely from the fever I am left in" (*Letters*
2:137). The fear that precipitates the denial sought is both
caused by and succeeded with the Keatsian "fever," equally
applied to both women and poetry and sometimes undistin-
guishable between the two.

In October 1819, a letter to Fanny Brawne that seems the
essence of the serpent/woman's power over the vulnerable Ly-
cius originates with the similarly vulnerable creator:

> My love has made me selfish. I cannot exist without
> you—I am forgetful of every thing but seeing you
> again—my Life seems to stop there—I see no further.
> You have absorb'd me. I have a sensation at the pres-
> ent moment as though I was dissolving—I should be
> exquisitely miserable without the hope of soon seeing
> you. I should be affraid [sic] to separate myself far
> from you. My sweet Fanny, will your heart never
> change? My love, will it? I have no limit now to my
> love—. . . . Do not threat me even in jest. I have been
> astonished that Men could die Martyrs for religion—I
> have shudder'd at it—I shudder no more—I could be
> martyr'd for my Religion—Love is my religion—I
> could die for that—I could die for you. My Creed is
> Love and you are its only tenet—You have ravish'd
> me away by a Power I cannot resist; and yet I could re-
> sist till I saw you; and even since I have seen you I
> have endeavoured often 'to reason against the reasons
> of my Love.' I can do that no more—the pain would
> be too great—My Love is selfish—I cannot breathe
> without you. (*Letters* 2:223–24)

Framed within the repeated lines that identify his love as "selfish," Keats's own egocentric "love" for Fanny Brawne here seems identical to what Lamia experiences with Lycius, whose own androcentrism will destroy their covert relationship. Brawne has "absorb'd" Keats, and he fears "dissolving," just as Lamia will at the poem's end. The facile sexuality that occurred through the metaphor of "dissolving" and "melting" in *Endymion* and "The Eve of St. Agnes," thereby creating identity, now threatens its loss. The masculine identity is in danger of being "dissolved," in both this letter and in "Lamia," and Keats final-izes this fear in the letter to Brawne, perhaps unconsciously, but certainly ironically, with a line from John Ford's *'Tis Pity She's a Whore*, in which he has "endeavoured often 'to reason against the reasons of my Love' " (1.125). It is the same lack of reasoning that will afflict his creation Lycius, who falls prey to a beautiful illusion cloaked in a "borrowed identity" of mortality.

Letters such as these compel many critics to see direct causa-tion between Keats's relationship with Fanny Brawne and the creation of Lamia. I agree with Douglas Bush, however, that "Lamia" is not totally allegorical, that Lycius is "a projection of only one part, and not the strongest part, of Keats himself" (161). Keats believes he has given up his "strongest part" to Brawne, however, and thus the reader must presume that his relationship with her most probably does have an effect on "Lamia" thematically. But she is not the primary, and far from exclusive, reason for Lamia's complexity. Too many of the poems that precede this one, and certainly the two that follow, written during the same frustrating relationship, made even more so by time, argue against such ill-founded logic. And despite the facile connection between Fanny and Lamia that may be invoked by some, the complexities that make up Lamia, as indeed those that make up his vision of Fanny, too, belong more to Keats than to either of the women. There are, of course, echoes of his doomed relationship with Fanny Brawne within the poem, as there must be, and I shall discuss those that I see within the chapter, but the primary concern in this poem and every other is Keats and the imagination, and any other reading would unfairly reduce the poet to a shadow of his own knight-at-arms, and the distinction between the past and present male figure is too clear from the beginning of the current poem to allow such a reduction.

A brief tale of Hermes and the nymph he pursues opens "Lamia" and is not found in the story of Lamia and Lycius that appears in Burton's *Anatomy of Melancholy* from which Keats derived his poem. The addition is significant. As an Apollo of reduced proportions, chasing but not capturing fleeing women, Hermes's role here is to introduce the poem by concentrating on it through the fairy-tale dimensions of illusion. The poem will progressively become more concerned with the antithesis of these dimensions—mortality—until, at the end, death rather than transcendence occurs, reversing the common scheme of the early poems. The dream state of "Lamia" now defines the inherent difference between mortal and deity, between Hermes and Lycius, rather than offers, even temporarily, a synthesis of the two. Thus, this is the only poem in which dream participation leads to physical as well as spiritual death; to live in a dream, the odes have shown, one must already possess the prerequisite immortality, as Keats again makes clear in the Hermes episode.

Like Mnemosyne to Apollo's birth into godhood, Lamia acts as "midwife" to the tentative relationship between Hermes and the nymph and it becomes real, as "into the green-recessed woods they flew; / Nor grew they pale, as mortal lovers do" (1.144–45). Lamia's identity within the opening illusion, like Saturn's "real self" before the usurpation by the Olympians, is a powerful one because it belongs in this illusory realm.

But, while the "dreams of Gods" are still transcendent (1.127), Keats's interest now lies elsewhere—in the tenuous, and often tragic, bond between mortals and the elusive imagination, a bond made more palpable than ever before by the actual marriage between Lamia and Lycius, who, like Glaucus before him, is duped into believing he has found "more bliss than all / The range of flower'd Elysium" (*Endymion* 3.427–28) in a female who deceives. Thus, the tale of Hermes and the nymph is summarily dismissed, having shown the union that exists, by its very nature, as the antithesis to the one Lycius will find.

Charles Patterson calls the following description of Lamia, which introduces her to the reader as a serpent, "the ultimate in daemonic beauty, utterly beyond any 'standard law' of being or knowing" (193):

> She was a gordian shape of dazzling hue,
> Vermilion-spotted, golden, green, and blue;
> Striped like a zebra, freckled like a pard,
> Eyed like a peacock, and all crimson barr'd;
> And full of silver moons, that, as she breathed,
> Dissolv'd, or brighter shone, or interwreathed
> Their lustres with the gloomier tapestries—
> So rainbow-sided, touch'd with miseries,
> She seem'd, at once, some penanced lady elf,
> Some demon's mistress, or the demon's self.
> Upon her crest she wore a wannish fire
> Sprinkled with stars, like Ariadne's tiar:
> Her head was serpent, but ah, bitter-sweet!

She had a woman's mouth with all its pearls complete:
And for her eyes: what could such eyes do there
But weep, and weep, that they were born so fair?
(1.47–62)

The contradictory nature of Lamia begins immediately with
this description, certainly demonic in its protean ability to evoke
such various identities simultaneously: a "penanced lady elf,"
a "demon's mistress, or the demon's self." Lamia "seem'd" a
demon, but, unlike her demonic predecessors, la belle dame
and the nightingale, even as a serpent she possesses a vulnera-
bility manifested by her eyes that, like Burton's earlier descrip-
tion of them as the "chief seat of love," "weep, and weep," an
ameliorating attribute because it is a human one, and not found
in either of Lamia's predecessors who existed wholly in the
realm of the Apollonian imagination that forsakes the earth.
While Melancholy "dwells with Beauty" that "must die" (21),
joy that is always "bidding adieu" (23), and pleasure that turns
to poison, the "rainbow-sided" Lamia displays "silver moons,
that, as she breathed, / Dissolv'd, or brighter shone, or inter-
wreathed / Their lustres with the gloomier tapestries." She is
at once the waxing and waning of female power.

Despite her protean abilities, however, the reader is advised
of her true and fundamentally unchanging nature when:

Left to herself, the serpent now began
To change; her elfin blood in madness ran,
Her mouth foam'd, and the grass, therewith besprent,
Wither'd at dew so sweet and virulent;
Her eyes in torture fix'd, and anguish drear,
Hot, glaz'd, and wide, with lid-lashes all sear,
Flash'd phosphor and sharp sparks, *without one cooling tear*.
The colours all inflam'd throughout her train,
She writh'd about, convuls'd with scarlet pain.
(1.146–54, my italics)

The most significant aspect of Lamia's transformation is that
the tears she shed while a serpent, ameliorating and human,
have now, in the process of her actually becoming human, all

dried up, leaving her eyes "in torture fix'd." In place of the salutary "cooling" tears, Lamia's eyes are "hot, glaz'd, and wide," and the pain is "scarlet," brought about by writhing rather than crying.

"Scarlet" pain is one that is alive with passion. Lamia is a "scarlet woman" in her transformation, but the passion that accompanies such an identification leaves her more vulnerable than she has a need to be, because in the hands of the female passion can be destructive to the male. But as with all women branded as "scarlet," their "crime" is their sexuality and it is one that requires a male accomplice. And like the vulnerable Ariadne whose constellatory "tiar" becomes a part of Lamia's own characteristics,[2] the sensuality of the serpent/woman becomes an irresistible lure to the emotionally besotted Lycius. Lamia appears to be unconscious of her sexuality, a trait not found in any of the other females who were imbued with it except Madeline, who was "duped" herself but was happily granted restoration rather than destruction. It is this unawareness that makes Lamia vulnerable and it is her vulnerability that attracts Lycius.

Lamia's sexuality, unlike that of la belle dame, is entirely dependent on her union with Lycius and thus is not something she uses as a weapon against him. She is, after all, the one who is infatuated with him, pursues him, and is willing to transform herself for him. She is an illusion but, unlike her destructive predecessor, is willing to accommodate the mortality that defines both her lover and her own desires.

Such accommodation is seen when Lamia is "undrest / Of all her sapphires, greens, and amethyst, / And rubious-argent" (1.161–63), luxurious trappings that would characteristically belong to the illusory female, but that she surrenders to her new mortality. But when "of all these bereft, / Nothing but pain and ugliness were left" (1.163–64), attributes that, up to this point, have not been applied to Keats's females—even the demonic ones. Lamia's "undressing" is shockingly different from Madeline's, whose similar divestment of "warmed jewels" and "rich attire" leaves her even more illusory, "half-hidden, like a mermaid in seaweed" (228, 230, 231), an act of transformation (and undressing) that clearly enhances rather than destroys her female characteristics. At the present stage of Keats's career, however, mystery transforms itself into falsehood. And Lamia's transformation is similar to Spenser's own personification of the "face of falsehood" in *The Faerie Queene*: Duessa, who, when stripped of "ornaments that richly were displaid," is revealed as a withered hag, "ill favoured, old, / Whose secret filth good manners biddeth not to be told" (1.8, 36.8–9). Duessa's transformation exposes the most "ugly shape" seen by any "living creature" (1.8, 47.9), and she flees. "Lamia" was written at a time when Keats, like Spenser, was becoming increasingly concerned with appearance versus reality, especially when it pertained to the female, fostered not only by the increasing demands he places on the imagination, but also probably by the increasingly androcentric demands he believes he must place on Fanny Brawne as well, to be the object of his own "self-possession" that he fears losing.

The obvious difference between the transformations of Duessa and Lamia is in the respective male lover's ideas regarding his own "self-possession." When Duessa's falsehood is finally exposed to her erstwhile lover, the Red Crosse Knight, he reacts appropriately, as both lover and hero, but it is Lamia's continuing ability to deceive, aided by Lycius's ability to be duped, that leaves the present lover content with the illusion rather than the reality. It is a fear that Keats himself had over Fanny Brawne, as relentlessly exposed in the letters, a fear that accompanies Lycius's inability to recognize reality until it is too late to save himself.[3]

The recognition of an intrinsic complexity that continues to distance the female further and further from the "pure Goddess" who inhabited Keats's "boyish imagination," again most likely exacerbated by his relationship with Fanny Brawne, nevertheless allows (or compels) Keats to make Lycius a more culpable figure in the ensuing tragedy than he has made any of the other heroes, even the very culpable knight-at-arms.

Lycius is not merely a hapless victim of Lamia's deceit but, instead, is the predecessor of the dreamer in "The Fall of Hyperion," a member of the "tribe" (1.167) who "[thoughtlessly

slept] away their days" (1.151). And his "thoughtlessness" be-
gins when he is about to meet Lamia:

> Over the solitary hills he fared,
> Thoughtless at first, but ere eve's star appeared
> His phantasy was lost, *where reason fades*,
> In the calm'd twilight of Platonic shades.
>
> (1.233–36, my italics)

Unlike Keats in his relationship with Fanny Brawne, Lycius
cannot even make a nominal attempt to temper the love that is
in danger of consuming him with "reason," for his reason,
like the nightingale's song, "fades." It is the prerequisite to
subsequent control by the illusory imagination. But while the
speaker of the nightingale ode is only frustrated rather than
destroyed by the break from the illusion, Lycius's exchange of
reason for fantasy will prove fatal. As the females grow more
powerful and problematic, the male grows weaker and more
susceptible to them. It is the traditional "sexual hierarchy" that
becomes dangerously reversed in Keats's poetry, a hierarchy
that is so entrenched in masculine literature, "its sexual asym-
metries so severe, the desires of its characters so invariant, that
[regardless of where it begins, it tends] to the same conclusion:
the dominance of one man, the helplessness of all women"
(Chase 48).[4]

The tragedy of this reversed hierarchy emanates from the
fact that, as Patterson says of Lycius's "thoughtlessness," "Lycius
is about to make the mistake of complete attachment to some-
thing that lacks the substantiality and concreteness necessary
to make it suitable for the human consciousness as now consti-
tuted" (199). Like Lorenzo before him, Lycius's "complete at-
tachment" will be manifested as an infantile dependence, but
unlike Isabella, Lamia cannot offer nurturance. It is this insub-
stantiality that delineates the final difference between the trag-
edy of the speaker of the nightingale ode and that of Lycius.
For when imagination is discovered to be a "deceiving elf," as in
the ode, there still remains an identity, albeit not transcendent,
because of the senses that are left. But because it is Lycius's

reason (that is, his senses) that has faded, he is left in the realm of illusions, devoid of identity because he is mortal. It is, ironically, because of Lamia's constancy to him rather than desertion that Lycius is irrevocably destroyed. In "La Belle Dame sans Merci" and "Ode to a Nightingale," the tragedy originates with the belief that the two realms can be fused; in "Lamia," it derives from the knowledge, which comes too late, that they cannot be. It is a conscious change in perspective on Keats's part not fully achieved in his life outside of poetry, even when his life involved Fanny Brawne.

Keats had always harbored feelings toward women that were as ambivalent as his female figures themselves. While he publicly revered the female as deity in his poetry, privately, in letters to friends, he frequently castigated them, as in the early letter to Bailey in which Keats confesses that when he is "among Women [he has] evil thoughts, malice spleen—[he] cannot speak or be silent—[he is] full of Suspicions and therefore listen to no thing" (*Letters* 1:341). He admits that he does not have such feelings when he is among men. His male peers are, to Keats, the portrait of strength, normalcy, and, most important, unambiguity. That is precisely why the female is his metaphor for the imagination, and why she has become Lamia.

The serpent/woman comes dangerously near to Keats's own complex ideas regarding the female, making the relationship between hero and goddess more difficult to sustain, and much more difficult to resolve. It is this new complexity that forces Lycius, whose gender is not defined as ambivalent by Keats, to take on the same ambiguous nature as seen in the present female, and with it, he acquires a larger portion of the culpability than his predecessors did.

Schapiro compares Lycius to a Byronic hero, "victim not only of the woman's ambivalent nature but also of his own. . . . the destructive rage is located in the self, in the nature of his own love as well as the woman's" (33). The "destructive rage" here is one that recognizes the illusion and its inherent dangers (Lycius eventually suspects Lamia is not mortal, and believes she may be a "descended Pleiad" [1.265]), but chooses it above the reality.

Waldoff extends Schapiro's remarks by suggesting that Ly-
cius's culpability lies in the fact that his love, like the self-
ascribed "selfishness" that Keats has attributed to his own love
for Fanny Brawne, is "ultimately a form of self-love": "When
he looks into her eyes, he sees himself 'mirror'd small in para-
dise,' and he calls her 'My silver planet' as if she were a planet
in orbit around him as a sun, calling attention to his brilliance"
(167–68). Of course, the planetary metaphor was introduced
by Keats as an intrinsic part of Lamia herself: "full of silver
moons," indicating her own erratic changeability, but it is nev-
ertheless clear here that the vision that was heightened in *En-
dymion* and destroyed in "La Belle Dame" becomes, in this poem
of male egocentricity, merely reflectory. Like Narcissus who
becomes enamoured of the illusion of himself that he sees
reflected in the water, Lycius, too, falls in love with the reflection
of himself rather than the reality of Lamia.

Lycius is described as "blind" or "blinded" three times in
the poem, and, in fact, the only character to possess vision
is Apollonius, a figure to whom Lemprière attributes great
knowledge and wisdom (68),[5] but who to Lycius appears as "the
ghost of folly haunting [his] sweet dreams" (1.377). Apollonius
"haunts" Lycius because he alone has retained his "quick eyes"
(1.374), unimpaired by either the "torture fix'd" of Lamia's or
the illusions of Lycius. His description recalls another old man,
the "ancient Beadsman" of "St. Agnes." But despite the Beads-
man's advanced age (he is the only other aged man in Keats's
poetry), he displays none of the wisdom of Apollonius. With
his "numb" fingers and "frosted breath," he is instead an image
of age approaching death, and thus his role in the earlier poem
is little more than portentous. But both old men, by their age
alone, convey the overthrow of passion in favor of ritualized
reason. It is an attempted coup that did not succeed in "St.
Agnes," but in this poem, the female, as well as the passion she
embodies, will be summarily destroyed.

Because the female has become illusory in the poetry, the
relationship between the man of reason, Apollonius, and Lamia
is antagonistic. It is a battle over not only the control of the
female but over the control of Lycius as well.[6] Because Apollo-

nius is described as "philosophic" (1.365), and Keats has become "convinced more and more that" the philosopher is second only to the writer as "the most genuine Being in the World" (*Letters* 2:139), illusion must succumb in this poem to the wisdom of Apollonius's reality. It is an outcome neither desired nor considered possible by Keats via the symbols of religion and age in "St. Agnes."

M. R. Ridley contends that the ending of "Lamia," whereby the relationship between goddess and mortal is unequivocally destroyed, is an indication of Keats's "growing up" (264), of his denouncing illusions altogether. This contention will be further validated in "The Fall of Hyperion," and, despite its often ambiguous language, there is much in "Lamia" to corroborate this reading. Regardless of her oft-cited moments of vulnerability that make her more sympathetic, Lamia is, like la belle dame before her, the quintessence of the unbridled imagination. She offers no resolution to the complexities that characterize her because there is none. The ending portrays the "inevitable necessity" of the replacement of illusion with reality (Stillinger, *Hoodwinking* 47), the only way to resolve the complexities.

Marriage, so frequently the metaphor for the fusion of the two realms, cannot work here as it did in *Endymion* and as the symbolic union of "To Autumn" will. Unlike Cynthia, who is the supreme exemplar of immortal beneficence because she does not long to be mortal, and unlike the figure of "To Autumn," who does not long for celestial powers, and in whom sexuality is subdued into asexual serenity, Lamia presents a confusion of boundaries because she herself is a willing product of the two discrete realms. As a serpent, she is immortal; as a counterfeit woman, however, she has falsely acquired the characteristics of a mortal. Such lack of true and harmonious identity makes her, unlike la belle dame, vulnerable and therefore pitiable, but it cannot erase the fact of her origin. La belle dame's lack of vulnerability was a result of her unacceptance of either realm wholly rather than an embracement of both. There was no "confusion" in her character, only indifference. But the emphasis in the relationship between Lamia and Lycius is on unweaving rather than "weaving," on rigidity rather than "dissolution," terms that, until now, most commonly signified the fusion that Keats sought, frequently through sexual union.

The sexual act in "Lamia" is metaphorically explicit, as it is in most of the poems whose characters seek immortality, but not only does it fail to achieve the desired union once again, it is also as transitory and insubstantial as Lamia herself. As Lycius

> harbour'd in
> That purple-lined palace of sweet sin,
> His spirit pass'd beyond its golden bourn
> Into the noisy world almost forsworn.
>   (2.30–33)

Lycius is willing to give up sex with Lamia for the same "noisy world" of "busy common-sense" ("Indolence" 40) that the poet immersed in indolence wished to avoid. "A moment's thought," Lamia realizes, "is passion's passing bell" (2.39), emphasizing the dichotomy between thought and sensation that informs the poem. The act of sex as a metaphor for creation, like poetry, can only be carried out through what Keats refers to as the "silent Working" of "the simple imaginative mind" (*Letters* 1:185), and Lycius will destroy the silence first by making demands of his lover. He tells Lamia he is thinking of "how to entangle, trammel up and snare / Your soul in mine, and labyrinth you there / Like the hid scent in an unbudded rose" (2.52–54). Lycius wants to turn Lamia's insubstantiality into something very real through his desire to reverse her obvious sexual identity into that of an "unbudded rose," a "virgin purest-lipp'd," whom he will display to the "noisy world." But the only way sin can remain "sweet" is by remaining private. The lines that depict the lovers' sexual encounter create a shrine to privacy—the word "harbour," even as a verb, the "palace," and the "golden bourn" all illuminate the idea of lush enclosure and separation from the outside world. As sexual intercourse itself can be seen as "enclosure" to the male, albeit sometimes a frightening one, there is a portentousness to these lines of a secret and sacred place about to be violated by outside and alien forces.

By virtue of her insubstantiality, Lamia is not only the perceived means of restoration to Lycius, but the object to be restored as well and such restoration must be, to the male who enjoys "reflection" more than perspicacious vision, performed in public. Thus the desperate attempt to "entangle, trammel up and snare" is one that Lycius hopes will publicly make his lover, and the relationship, a permanent part of his life—his identity—and it will be achieved by placing the burden of the responsibility on the female.

And, like Lycius, Keats, too, places the responsibility for his own identity on Fanny Brawne—an obvious reason for his exposed battle with uncertainty over their relationship. Her behavior is always, according to the desperate Keats, nothing less than a barometer of her feelings for him and the degree of his own "self-possession." As most fledgling lovers, Keats had trouble distinguishing love's object from the emotion itself; Brawne came to symbolize and internalize the emotion of love to Keats, and thus its pain as well.

"You must be mine to die upon the rack if I want you," Keats tells Brawne in a letter of May 1820 (*Letters* 2:291), an eerily similar demand to the one Lycius will make to Lamia, which does, in fact, cause death.

From the demands that Lycius makes to his lover comes the disastrous scheme of making Lamia "real" by making their marriage public. Keats makes it patently clear that Lycius's desire to exhibit Lamia to the Corinthians emanates from a need for self-aggrandizement rather than from love of Lamia, because the "purple-lined palace of sweet sin" is no longer enough for Lycius, whose desire to see himself "reflected" is not being met by the solitariness of the "silent Working" of either sex or the imagination.

Lycius's decision to display Lamia to the public is one that weakens her until she is "all subdued" and has reluctantly "consented to the hour / When to the bridal he should lead his paramour" (2.82–83). As the priest led the heifer to slaughter on the frieze of the Grecian urn, "all her silken flanks with garlands drest" (34), Lycius will lead Lamia, "veil'd, . . . heralded along / By strewn flowers, torches, and a marriage song"

(2.108–9), in a ritual of masculine control that will prove to be as disastrous to the lovers as it had been to the heifer. Marriage is perverted, and the traditional marriage veil, symbol of both innocence and privacy, will be violently and noisily rent.

Patterson writes that Lycius's actions here manifest a "transposition of values" (209), caused by his own vanity, one which emanates from his desperate need to control. Lamia's own desperation at this point stems from "how to dress/ The misery" of Lycius's actions "in fit magnificence" (2.115–16). Another facet of her personality that makes Lamia vulnerable is her passivity here. Fitting the male's perception of the ideal female, she truly wants to please her lover—at the expense, even, of their own best interests. Thus Lamia obeys, but "silently paced about, . . . / In pale contented sort of discontent" (2.134–35).

As a putative mortal female, Keats contends, "she lov'd the tyranny" (2.81), and thus is "contented" in her obedience. But as the immortal she truly is, unused to submission and more wary of the consequences than is Lycius, she remains "discontent[ed]." Through the attempts at gaining mortality that have weakened her, she does not have the power, as Melancholy did, to sustain the contradictions. Her actions, therefore, manifest not so much a "transposition" of values, as those of Lycius, but a helpless surrender to their confusion.

The "dreadful guests" will "spoil [Lamia's] solitude" (2.145), the quiet that must exist for the imagination to survive. Food again serves as prelude to change in this poem, as it had in "St. Agnes." It is not an intimacy that will be created this time, though, for the feast will be devoured rather than left uneaten, and the oral gratification will be that of the intrusive guests rather than the lovers. They are offered "baskets of bright osier'd gold . . . / High as the handles heap'd, to suit the thought / Of every guest" (2.217–19). Unlike Lamia, who spurns thought, and Lycius, whose "reason" had "fad[ed]" upon meeting Lamia, the guests are characterized by their individual "thoughts," the act of reasoning that has already been identified as "passion's passing bell." They are the "noisy" world, who, with "busy brain[s]" (2.150), will destroy the solitude and privacy that Lamia has tried to sustain. But, most importantly, the guests are the harbingers of Lamia's own destruction, for among them is Apollonius, from whom "all charms fly" because he "will clip an Angel's wings, / Conquer all mysteries by rule and line, / Empty the haunted air, . . ." and finally "unweave a rainbow" (2.229, 34–37). The catalog of perfunctory masculine rites—to "clip," "conquer," "empty," and "unweave"—precipitates the end to illusory love and to the female's "charms" that were born from the "pain and ugliness" of her transformation from serpent to woman. Masculine rites cannot save the male, however. Like Apollo's birth in "Hyperion," Lycius's death is necessary to elucidate the end of a poetic era. "Cold philosophy" (2.230) will unweave the "beauteous wreath" (1.84) that is Lamia, but as Keats has learned from her predecessors, this is the only solution to the otherwise insoluble feminine character.

Further evidence of Lamia's own ambiguous identity occurs when she becomes the only female of Keats's poetry to lose (rather than give up) her vision, a loss usually sustained exclusively by the male in the poetry. Lycius asks Lamia whether or not she knows Apollonius:

> Poor Lamia answer'd not.
> He gaz'd into her eyes, and not a jot
> Own'd they the lovelorn piteous appeal:
> More, more he gaz'd: his human senses reel:
> Some hungry spell that loveliness absorbs;
> There was no recognition in those orbs.
> (2.255–60)

As there is no "recognition" of Lycius in Lamia's eyes, neither is there a reflection in which he can find comfort for his own egocentricity. Thus the advice given in the "Ode on Melancholy," to "feed deep, deep upon [the mistress's] peerless eyes" (20) in order to counteract the effects of mortality is not applicable here. As one without vision, Lycius's only form of sustenance has been Lamia's own ability to see, but her eyes, in effect, have once again become those of the serpent—"in torture fix'd." And for the first time in the poetry both the imagination and the speaker have become mutual victims of blindness.

Finally, the eye of Apollonius "like a sharp spear, went through [Lamia] utterly, / Keen, cruel, perceant, stinging" (2.300–301). There can be no doubt about the destruction here. It is both phallic and all-encompassing. The masculine rites of Apollonius have destroyed the serpent with a weapon of phallocentric proportions that resembles the serpent herself when erect, poised to strike.[7] It is a violent exorcism that Apollonius performs, and the female has surrendered to the male through alienation of her self from herself. It is an exorcism that destroys the victim as well as the demon, however, because it is a mutual "possession," thereby confusing the boundaries between guilt and innocence.

The final symbol of the transformation of the female from maiden to demon is the marriage robe itself. Intended to symbolize unity, it becomes instead the icon of separation here, as Lycius is "wound" in the robe as a corpse in its shroud: "no pulse, or breath they found, / And in its marriage robe, the heavy body wound" (2.310–11).

The masculinity that informed the poem and conquered imagination in the figure of Apollonius continues to usurp Lycius's identity in death—no longer the androcentric male, Death, instead of the female, has degendered him, and he is at the end only a "heavy body" referred to as "it." Thus while beauty is an illusion in "Lamia," and the goddess vanishes at the end to prove it, death is real, and, Keats insists, fitting retribution to one who cannot distinguish between the two.

In "The Fall of Hyperion" to follow, Lycius is reanimated, so to speak, in the character of the dreamer, but the father figure of Apollonius is replaced by the most powerful (and real) female thus far, the goddess Moneta, who will reclaim the boundaries that have been lost between dreams and reality by restoring the dreamer's vision and redefining his identity.

"The Fall" and "Autumn"
The Final Relationship

This chapter will focus on Keats's last two major works—"The Fall of Hyperion" and "To Autumn"—considered together because their individual creations are so profoundly intertwined, and thus, so too is their individual greatness.[1] As many critics have noted, each poem concerns a fall—the first, that of a poetic ideal, whereby Hyperion allegedly surrenders to his successor, Apollo, and the second of a seasonal ideal, in which summer reluctantly succumbs to autumn. Both poems exist at the far end of the process intrinsic to the creation of the female and manifest the poet's final attempts at an imagination able to escape mutability.

They are the poems that at last come between the poet and death, and portray the "knowledge of contrast, feeling for light and shade" (*Letters* 2:360) that Keats realized necessary not only for a poem but for life. They are the fragile and tragic "good bye" that Keats can "scarcely bid" Charles Brown in the same letter. Like the Fall in Genesis, these final poems indicate an end that serves simultaneously as a beginning, a felix culpa that promises new knowledge. It is the final portrait of the female that evokes the new and final knowledge. It is a knowledge that, like Keats prematurely wished of Lamia's, "smote, [yet] still guaranteed to save" ("Lamia" 1.339). The female at this last phase of the process from which she derives life is ultimately the only salvation possible to the poet who looks "upon fine Phrases like a Lover."

The need to believe in the constancy that these last poems promise is profoundly important at the end of the poetics, and one that Keats felt was denied him in the last days of his life.[2] But the female of these poems, at once admonitory and forgiving, serves to Keats, at least for now, as the perfect receptacle for that need.[3] In the dual figure of Moneta and Autumn, she becomes a process within herself, the maternal and desexualized, and finally degendered, apotheosis of both the "agonies, the strife / Of human hearts" ("Sleep and Poetry" 124–25) and the "bosom of a leafy world" where finally "we rest in silence" (119–20). The need becomes a faith, and the process that invokes it begins, as it had in "Hyperion," at the point of decimation of the Titans—the giant race of fallen deities who are able to promise only mutability to the poet who strove to escape it.

In the second "Hyperion," the grief of the Titans, which left them impotent in the first, succumbs to a new knowledge that gives identity not to Apollo, who is again dismissed at the end, but to the dreamer himself.

I

Begun as a revision to "Hyperion" in July 1819, and finally abandoned on September 21, "The Fall of Hyperion" takes the dream world that the mortal Lycius, among others, had disastrously attempted to enforce into reality, and makes it the setting for the poem itself. The dream in "The Fall" is reality, a reality that supplants all else. The dreamer, that is, never returns from it, as do virtually all the other heroes of the poems who were dreamers by choice rather than by name as the hero is here.[4] Even Endymion, who finally achieved and sustained the dream state, fully recognized it as one opposed to reality.

The dreamer of "The Fall" does not consciously invoke the dream, however, as Endymion and the other heroes had, but receives it through eating and drinking, actions that make it an integral part of him, an identity, gained through the maternal:

> I ate deliciously;
> And, after not long, thirsted, for thereby
> Stood a cool vessel of transparent juice,
> Sipp'd by the wander'd bee, the which I took,
> And, pledging all the mortals of the world,
> And all the dead whose names are in our lips,
> Drank. That full draught is parent of my theme.
> (1.40–46)

While "pledging" mortality, the dreamer transcends it. Like Eve, he eats forbiddenly.[5] While it is nowhere expressly acknowledged as "forbidden," it is the precursor to a fall, and the "parent of [the dreamer's] theme." And like the early Endymion, the "parent," so to speak, of Keats's own theme, who "felt endued / With power to dream deliciously" (*Endymion* 2.707–8), the dreamer, whose own powers will issue from it, "ate deliciously."

Like Keats, the dreamer will become subjugated by his own creation that he has internalized through the act of eating. And the outcome will be a "knowledge enormous," but a salutary rather than destructive one. With her "fine spell of words" (1.9), Moneta will admonish the dreamer into understanding.[6] As the most powerful female of the poetry she is also the most articulate. She is not, like Apollonius to Lycius, merely censorious; as the personification of "cold philosophy" ("Lamia" 2.230) and masculine ritual, he embodied the knowledge distinct from the imagination and could only condemn Lycius to an unambiguous death. Moneta threatens the same condemnation but, by virtue of her gender and thus connection with the imagination, she can also offer its counterpart, salvation. She not only exposes the wound but she applies the balm as well, for hers is a "minist'ring" power (1.96), and the food here, unlike that given and taken away by la belle dame, is a reality. The dreamer is sated rather than starved, attesting to the goddess's maternal and life-giving identity.

Unlike the knight-at-arms who existed at the nadir of poetic creativity as well as the devolution of the female figure, the dreamer is neither seduced, deceived, nor diseased. The goddess is closest thus far to the maternal ideal and is therefore liberated from the sexuality that has proven destructive in the previous poems. Her liberation gives the male his, and she will allow the dreamer a rebirth that, like Apollo's, derives from the female as mother rather than lover who must be controlled. It is the identity denied the knight-at-arms because la belle dame's powers stemmed from her sexuality, a force that Keats now deems more destructive than creative. Moneta exists as neither a literal nor metaphorical lover to the dreamer, so the need for control, leading to the familiar dilemma of irresolution, dissipates.

There is not much chance of the current male figure "controlling" any female, much less the exquisite Moneta. Corresponding with the poetry's most powerful female is its weakest male. Once the trait of the male exclusively, "self-possession" has become the defining characteristic of the female, and the male hero is progressively alien, first with the physical death of Lycius and here with the absence of a name, to the final poem in which he does not exist. Ross writes that "The Fall" "retreat[s] into the private self"; set in a dream, the poem is more of musing than discourse, and Keats "falls, from the very first word, into the obtuseness of private language" ("Fragmented Word" 129). The "private self" is not a masculine one, and neither is it the creative female.[7] Like his literary counterpart, Alice of the dream world of Wonderland, the male must "eat" to find the power to act. He is, as was the poet of "Indolence," befuddled with indirection rather than frantically grasping for lost identity as most of his predecessors were, expressed later in his apparent indifference to his own death: "What am I that should be so sav'd from death?" (1.138). And the "obtuseness" of the language becomes a part of himself, causing the setting to seem more barren than that of a "dream" should be. It is only with the appearance of Moneta, and the direction she internalizes for the dreamer, that the setting becomes recognizably mythopoeic. She comes as a

> small warm rain [that]
> Melts out the frozen incense from all flowers,
> And fills the air with so much pleasant health
> That even the dying man forgets his shroud.
>   (1.98–101)

Homans writes that the mother figure is the "most powerful feminine figure in Romantic poetry" (14). Moneta has gone beyond not only the boundaries of the feminine, however, but she surpasses even the masculine excesses of patriarchy that are variously uncovered in the poetry, making her, in Keats's idiom, the most powerful figure of either gender.

Although she is twice called "Mnemosyne," Moneta is far
removed from the goddess of "Hyperion." As a preserver of
old knowledge, of memory, Mnemosyne can offer only the past
to Apollo and he finds her unable to answer his question,
"Where is power?" (3.103). "Memory should not be called
knowledge," Keats writes to Reynolds on February 19, 1818
(*Letters* 1:231), and Moneta, the epitome of power that derives
its strength from the future as well as the past, tells the dreamer:

> "My power, which to me is still a curse,
> Shall be to thee a wonder; for the scenes
> Still swooning vivid through my globed brain
> With an electral changing misery
> Thou shalt with those dull mortal eyes behold,
> Free from all pain, if wonder pain thee not."
>   (1.243–48)

The ability to articulate her power rather than compel the
dreamer to "read / A wondrous lesson in [her] silent face"
("Hyperion" 3.111–12) presents Moneta as an active rather
than passive force as Mnemosyne was. Moneta will lead the
dreamer into either salvation or damnation at the end of this
process of acquiring knowledge, and, unlike any of the poems'
previous females, Moneta causes the male immediate fear
rather than joy:

> As near as an immortal's sphered words
> Could to a mother's soften, were these last:
> But yet I had a terror of her robes,
> And chiefly of the veils, that from her brow
> Hung pale, and curtain'd her in mysteries
> That made my heart too small to hold its blood.
>   (1.249–54)

The "terror" the dreamer has of her appearance, in direct
contrast to the reality of her maternally softened words, makes
Moneta's purpose, unlike Cynthia's to Endymion and Mnemo-
syne's to Apollo, suspect to the male who appears at this point
to be the most vulnerable of all the poetry, having experienced

how wide the schism can be between appearance and reality in "Lamia." He is thus too vulnerable and self-protective to be called a "hero" and is truly defined by the perverse appellation of "dreamer"—he is what he does. The goddess is "curtain'd" in "mysteries" that make not only the female herself a mystery, but her immediate surroundings as well, the surroundings that have become frighteningly alive with her sudden appearance. And it is these surroundings, and the robes and veils and "Maian incense" (1.103), that the dreamer is afraid of being drawn into. Moneta is not simply a figure—she is a presence, and the dreamer will not stand too close for fear of being engulfed by her. He is the first male to be initially afraid of a relationship with the female rather than an active seeker of it.

The active presence that informs Moneta is one that is aptly characterized by Vendler as being a recognizable similarity between the maternal goddess and her predecessor, Spenser's Dame Nature in the "Mutability Cantos." Like Nature, Moneta wears an "ambiguous veil" (206), and it is this ambiguity that curtains her in mystery that the dreamer fears. Behind the veil could lurk another belle dame, who will irreparably shatter the dream, taking away both his food and his power, and leave the dreamer "alone and palely loitering" ("La Belle Dame" 46) by turning the Edenic landscape into the fairy child's "cold hill's side" (44). Vendler writes that Keats borrows the "splendor and beams (as well as terror and veils) for Moneta" from Dame Nature (207), thereby making the maternal connection between the goddesses real. Certainly Nature, with her ambiguous veil, "so by skill devized, / To hide the terror of her uncouth hew / From mortall eyes that should be sore agrized,"[8] seems a plausible prototype of Keats's goddess, especially since the latter will become the figure of Autumn, Keats's own Dame Nature.

But at this early point in the poem, Moneta is more a source of fear than a mother figure to the dreamer, a fear that stems from his own uncertain identity rather than hers. Another of Spenser's veiled figures may be more accurately compared with Moneta at her first appearance to the dreamer, one whose characteristics include both the dreaded sexuality and its counterpart, female ambiguity—the veiled Venus, from *The Faerie*

Queene, whom Paglia also suggests as Moneta's precursor (387). Unlike Dame Nature, Venus is in a temple, "all with frankensence ... / And odours rising from the altars flame" (4.10.37.2–3). Like the "marble balustrade" of Moneta's temple (1.91), Venus's contains "an hundred marble pillors" (4.10.37.4). "In the midst" of her temple, "the Goddesse selfe did stand / Upon an altar of some costly masse" (4.10.39.1–2). She is "covered with a slender veile afore; / And both her feete and legs together twyned / Were with a snake, whose head and tail were fast combyned" (4.10.40.7–9). She is a terrifying specter, although the terror is not explicitly stated, and much of it derives from her mythical identity as goddess of both love and lust. It is this two-horned sexuality and the debilitating need to control the female that has terrorized Keats's previous heroes, not the asexuality embodied in the figure of an earth mother such as Dame Nature.

Spenser continues:

> The cause why she was covered with a vele,
>   Was hard to know, for that her Priests the same
>   From peoples knowledge labour'd to concele.
>   But sooth it was not sure for womanish shame,
>   Nor any blemish, which the worke mote blame;
>   But for, they say, she hath both kinds in one,
>   Both male and female, both under one name;
>   She syre and mother is her selfe alone,
> Begets and eke conceives, ne needeth other none.
> (4.10.41)

Spenser's hermaphroditic Venus, having "both kinds in one," able both to conceive and beget in one fluid sexual continuum that, like the snake at her feet, symbolizes the cycle of regeneration, will evolve into the androgynous Dame Nature, just as Keats's veiled Moneta will become, by virtue of her ability to combine the realms of earth and heaven, and thus assure Keatsian regeneration, the figure of Autumn. Whereas the sexual act has previously been the immediate channel to the imagination and thus knowledge (albeit a frequently destructive one), Moneta's is the ultimate knowledge that is transcendent and

parthenogenic, desexualized into a figure who neither needs
nor desires the vulnerability of the male for her identity. As
both "Fatal" and "Ideal" Woman, Moneta is, as Spenser calls the
veiled Venus, the "Great God of men and women" (4.10.47.7).

As Sandra Gilbert and Susan Gubar point out, however, the
veiled female figure "reflects male dread of women" and the
uncertainty of whether the female will "haunt" or "inspire"
him (472). It is an uncertainty exacerbated here into fearful
proportions by the fact that it is an obviously powerful goddess
who hides her face from the male, and thus the mystery seems
too great for the mortal to bear, and may turn his characteristic
"dread" of women into an impotent stupor.

The possible danger is necessary to the dreamer, however,
if he is to acquire the knowledge that will turn him into a poet.
Because it records all human emotion, the face, and especially
the eyes, contain the source of that knowledge, and thereby
power, to Keats. Moneta's closest predecessor, the veiled god-
dess Melancholy, has "no shape distinguishable," as Van Ghent
states (211), indicating an ambiguous knowledge to be gained
at best. Mnemosyne, on the other hand, is represented as a
"robed form" and a "supreme shape," but her face is visible at
her appearance; Apollo says to her, with none of the fear of
the dreamer: "Goddess! I have beheld those eyes before, / And
their eternal calm, and all that face" ("Hyperion" 3.59–60).
Unlike Moneta's hidden eyes, Mnemosyne's are visible and
salutary from her inception. The goddess of the first "Hype-
rion" embodies none of the contradictions that characterize
both the succeeding poem and its goddess. Moneta is no longer
a "lifeless abstraction," as Sperry calls Mnemosyne, but rather
"the supreme embodiment of the poetic conscience and hu-
manitarian concern" (313).

Moneta is more the finished portrait of the goddess Ops
in "Hyperion" than of Mnemosyne, who symbolizes human
suffering by "uplifting her black folded veil" and revealing
"pale cheeks, and all her forehead wan, / Her eye-brows thin
and jet, and hollow eyes" (2.113–15). Like Moneta's, Ops's is a
feminine rather than masculine ritual of suffering that leads
to knowledge. "All clouded round from sight" at her initial

appearance in "Hyperion," Ops is, like Melancholy, of "no shape distinguishable, more than when / Thick night confounds the pine-tops with the clouds" (2.78, 79–80). And, although her presence will be supplanted by Mnemosyne in that poem of passive acquisition of knowledge, her shape will be made exquisitely "distinguishable" in the figure of Moneta.

It is indeed a momentous vision that Moneta's parted veils disclose, containing, as Bate says, "both the remorseless accumulation of suffering and also its transcendence" (600). The dreamer sees:

> a wan face,
> Not pin'd by human sorrows, but bright blanch'd
> By an immortal sickness which kills not;
> It works a constant change, which happy death
> Can put no end to; deathwards progressing
> To no death was that visage; it had pass'd
> The lily and the snow.
>
> (1.256–62)

"Deathwards progressing / To no death," the same process without end that will inform "To Autumn," is the defining characteristic of the goddess of new knowledge. Following his initial fear, the dreamer recognizes her as the maternal figure she is who not only promises the destruction of death but will grant its redemptive counterpart, rebirth, as well. It is a cycle that can be offered to the male only by the female, as masculine identity both rests upon and emerges from it. The concept of an ideal poetry becomes better able to be realized now as it derives from the power of the ideal female who parallels it.

As many critics have pointed out, the setting of "The Fall" is an "internal landscape," and thus the danger of the "self-destructive solipsism" that befell the knight-at-arms is paramount here to the dreamer, as the "language feeds upon itself" (Yaeger 50), and the question of identity that has haunted all the poetry of 1819 resurfaces. The articulate Moneta, who rescues both the dreamer and the language by embodying the ideal imagination that coheres rather than alienates, is the only female of the poetry capable of granting an identity that will do the same. It is a frightening aspect for the poet who claims to "class women" in his poetry with "roses and sweetmeats,—they never see themselves dominant" (*Letters* 2:327).[9] Moneta is undeniably "dominant," a characteristic acquired not only through her ability to encompass and articulate both suffering and redemption, but, of primary importance, through the promise of identity that accompanies the ability.

Keats's heroes have been seeking identity since the poet of "I stood tip-toe" asked, "Was there a Poet born?" (241). And Endymion soon joined the all-male chorus with the question, "What is this soul then?" (4.475). Since Moneta is the only female able both to grant and sustain the identity sought, she is an evolution rather than a repetition of the theme, and the male's identity, in a desexualized female, comes from her brain, which as Van Ghent notes, is analogous to the womb (236). No longer simply a receptacle for the world's memory, the *Anima Mundi* (Van Ghent 235), as Mnemosyne's had been, the female mind becomes "admonisher," and memory acquires the ability to create, to learn from the past in order to warn against the future. The "hollow brain" of Apollo, wherein the "creations and destroyings, all at once / Pour[ed]" (3.116–17) in order to deify him, has been transferred to the goddess herself, and the dreamer "ached to see what things the hollow brain / Behind enwombed" (1.276–77), in language that seems not yet able to let go of sexuality. With the transfer comes not only her own transformation from passive to profoundly active, but, with the brain now an organ of procreation, the "new grown" thoughts that emerged tentatively in "Psyche" have come to fruition, and the "life of sensations" for which the poet once longed has become the chaff. The dreamer will gain identity from the "high tragedy" that exists within Moneta's brain, and thus the sorrow of the Titans in "Hyperion," which left them frozen in immobility, becomes, in the figure of Moneta, a power of redemption. The human becomes inextricably entwined with myth, and the result is that the ruin of the Titans is no longer a mere abstraction but is proven upon the dreamer's pulses.

The poet who suffered previously because he could not

leave the earth now suffers in unison with it. It is a healing
transformation that begins when Moneta calls the dreamer "a
dreaming thing / A fever of thyself" (1.168–69). The oxymo-
ronic "feverous relief" of poetry that Keats frequently refers
to can be eliminated only through the "extensive knowledge"
of the most powerful of his female figures, a product herself
of the Keatsian love of oxymora, of language that "feeds upon
itself."

"Think of the earth" (1.169), the goddess admonishes the
dreamer, a reminder that, as Stillinger says, "except in inciden-
tal details the poetry of the earth [is] still missing" (*Hoodwinking*
64). The remembrance of the earth is the first step that must be
taken to cure the fever, always symptomatic of an imagination
brought "beyond its proper bound." Moneta warns the
dreamer that there is no "bliss even in hope" for him, no
"haven": "Only the dreamer venoms all his days, / Bearing
more woe than all his sins deserve" (1.170, 171, 175–76).[10] It is
a truth that must be internalized for the dreamer to become a
poet, and it is the "pain of truth" that, as Oceanus says in the
first "Hyperion," is "the top of sovereignty" (2.202, 205). The
god urges the Titans to "receive the truth, and let it be your
balm" (2.243), and Moneta distinguishes the poet from the
dreamer as one who "pours out a balm upon the world" (1.201).
It is within this truth, articulated by Moneta but sounding very
much like Keats himself, that the dreamer will gain identity, by
the ability to recognize the distinction, a recognition that he
will acquire through the internalization of the Titans as well as
his own suffering. The fever that made the act of creativity
analogous with flight in the early poems is transformed here—
from passion to compassion—through the female who acquires
power more from being an icon of divine humanity than being
an immortal.

Schapiro writes that the "most prominent and powerful im-
ages [in "The Fall"] all portray a woman's compassion—Mone-
ta's face, Saturn with his bowed head, 'listening to the Earth /
His ancient mother, for some comfort yet', the goddess with
hand 'pressed upon that aching spot / Where beats the human
heart, as if just there, / Though an immortal, she felt cruel

pain' " (59). It is finally the female freed from sexuality, and
from being coercively defined solely in masculine terms, who
can offer a redemptive rather than solipsistically destructive
pain to the poet, a pain that originated with his own masculinity.
The morbid belle dame and the females of the odes who disre-
garded the male's sorrow have led not to the cessation of life
and the absence of human identity that seemed inevitable and
was even overtly desired, but to its redemptive counterpart that
sustains the joy by separating it from the pain. Through the
compassion of the female, it is the "fever" that is eliminated
rather than the "relief."

In his famous "Mansion of Life" letter of May 3, 1818, Keats
elucidates the need to separate joy from pain:

> I compare human life to a large Mansion of Many
> Apartments, two of which I can only describe, the
> doors of the rest being as yet shut upon me—The first
> we step into we call the infant or thoughtless Cham-
> ber, in which we remain as long as we do not think—
> [we] are at length imperceptibly impelled by the awak-
> ening of the thinking principle—within us—we no
> sooner get into the second Chamber, which I shall call
> the Chamber of Maiden-Thought, than we become in-
> toxicated with the light and the atmosphere, we see
> nothing but pleasant wonders, and think of delaying
> there for ever in delight: However among the effects
> this breathing is father of is that tremendous one of
> sharpening one's vision into the heart and nature of
> Man—of convincing ones nerves that the World is full
> of Misery and Heartbreak, Pain, Sickness and oppres-
> sion—whereby This Chamber of Maiden Thought be-
> comes gradually darken'd and at the same time on all
> sides of it many doors are set open—but all dark—all
> leading to dark passages—We see not the ballance of
> good and evil. We are in a mist—*We* are now in that
> state—We feel the "burden of the Mystery." (*Letters*
> 1:280–81)

When we finally leave the "infant or thoughtless Chamber," as
Keats left his early poems of "leafy luxury," "impelled by the

awakening of the thinking principle," we convince ourselves that, as he did in the odes, "the World is full of Misery and Heartbreak." Like the poet who dwells within this illusion, "we are in a Mist." We feel the "burden of the Mystery," but it is not enough, this letter (and Moneta) admonishes, simply to escape it. Rather, like life itself, it must be undergone.

A curious hierarchy of the male to the female, not particularly Keatsian, occurs in this early letter. While the second chamber, the one that succeeds the embryonic "thoughtless" chamber, is defined as of "maiden-Thought," seemingly a virginal precursor to Moneta, the vision that originates with it is "fathered" rather than "mothered." To the early Keats, who defined the female primarily as an aberration of his male self, vision into "the heart and nature of Man," he believes, will come from a father figure rather than from one like the maternal Moneta, a figure who was absolutely foreign to the poet at the time of this letter.

But Moneta's presence is now real, created from the perceived inadequacies of her predecessors and the pain involved in that perception, and in the final great ode of autumn, the dreamer turned poet will indeed "think of the earth"—an earth no longer considered a hindrance to the imagination but, rather, the serene counterpart to a relief that could only be called "feverous" before.

II

The only "mist" that appears in "To Autumn" is a natural one—"season of mists and mellow fruitfulness" opens the final major poem, one so rich in the abundance of the earth that it seems a direct acknowledgment of Moneta's admonition to "think of the earth." "To Autumn" is the result of the poet's internalization of the sorrows of the earth experienced in "The Fall," and it exemplifies the creative process produced by this sorrow.

The poem again focuses on regeneration, but the figure here is exquisitely different from any who have come before. There is no direction in which the Ideal Female, as Moneta, may evolve except in one that not only desexualizes her but degenders her as well. Through this degendering, Keats discovers a way to transform the ephemerality that has characterized all the poetry's females into the permanence he has sought through them from the beginning. The androgynous figure of "To Autumn" derives from the personification of Keats's desire, first implemented in the portrait of Moneta, to rid his females of a sexuality that threatens. This figure is a "close bosom-friend" of Apollo (2), reinstated as the sun here, and always a figure of ambiguous masculinity in Keats's works. The fever that previously manifested itself through sexual imagery is gone, and in its place emerges an androgyne whose identity, like that which the dreamer himself acquired, derives from both wisdom and compassion, two discrete traits of the male and female respectively, rather than from the sexuality that Keats now perceives to set up boundaries to the genders rather than synthesize them into one.

Ward says of "To Autumn," "It is Keats's most characteristic because most impersonal poem. The poet himself is completely lost in his images, and the images are presented as meaning simply themselves: Keats's richest utterance is the barest of metaphor" (322). Despite the fact that the poet is indeed "lost" in the images, the poem seems to be the most "self-possessed" of all, but the difference is that the "self" is finally not a male, nor even a poet. What is being so assuredly "possessed" here is a moment in time, free of the trappings of masculine lineage that have so utterly consumed all previous moments that the poet himself wished to take possession of. It is not time itself that is portrayed here, but rather a single, independent moment, with neither past nor future; time, like gender, has become irrelevant.[11]

"To Autumn" has neither an explicit speaker nor an intrinsic hero—nothing, that is, to doubt the presence of the figure. Vision is not in danger of being lost, nor is there a declaration of vision to counteract the possibility of its being a dream. There is no need for affirmation because the question that exists in the poem, "Who hath not seen thee oft amid thy store?" (12), leaves no doubt of the reality that informs the work. Fecundity, or "advanced pregnancy" (Paglia 382), assures the regeneration begun in "The Fall," but there is no indication of the prerequisite sexuality. Sexuality is unnecessary because the female has become the "feminized male self, internalized by the poet" (Paglia 388). Autumn is a presumption, with no need of verification; it is the female's power that the poet has sought, and, with this poem's locus of degendered objectivity that becomes supremely subjective, its attainment is celebrated.

The setting here is not the prelude to an epiphany, as it had been in "The Fall," but is the epiphany itself, indicative of Keats's "philosophical understanding that this is the only real world we have" (Stillinger, *Poems* 477), as well as his final recognition of the truth of the "only real" identity he has as well.

All explicit language that Keats previously struggled to contain the elusive imagination is, as Vendler says, "modestly restricted to the 'sometimes' and 'oft' of the rewarded quest and to the 'now' of the dispersed creatures"—that is, to the moment itself (278). The past has been stretched into the present, and will extend, with the "last oozings" of the "cyder-press" (22, 21), into a future and, like the "vines that round the thatch-eves run" (4), will "bend" (5) back upon itself, back into the transcendent present. It is, in Keats's terminology, a "melting" of identities between poet and creation, and the intrinsic circularity of this ode, unlike that of the Grecian urn, promises regeneration rather than confusion because the frantic, androcentric questions of the speaker of that ode have been replaced with the simple statement of corrected vision.

The specter of dissolution that has threatened all of the poetry's heroes since "Hyperion" is itself dissolved, as the "hook / Spares the next swath and all its twined flowers" (17–18) rather than harvests it, compellingly different from the act of destruction portrayed by the traditionally male figure of Autumn. The liquidity of the language, the "oozing" that is equally oral and sexual, but far removed from phallic, ensures a lack of finality in the "full-grown lambs" (30) as well as the full-grown poet.

With this poem Keats has realized the serenity for which he expressed a desire in his letter of September 21, 1819, to George and Georgiana:

> Some think I have lost that poetic ardour and fire 'tis
> said I once had—the fact is perhaps I have: but in-
> stead of that I hope I shall substitute a more thought-
> ful and quiet power. I am more frequently, now, con-
> tented to read and think—but now & then, haunted
> with ambitious thoughts. Quieter in my pulse, im-
> proved in my digestion; exerting myself against vexing
> speculations—scarcely content to write the best verses
> for the fever they leave behind. I want to compose
> without this fever. I hope I one day shall. (*Letters*
> 2:209)

The only means by which he may rid himself of the fever is
through the female, who, in her destructive form, represents
the fever itself. Thus in the only major poem of Keats's later
career that does not attempt to coerce a state of permanence
into being, the fever that consumed Endymion, the knight-at-
arms, and the dreamer is irrevocably abated. And the female,
once source and embodiment of the poet's "vexing specula-
tions" now sits "careless on a granary floor, / . . . hair soft-lifted
by the winnowing wind" (14–15). As in "Indolence," the mood
is a degendered one, but it is androgyny rather than "effemi-
nacy" that is the result.

The mystery that previously defined her has been penetrated
by the poet's ability to let go of his need to comprehend it, the
Negative Capability of faith replaces androcentric doubt, and
the dreamer's inspired vision in "The Fall," that of seeing "as
a God sees" (1.304), is the controlling metaphor of "To Au-
tumn." There are no gods in the poem, but godlike vision, a
vision that evokes, as Wordsworth calls it in the immortality
ode, "the faith that looks through death," a "primal sympathy /
Which having been must ever be" (187, 183–84). And Keats's
Autumn is a "primal sympathy" as well, having appeared in the
earlier poems largely as the poet's antagonist. But in "Lamia"
the serpent/woman seeks plenitude and magic in "the store
thrice told / Of Ceres' horn" (2.186–87) and in both Hyperions,
Saturn bemoans the loss

> Of influence benign on planets pale,
> Of peaceful sway above man's harvesting,

> And all those acts which Deity supreme
> Doth ease its heart of love in.
> ("Hyperion" 1.108, 110–12; see "Fall" 1.414–17)

Thus the embattled figure of the earth, who promises final reconciliation of not only Saturn's but Keats's divided self, has, in fact, been a silent part of the salutary process all along, and every other female, mortal or immortal, now seems derived from her.

There will be no more songs of spring; nor, though, will there be another song of winter, as "La Belle Dame sans Merci" had been, a song that, because of the profound loss of the imagination, was transformed into silence. The song of autumn is one of plenitude:

> Then in a wailful choir the small gnats mourn
>   Among the river sallows, borne aloft
>   Or sinking as the light wind lives or dies;
> And full-grown lambs loud bleat from hilly bourn;
>   Hedge-crickets sing; and now with treble soft
>   The red-breast whistles from a garden-croft;
>   And gathering swallows twitter in the skies.
>   (27–33)

A euphony of nature defines and accompanies the plenitude. It is a celebration of life without end, of music that will not cease. The "small gnats" who "mourn / Among the river sallows" complete the process of mourning begun by the Titans, and mourning becomes an invocation. The "gathering swallows," unlike the nightingale before, whose disembodied voice was "buried deep," remain at the end to "twitter in the skies." Nothing remains hidden in this final ode, as so little of Keats's previous dogma remains pertinent here.

Ricks calls this last stanza "a large intimation of a parallel . . . between human and non-human life, taking part in each other's existence" (210). The realms will finally remain comfortably separate, "taking part" in each other, as the figures of Autumn and Apollo do, rather than frantically enjoined, as the poet has so often attempted.

Sperry writes: "ripeness is fall" (336), and "To Autumn" celebrates not only the fruition of the season, but also of Keats's poetics, the "ripeness" of the imagination. It is, first and foremost, a poem of restoration despite its new creation of the androgyne. And, ironically, the symbol of permanence that Keats sought throughout most of his career within the feverous realm of the imagination that denies the earth is discovered within his acceptance of it, a mature reworking of the too-facile immortality of Endymion.

Lau observes that for most of his career Keats emphasizes suffering "as a means to some happier state of being, rather than as a permanent feature of the human condition," and because of this Keats could not, until Moneta and Autumn, find a figure who adequately represented his belief in the "inevitability and importance of suffering" (330). With these final works Keats discovers, however, that suffering is integral to the human condition, and the human condition is integral to the imagination. The roles that both suffering and pleasure play in these final two figures of the imagination are finally almost indistinguishable from each other as they involve a continuum that cannot progress without both. These final poems and the knowledge that enlivens them become a part of Keats's canon within a matter of weeks but the wisdom contained within both extends beyond a lifetime.

Conclusion

In her discussion of American male writers, Heilbrun comments that the reason for so few "women heroes" in their works is that "the fear of the loss of masculinity is so extreme that any recognition of a feminine self is unbearably threatening" (74). Women have long been ancillary figures in the male imagination even when they serve, as they frequently do, as its focus. The control and subjugation of a woman character through literature is an exertion of male creative authority, an authority that often becomes immortalized.[1]

The females of Keats's poetry ultimately do become "heroic," however, largely because they are not to be taken as women per se. The "feminine self" that Keats reveres is more precisely the icon of everything he had hoped to find in women but could not. Keats's female figure is finally desexualized because he needs her to be a reflection of his own self; she is the recreation of what Keats, perhaps like most men of western culture, is socially indoctrinated to expect (and need) from the female. The exploitation of the female, as Keats pursues it in his poetry, thereby augments masculinity rather than threatens its loss. She is defined by the boundaries of male understanding, and when the male does not have the necessary understanding, he recreates her identity to fit within the already established boundaries. It is this recreation that delineates the evolution of the female character in Keats's poetry.

Keats's vision of women in his poetry reflects the predominant male vision toward women in life. There is the ever-present duality between a vision of the female as a subject in works of art, which tends to romanticize and alienate her even further from the male sensibility, and the more prosaic vision of the female as objective reality—as faithful wife or patient mother. This perceived duality, so frequently manifested in Keats's females, is transferred, for easy categorization, from the male's vision of her to the intrinsic definition of the female herself.

An example of Keats's own dual vision of the female, which shows it to be his vision rather than her reality, occurs in September 1819, shortly after he created the exquisitely powerful Moneta. He finds and takes pains to copy a lengthy misogynous parody of love and the woman's role in it into a letter to his brother George. It is from Burton's *Anatomy of Melancholy*, and it begins: "Every lover admires his Mistress, though she be very deformed of herself, ill-favored, wrinkled, pimpled, pale, red, yellow, tann'd, tallow-fac'd, have a swoln juglers platter face, or a thin, lean, chitty face, have clouds in her face, be crooked, dry, bald." Burton goes on to represent the mistress in a bawdy caricature, and Keats relentlessly transcribes every word of it into his letter. His own delight in sharing the statement is obvious in his prefatory remark to George that he had been "reading lately Burton's Anatomy of Melancholy; and I think you will be very much amused with a page I here coppy [*sic*] for you. I call it a Feu de joie round the batteries of Fort St Hyphen-de-Phrase on the birthday of the Digamma." At the end of the lengthy diatribe Keats tells his brother, "This I th[i]nk will amuse you more than so much Poetry" (*Letters* 2:191–92).

Despite the delight in sharing such ribald humor with his brother, restricted to the confidence of another male who would, without question, understand and appreciate it, Keats defines the female in his poetry as the necessary embodiment of an imagination that sustains the masculine creativity, that frequently terrifies but never "amuses." While the actual woman too often reminded Keats of early disappointments and lifelong doubts, which most likely contributed to his obvious enjoyment of "dirty jokes," the woman produced by his imagination could, by virtue of her ability to change through him (and with him), turn his frightening masculine failures into the channel of at least poetic success.[2]

The woman's changeability in the poems from healer to

destroyer and back again underscores Keats's own confusion about a man's role vis-à-vis woman, although the poet believes such female inconstancy indicates, conversely, woman's confusion and petulance about her role vis-à-vis man. A man frequently does not see himself as even having a "role" in a love relationship with a woman that does not originate with her own behavior. He is more an observer of his own (and her) actions in the relationship, as Keats is of his female figures. As woman is objective love, she is also, by extension, the creator of its need, and Keats's own retrospective confession that he once thought the woman a "pure Goddess" who slept in the "soft nest" of his mind (*Letters* 1:341) makes him not only a receptacle of that need but the ultimate observer of it. Portrayed in "To Autumn" as "sound asleep, / Drows'd with the fume of poppies" (16–17), the figure of the final poem is as close as Keats can come to the "sleeping goddess" of his youthful fantasies, but the mature poet has lost the desire for a lovers' relationship.

The figure of "To Autumn" is the imaginative counterpart to the human Jane Cox, about whom Keats says: "I like her and her like because one has no sensations—what we both are is taken for granted" (*Letters* 1:395). It is a presumption of identity, what Keats calls "disinterestedness" (*Letters* 1:293, 2:79), a trait he gives the ideal poetry as well as the ideal female, that informs both the final figure and the creator at the final stage of the poetics, and sexuality is no longer necessary. Keats's poetry painstakingly creates the Ideal Female—a sublimely masculine act—and by transferring his expectations of women from human to ethereal figures, Keats finds cathartic relief rather than the "feverous relief" (*Letters* 1:370) he had previously hoped to find from both his fear of women and his frustrated hopes regarding them. The ideal does finally replace the real.

Notes • Works Cited • Index

Notes

Introduction

1. As example of the perceived duality of women that pervades the man as well as the poet, Keats tells his sister-in-law, Georgiana, of Jane Cox, whom he calls a "Charmian": "I should like her to ruin me, and I should like you to save me" (*Letters* 1:396).

2. Contrary to my thesis, Evert contends that Keats made the masculine god (rather than the goddesses) "functionally representative of his own experience and reflection" (38). Donald H. Reiman agrees that Apollo is consistently Keats's metaphor for poetry, and to discount the female even further from the creative process, sees Cynthia/Diana as "the goddess of dreams and sleep, as opposed to imagination and poetry" (666n). In the very early poems, those published in 1817 especially, the masculine Apollo was certainly representative of both poetry and poet to Keats, a reason for his characterizing the females as ineffectual maidens who serve as little more than part of the scenery. But as Keats's personal (rather than conventional) symbol of poetry, Apollo simply did not last as representative of the transformative imagination.

3. The misogyny inherent in both Apollo and Keats will help produce the females that many critics refer to as "femmes fatales," the physical and feminine embodiment of an imagination that attempts desertion of the earth, of replacing the Dionysian principle of beauty with the Apollonian of knowledge.

4. Kate Millett claims that Keats "started it all with that fatal woman . . . who kept her knight hanging about disconsolate and 'palely loitering' " (148).

5. The critics who have, in one way or another, come closest to what I am doing are Mario D'Avanzo, who devotes the second chapter to Keats's use of the female as metaphor for the imagination but does not discuss, as I do, the process of evolution from meek to threatening; Barbara Schapiro, who explores la belle dame and Moneta psychoanalytically; Dorothy Van Ghent, who,

by virtue of her analysis of myth, gives more than usual attention to the later goddesses; Beth Lau, whose thesis explores the drama of knowledge and sorrow that informs the later goddesses; and the collection of essays that make up *Romanticism and Feminism*, ed. Anne K. Mellor (Bloomington and Indianapolis: Indiana UP, 1988), which discuss the search for masculine identity through the feminine.

1. "A Leafy Luxury": *Poems* of 1817

1. I shall not be taking into consideration every poem of the first volume, only those that most clearly express Keats's early attitude toward the use of the female figure as representative of the imagination.

2. See Brown's account in *The Keats Circle*, vol. 2, ed. Hyder E. Rollins (Cambridge, MA: Harvard UP, 1965), 52–97. To be absolutely fair to Keats, however, he does not see the females that populate his poetry as literal "women," and thus the statement does contain verity from the poet's perspective. The statement, like the poetry itself, attempts to replace the real with the ideal.

3. As vision will progressively become the metaphor for knowledge in the poetry, the direction in which the eyes gaze will evolve with the female. Innocence will consistently be depicted in a gaze that focuses either downward, on the earth, or upward to heaven, until Moneta's eyes of "visionless entire . . . / Of all external things" ("The Fall of Hyperion" 1.267–68).

4. Merlin Stone discusses the supersession of the female deity by the male and the traditional role of the male as provider of light. The mythical battles between male and female deities are invariably battles between light and darkness—between knowledge and errant emotion. Yet, as Stone points out, even when the male priests took over the sites of divination from the goddesses, "it was still priestesses who most often supplied the respected counsel" (203). As Keats's poetry will attest, this is an observation that he was fully aware of.

5. According to *Lemprière's Classical Dictionary*, Cynthia (or Diana) "had such an aversion to marriage that she obtained from her father the privilege of living in perpetual celibacy, . . . she forgot her dignity to enjoy the company of Endymion" (228). Her power, unlike the very sexual goddesses to come, traditionally derives from celibacy, probably one of the reasons Cynthia will be abandoned in later poetry.

6. Traditional courtly love, whose tenets include songs and poetry to the female rather than actual contact with her, is a way that the male, as the poet does here, may distance himself from his beloved, thereby avoiding the pain that frequently accompanies sexuality. When the conventions of courtly love are forsaken, as in "La Belle Dame sans Merci," the results are disastrous.

7. As the females change, so will the connotations (and ramifications) of the "thrall." The thrall in which la belle dame holds the knight will be an entanglement of deadly proportions because the female herself has become deadly at that point. The mortal speaker, the male hero, will have changed very little, however, as he continues to seek a stable identity through the persistent instability of the females.

8. An imagination pejoratively described as "bloomy" cannot hold the attention of the male for long, and it certainly cannot grant him identity. In its stern beckoning of the poet away from such scenes, the imagination seems more disciplined at this point than the creator.

9. As Dickstein points out, the "common Elizabethan pun on 'die' testifies that there is nothing novel in Keats' association of loss of self with an intensity of pleasure" (42), but it certainly does testify to Keats's idea of sexuality as omnipotent in the creation of poetry. The loss of self through "dying," as will be seen later in "Hyperion," is analogous to the creation of the "camelion Poet," which is auto-erotic in that it is "every thing and nothing" (*Letters* 1:387).

2. *Endymion*: "He awoke and found it truth"

1. These lines are very similar to the dialogue in Shakespeare's *Romeo and Juliet* between Romeo and Mercutio about Romeo's dreams (1.4.95–103). In a letter to J. H. Reynolds dated July 13, 1818, three months after publishing *Endymion*, Keats writes, "Believe me I have more than once yearne'd for the time of your happiness to come, as much as I could for myself after the lips of Juliet" (*Letters* 1:325). Because dreams are so significant to this stage of the imagination (and the "lips of Juliet" so prominent in his thoughts), it is quite possible that Peona's lines are a conscious allusion to Mercutio's speech, one that, like hers, both admonishes and foreshadows.

2. In the original text, as Garrod makes clear in his edition of Keats, Peona is "a most tender lass" as well (1.408), making her

even closer in stature and identity to the maidens of 1817 before Keats's revision of her (*Poetical Works* 76n).

3. Goldberg notes that Cynthia is not the traditional symbol of chastity in the poem, but that "through Keats, she emerges as the embodiment of eternality, immortality, perfect beauty . . . [in whom] beauty can remain a joy forever" (21). Cynthia appeared earlier, in "Sleep and Poetry," but was not the predominant figure she has become here. This second time, Keats has made the moon goddess the symbol of the only type of permanence his early imagination can render, a symbol which will evolve into the necessary replacement of Cynthia by more powerful goddesses and the transference of her wisdom to them.

4. Compare Endymion's awakening to the unreality of his vision to Madeline's abrupt awakening to the reality of Porphyro ("The Eve of St. Agnes" 328–33). The dreamers' responses are similar; the differences lie in the situations that evoke them and in Keats's own changing perception of the dreaming state (to be discussed in chapter 3).

5. The morbidity of that poem makes such a statement about "Isabella" somewhat difficult to defend, however, especially since, after his death, Lorenzo's ghost does seek reanimation and thus redefines Isabella from mortal to at least novice "enchantress." It is probably safe to say, therefore, that "love" does not exist in the poetry outside "Ode to Psyche." Even in the final poems of restoration, the prevailing emotions are fear ("The Fall of Hyperion") and friendship ("To Autumn").

6. As I have stated, however, the idea of the female figure becoming a "femme fatale" is unsatisfactory to me. The appellation is one that defines her in strictly androcentric terms because she becomes not a powerful figure per se, but powerful only in relation to her destructiveness to the male.

7. Frederick Beaty writes that Keats introduces the Indian maiden because of her own "intense suffering from which she has learned the importance of love." Keats is thus able to justify "sorrow as a means of stimulating imagination" (182). This is probably an oversimplification because, while the Indian maiden has certainly learned the importance of love, it is never clear, in the supernatural processes of development that inform the poem, whether or not Endymion has. He remains torn between the two

females until the end. But Keats will eventually use human sorrow as the primary means to the imagination regardless of justification.

3. The Mortal Females: Isabella, Madeline, and Bertha

1. Lionel Trilling elaborates on Keats's statement: "Keats, who thought of women as exempt from the moral life of men, and therefore not to be held responsible or guilty, conceives the problem of evil with particular reference to them. . . . that *women* should 'have cancers' is to him a conclusive instance of the unexplainable cruelty of the cosmos" (40). Perhaps this perception is more a product of Trilling's own beliefs in the society of the 1950s rather than a correct reading of Keats, however. As the agent of the imagination, the female as persona is certainly characterized as "moral." (Poetry is, after all, the most "genuine" thing in the world to Keats, except for philosophy [*Letters* 2:139].) And the mortal female, of whom Keats and Trilling speak, seems consistently to be held morally "responsible or guilty" in these poems and in Keats's life. The juxtaposition of women and cancer with his own "dying day" in the letter seems to connote more a ranting against mortality than a championing of women.

2. A nurse will also play surrogate mother to Madeline in "The Eve of St. Agnes," aiding in the maiden's own transformation from child to woman by allying herself with Porphyro, who will be the unusual male catalyst (and perpetrator) of the transformation.

3. This statement excludes Byron, who found madness more romantic when it occurred in the male, especially in the male speakers who were his own alter egos. In *Manfred* it is seen by Byron as a liberating experience, however, and could thus be considered a part of his own feminized self.

4. As previously noted, Madeline will be an exception to such a description. She is the only one of the mortal females not to be "abandoned" by either the male or the imagination.

5. In the later unions of mortal with immortal, it will be important that the male be the mortal, thereby vulnerable, half of the pair, because he will be the one seeking change through the invulnerable female.

6. Although it will serve as theme and backdrop to the next two poems, "The Eve of St. Agnes" and "The Eve of St. Mark," religion will continue to prove ineffectual to mortal suffering. In a continu-

ation of the theme begun here, the powers of religion will be inferior to those of imagination.

7. The medieval setting is important to Keats's final complete poem that focuses on the mortal female as discussed by Frances Gies and Joseph Gies: "Medieval ambivalence . . . simultaneously placed woman on a pedestal and reviled her as the incarnation of evil" (37). Religion is a major force in the dichotomy of the female, as the two dominant figures in the church's domain, Eve and Mary, prove the point.

8. Paglia is referring here to Spenser's male figures, and calls voyeurism "one of the most characteristic moods of *The Faerie Queene*" (189). Voyeurism is a characteristically male activity, originating from the concept of male as subject and woman as object. Porphyro's own voyeuristic tendencies help make his own role in the poem undeniably that of subject, one perhaps difficult to give up, as the tendencies to spy on Madeline continue even when he exits the closet and goes to her bedside where her sleeping affords him more opportunity to watch her unnoticed.

9. For further discussion of the significance of Porphyro's name, see Marcia Gilbreath, "The Etymology of Porphyro's Name in Keats's 'The Eve of St. Agnes' " (*Keats-Shelley Journal* 37 [1988]: 20–25).

10. Keats's need for human passion in his poetry will be forcefully reiterated in the "Ode on a Grecian Urn," a symbol that, like religion, can offer only lifeless ritual. It is a deficiency that he will again acknowledge in terms of coldness, as he calls the urn "cold Pastoral!" (45).

11. Like the machinations of *Endymion*, however, the imagination that saves the lovers in the end will be more supernatural than creative.

12. Lemprière recounts that Tereus "offered violence to Philomela, and afterwards cut out her tongue, that she might not be able to discover his barbarity, and the indignities which she had suffered" (519). Through her own lack of vision, Madeline will not "discover" Porphyro's own "offered violence" until after it has been "received." Lack of vision is analogous to voicelessness here, as it will be in "La Belle Dame sans Merci." The male will fall prey in the later poetry, however.

13. Both Levinson (*Allegory* 158) and Earl R. Wasserman (*The Finer Tone: Keats' Major Poems* [Baltimore: Johns Hopkins Press, 1953]), in his lengthy discussion of the poem (97–137), suggest

that the lovers have died (and become mythologized) at the end, thereby making the problematic ending a moot issue.

4. "Ripe Progress" and "Horrid Warning": The Goddesses of "Hyperion" and "La Belle Dame sans Merci"

1. Unable to continue with "Hyperion," Keats took time off from it to write "The Eve of St. Agnes," which is most likely why the Titans of this poem seem like human counterparts to the lifeless statuary of "St. Agnes." The bulk of "Hyperion" was written after the previous poem, and the inherent difficulties with it speak to the burgeoning difficulties with the new poetic direction Keats pursues.

2. Hirst writes that because the Greek words for both *Saturn* and *time* differ only in a single letter (*Kronos* for *Saturn* and *chronos* for *time*), the defeat of the Titans is a defeat not of mortality because the Titans are not mortal, but of time itself (94). While the Titans are as close to mortal as immortals can be, as Van Ghent points out, and as their overthrow makes clear, I agree that time is indeed a part of the loss here, as will be so exquisitely apotheosized in "To Autumn," but time is also a defining and limiting characteristic of mortality itself.

3. The characterization of Saturn as a "stone" makes the battle a contrast between "the massive and changeless serenity of the Titan character [with that of Apollo] described in terms of intense emotional expressiveness and a grace that is feminine" (Van Ghent 190). The stone that is Saturn does certainly negatively compare to Keats's Apollo and seems to misplace the emotions that Apollo is sent to supplant.

4. Because *King Lear* was one of Keats's favorite works, it could not have escaped his notice that the only major character left alive at the play's end, Edgar, has survived by forsaking his own masculine identity, his "true self," and feigning madness.

5. Homans discusses the passivity of Milton's own Mother Earth, "giving birth to herself [and yet requiring] the active agency of 'Main Ocean' to complete the process" (16). In Keats, true parthenogenesis, begun in "Hyperion" with Mnemosyne, will not become valid until "To Autumn," in which it is neither male nor female but the process itself that creates.

6. As the first poem to succeed those concentrated on mortality, the emphasis of "Hyperion" remains more on the struggle to achieve permanence rather than on its actual achievement, on

"creating itself," that is. The poem depicts a painful death and birth but not the life to follow, remaining a fragment rather than a completed work. Its completion will be enacted in the poems to follow but will no longer focus on the burgeoning Apollo.

7. On his deathbed, Keats will call life after poetry a "posthumous existence": "I have an habitual feeling of my real life having past, and that I am leading a posthumous existence" (*Letters* 2:359). Like his Titans, the poet is simultaneously past change and in the midst of it.

8. The "wretched" state of the knight-at-arms is discernible in the earlier version, however, from another male's perspective—that of the disembodied yet masculine voice that interrogates the knight but then, like the lady herself, apparently leaves him. Elusiveness is thus a trait of both genders in this poem.

9. It is possible madness that the knight-at-arms attributes to the lady, retrospectively, through her "wild eyes," reminiscent of Keats's own "beauteous woman's large blue eyes / Gone mad" ("Dear Reynolds" 53–54).

10. In shutting the lady's eyes, the knight-at-arms seeks the lady's loss of vision and direction but loses his own instead. To shut her eyes also enforces a passivity upon the lady, imitative of sleep. The knight continues to attempt restriction through known, mortal means.

11. A female causes the Mariner's destruction as well, but she is described in terms of "otherworldliness" that can only be called ugly: "*Her* lips were red, *her* looks were free, / Her locks were yellow as gold: / Her skin was as white as leprosy, / The Nightmare LIFE-IN-DEATH was she, / Who thicks man's blood with cold" (3.190–94). Coleridge's emphasis on the first two instances of "her," articulated by the Mariner, is perhaps from the shock of encountering a woman of such deathly dimensions. The life-in-death female figure is compelled to be characterized as deathly ugly, though, because she seeks out the Mariner not for sex, as la belle dame does, but for ritualistic repentence. Both are equally destructive. Through his ordeal with the Fatal Woman and the ensuing ritual, the Mariner is left psychically as "starved" as the knight-at-arms and his predecessors have been physically. Starvation is frequently a metaphor for "outsider" status. M. K. Louis, for example, contends that Emily Dickinson "made her poetry out of hunger; hunger is implicit in the very texture of her spare language and desperate syntax" (355). An example of such language Louis uses is

particularly appropriate to the knight-at-arms: " 'Hunger—[is] a way / Of Persons Outside Windows' " (357).

5. The Odes and Keats's "Branched Thoughts"

1. In my discussion of the odes, I shall repeatedly refer to "La Belle Dame sans Merci" because I believe it had a significant influence on their creation. Not only do the odes, like their predecessor, contain themes of dreaming and wakefulness, of vision and nonvision, which lead to a doubtful sense of reality, but also both "La Belle Dame" and the odes portray a narrator who is an outsider to the symbol of the imagination, unable to bridge the profound gap between himself and the female. In effect, "La Belle Dame" and the odes are the first group of poems to contradict Keats's famous maxim on Adam's dream, whereby "what the imagination seizes as beauty must be truth—whether it existed before or not" (*Letters* 1:184), for these poems force the poet to the crucial realization that "truth" cannot be sustained in the presence of the imagination he now seeks.

2. Various critics have pointed out the implicit debate that is common to all of the odes, but it is where the debate finally takes the speaker that is crucial to discussion of the odes, and it is at this apex of activity that the differences emerge.

3. Through the creation of "Psyche," Keats also resurrects one of his most revered predecessors, Milton. It is frequently noted by critics that "Psyche's" "no shrine, no grove, no oracle, no heat / Of pale-mouthed prophet dreaming" is more than reminiscent of "No nightly trance, or breathed spell / Inspires the pale-ey'd Priest from the prophetic cell" from Milton's "Ode on the Morning of Christ's Nativity." John Hollander discusses the echoes between Keats and his predecessor and contends that in "Ode to Psyche," "Keats, too, asks his Muse to 'prevent' with his humble ode the canonical judgment of history, as Milton prays that his figurative orient gift be delivered before the merely opulent spices of the magi" (68). Whatever the actual reason for Keats having so obviously returned to Milton for the speaker's role in "Psyche," it is an intriguing circumstance that the poem to which he alludes is, in effect, an ode and offering to Christ—making a connection between the "hethen Goddess" (*Letters* 2:106) and the icon of Christian salvation seem undeniable.

4. In *The Quest for Permanence* (Cambridge, MA: Harvard UP, 1959), David Perkins points out the many suggestions of insub-

stantiality that exist within the "Ode to Psyche" as well, the one ode that does successfully control the imagination, but at the expense of the speaker's sexuality (226–28).

5. The ode's closing aphorism, so long debated, seems, like the urn's female shape whose powers prove specious, to "tease us out of thought" if we attempt to relate a message between it and ourselves. It seems to make the most sense if taken simply as a statement whose inherent circularity, like the urn's itself, leads us away from questions that have no answers. The significance of the last two lines lies, like the shape of the urn, in form rather than in meaning.

6. It is an interesting paradox that the figures come to life in this ode, as the speaker, who so frantically sought their animation in the previous ode, is in a state of deathly lassitude. While this ode probably rightly follows "Ode on Melancholy," although the precise dates are not known, it is thematically closer to "Ode on a Grecian Urn," and so I have chosen to discuss the remaining two odes in this order.

7. Keats had added another additional stanza to the beginning of the ode, one which he intentionally discarded before the poem was printed. That stanza, rich in phallic overture, is as follows:

> Though you should build a bark of dead men's bones,
>   And rear a phantom gibbet for a mast,
> Stitch creeds together for a sail, with groans
>   To fill it out, bloodstained and aghast;
> Although your rudder be a Dragon's tail,
>   Long sever'd, yet still hard with agony,
>   Your cordage large uprootings from the skull
> Of bald Medusa; certes you would fail
>   To find the Melancholy, whether she
>   Dreameth in any isle of Lethe dull.

The most significant aspect of this excised stanza, besides the plethora of dreadful male Gothic imagery, is the way its last line leads into the opening line as it now exists: "No, no, go not to Lethe," indicating that the extant poem is a desired series of options on how the listener may find Melancholy through life rather than through the death that consumes this omitted stanza.

The excised stanza also eliminates the idea of phallic sexuality as a way to find Melancholy, simultaneously eliminating the male speaker from the poem until he becomes a "cloudy trophy" at the end. The Medusa is "bald" in these lines of masculine power, thus, like Samson's haircut, depriving her of her threatened destructiveness, but in the images of female sexuality that follow in the remaining stanzas, the threat is still real.

8. Robert Cummings argues that the "mortality of beauty is not Keats's point [in the ode]—though he acknowledges that beauty must die. The peculiar melancholy edge of intense experience is its unaccommodatability, its being on the edge of what can be felt at all. The extremity of delight is generated by a suffering at the center; and the profoundest exploration of delight returns us to its origin in grief" (51–52). It is a circularity that reverses the order of things to come in "To Autumn," whereby the "profoundest exploration" of grief returns us to delight.

6. Lamia: The "Rainbow-Sided" Female

1. An interesting parallel to Keats's use of the serpent/woman is given by Stone in her discussion of the theory of archaeologist Stephen Langdon, who wrote that "the Goddess known as Nina . . . was a serpent goddess in the most ancient Sumerian periods. . . . She was esteemed as an oracular deity and an interpreter of dreams" (199). This definition of the lamia takes on greater meaning here when read in the context of Keats's new attitude toward dreams. On another terrifying female figure, Bertha Mason of *Jane Eyre*, Elaine Showalter writes that Bertha is "the incarnation of the flesh, of female sexuality in its most irredeemably bestial and terrifying form" (118). Bertha's devolution from woman to beast reverses the process undergone by Lamia, but the end result remains the same because of the overwhelming and errant sexuality uncovered in both.

2. The vulnerable Ariadne hanged herself following her abandonment by Theseus in one story. In others, "Bacchus loved her after Theseus had forsaken her, and gave her a crown of seven stars, which, after her death, was changed into a constellation" (Lemprière 80). While Lamia will not commit suicide, even for Lycius, her vulnerability aligns her with Ariadne.

3. It is the female's ability to elude and delude the male that makes her dangerous, her ability to change shape and character with ease. Auerbach points out that the mermaid evolves from the lamia figure, and believes that both "may typify the restoration of

an earlier serpent-woman, the Greek Medusa" (9). The various shapes are a history of transformation that defines the perceived feminine nature. Coleridge's Geraldine, whose undressing reveals "A sight to dream of, not to tell!" ("Christabel" 253), manifests the myth of transformation as well. Bullough recounts a twelfth-century rendition of the myth in the words of an abbot who spoke against admittance of women into the Premonstratensian order: "The wickedness of women is greater than all the other wickedness of the world, . . . the poison of asps and dragons is more curable and less dangerous for men than the familiarity of women. . . . we will on no account receive any more sisters to the increase of our perdition, but will avoid them like poisonous animals" (160).

4. Chase is referring here to the juvenilia of Charlotte Bronte rather than a male, but the Bronte sisters' own literary imagination was so immersed in the literature of the male romantics at that time, especially Byron's, that their adherence to the sexual hierarchy of which Chase speaks was more natural than imitative.

5. Interestingly, Apollonius is also described by Lemprière as "the first who endeavored to explain the apparent stopping and retrograde motion of the planets" (68), an indication of his own knowledge of and thus invulnerability to the "silver planet" that is Lamia.

6. The battle for control both pervades and subverts the actions of the characters. All literal action is taken as metaphor. For example, as Simpson says, when Lycius "begins the insidious process of trying to institutionalise his love for Lamia, to fix it within a stable social framework and to clip its wings, the first thing he asks of her is her name" (72). Control lurks underneath "love;" the blasé desire to procure a name from Lamia, any one we may presume, is, to Lycius, the source and manifestation of the control he seeks.

7. It could not escape anyone's notice that the serpent is more a phallic symbol than one of female fertility, yet the serpent is archetypally associated with the female when considered as evil. In its uroboric position, with tail in mouth, it has more "vulval" dimensions, but it is then a symbol of eternity—the timelessness that is again claimed by the masculine. Medusa and Eve notwithstanding, there seems to be more confusion to the lamia myths than simply that which emerges from the admixture of woman and serpent; if it is a sexually procreative image that is created from the fusion of serpent with female, then much of the confusion over the lamia's identity must rest with the male.

7. "The Fall" and "Autumn": The Final Relationship

1. Although Stillinger places "To Autumn" before "The Fall of Hyperion" in his edition of the poems, the dates we have for their composition are, I believe, too imprecise for definitive placement. "The Fall" was begun but not finished before "To Autumn," in July 1819, but Keats went back to it sometime in September ("To Autumn" was written September 19), and finally abandoned it by September 21. Thus it seems that the greater portion of "The Fall" had to have been written before "To Autumn."

2. In Joseph Severn's letter to William Haslam from Rome, of January 15, 1821, he says of Keats: "This noble fellow lying on the bed—is dying in horror—no kind hope smoothing down his suffering—no philosophy—no religion to support him—yet with all the most knawing desire for it—yet without the possibility of receiving it" (*Letters* 2:368).

3. I once believed the figure of Autumn was undeniably female, the goddess Ceres. I am now convinced that, while the feminine principle is a part of the figure, as I discuss in this chapter, the strictly female figure is no longer necessary to or even desired by Keats. What is important to the final figure is not gender but the process of poetic maturity that it inheres.

4. Besides the knight-at-arms, an obvious predecessor to the dreamer, this final male is the only one not given a specific name. Like the knight, he is identified by what he does.

5. Sperry discusses an implied similarity between Eve and the dreamer (318).

6. Lemprière attributes Moneta's admonitory and prophetic powers to her advice to the Romans to "sacrifice a pregnant sow to Cybele, to avert an earthquake" (422).

7. The poet's own "private self," that he communicates to Fanny Brawne in the letters he writes to her during composition of these final poems, is one of illness and disillusionment. In July 1819, Keats writes to her:

> You must have found out by this time I am a little given to bode ill like the raven; it is my misfortune not my fault; it has proceeded from the general tenor of my life, and rendered every event suspicious. . . . If through me illness have touched you (but it must be with a very gentle hand) I must be selfish enough to feel a little glad at it.

> ... I have been reading lately an oriental tale of a very
> beautiful color—It is of a city of melancholy men, all
> made so by this circumstance. ... each one of them by
> turns reach some gardens of Paradise where they meet
> with a most enchanting Lady; and just as they are going
> to embrace her, she bids them shut their eyes—they shut
> them—and on opening their eyes again find themselves
> descending to the earth in a magic basket. (*Letters* 2:130)

Like his dreamer, Keats is both fearful and desirous of the encoun-
ter with the "most enchanting Lady." He, too, is inert with indeci-
sion, an indecisiveness that finds itself ensconced in its own dream.
It is an inertia that originates with another and possibly simultane-
ous letter to Brawne, on July 11, 1819, which claims Keats to "have
of late been moulting: ... I have altered, not from a Chrysalis into
a butterfly, but the Contrary. Having two little loopholes, whence
I may look out into the stage of the world. ... The first time I sat
down to write, I [could] scarcely believe in the necessity of so
doing. It struck me as a great oddity—Yet the very corn which is
now so beautiful, as if it had only [taken] to ripening yesterday, is
for the market: So, why [should] I be delicate (*Letters* 2:128–29).
The vision that has been reduced to "two little loopholes" and the
corn that is harvested "for the market" will both be restored in
these final poems. The poetic restoration is one that the "private
self" of Keats could never achieve with Fanny Brawne, but through
the repeated correspondence of this self to her, he created at least
the symbols for such restoration.

   8. The rest of Spenser's description of Dame Nature, from
which Vendler quotes, is as follows:

> For that her face did like a Lion shew,
> That eye of wight could not indure to view:
> But others tell that it so beautious was,
> And round about such beames of splendor threw,
> That it the Sunne a thousand times did pass,
> Ne could be seene, but like an image in a glass.
>   (7.7.6)

As noted in the previous chapter, I believe Spenser's figure of
change is more an analogue to Melancholy than to Moneta, as
Vendler believes, because of the precise moment of suspended

activity that the previous goddess inheres, the same moment that informs "To Autumn," Keats's own invocation to the earth.

9. As previously discussed, this is indeed a peculiar comment from the poet who has, at the end of the process especially, made the female not only "dominant," but the title figure in "Isabella," "La Belle Dame sans Merci," and "Lamia." But, as is especially true now in the women around him, "with few exceptions," he always discovered some "inadequacy," even in Fanny Brawne (*Letters* 2:19n).

10. Curran observes that Moneta's denunciation of dreams questions "the very dream in which she appears" (218), perpetuating the ambiguity Keats has toward the imagination. The dream setting here, though, seems to be more transitional than ambiguous, serving as liaison between Lamia and the figure of Autumn to come.

11. The "moment" here is not like Wordsworth's "spots of time," which were transformatively powerful because of their ability to affect the poet's present; there is no "present" per se in this poem. Rather, it is like Blake's own "moment"—a single pulse of the artery, which both delineates and transcends past, present, and future.

Conclusion

1. Virginia Woolf cogently expresses the historical status of the woman as literary character in man's work as opposed to her reality in *A Room of One's Own*:

> Imaginatively she is of the highest importance; practically she is completely insignificant. She pervades poetry from cover to cover; she is all but absent from history. She dominates the lives of kings and conquerors in fiction; in fact she was the slave of any boy whose parents forced a ring upon her finger. Some of the most inspired words, some of the most profound thoughts in literature fall from her lips; in real life she could hardly read, could scarcely spell, and was the property of her husband. (45–46)

2. Levinson calls such transference by Keats "masturbatory": poetry that creates "a fantasy of pleasure without the death of perfect gratification" (*Allegory* 27).

Works Cited

Allott, Miriam. "'Isabella,' 'The Eve of St. Agnes' and 'Lamia.' " *John Keats: A Reassessment*. Ed. Kenneth Muir. Liverpool: Liverpool UP, 1958.

Auerbach, Nina. *Woman and the Demon: The Life of a Victorian Myth*. Cambridge, MA: Harvard UP, 1982.

Baker, Jeffrey. *John Keats and Symbolism*. New York: St. Martin's, 1986.

Bate, Walter Jackson. *John Keats*. Cambridge, MA: Harvard UP, 1963.

Beaty, Frederick. *Light from Heaven: Love in British Romantic Literature*. DeKalb, IL: Northern Illinois UP, 1971.

Beauvoir, Simone de. *The Second Sex*. Trans. H. M. Parshley. New York: Vintage, 1974.

Blake, William. *The Complete Poems*. Ed. Alicia Ostriker. New York: Penguin, 1977.

Bullough, Vern L. *The Subordinate Sex*. New York: Penguin, 1974.

Burton, Robert. *The Anatomy of Melancholy*. Philadelphia: Moore, 1854.

Butler, Marilyn. *Romantics, Rebels and Reactionaries: English Literature and its Background 1760–1830*. Oxford: Oxford UP, 1982.

Chase, Karen. *Eros and Psyche: The Representation of Personality in Charlotte Bronte, Charles Dickens, George Eliot*. New York: Methuen, 1984.

Coleridge, Samuel Taylor. *The Portable Coleridge*. Ed. I. A. Richards. New York: Viking, 1950.

Cummings, Robert. "Keats's Melancholy in the Temple of Delight." *Keats-Shelley Journal* 36 (1987): 50–62.

Curran, Stuart. *Poetic Form and British Romanticism*. Oxford: Oxford UP, 1986.

D'Avanzo, Mario. *Keats's Metaphors for the Poetic Imagination*. Durham, NC: Duke UP, 1967.

Dickstein, Morris. *Keats and His Poetry: A Study in Development.* Chicago: U of Chicago P, 1971.

Evert, Walter. *Aesthetic and Myth in the Poetry of Keats.* Princeton, NJ: Princeton UP, 1965.

Ford, John. *'Tis Pity She's a Whore.* Ed. N. W. Bawcutt. Lincoln, NE: U of Nebraska P, 1966.

Gaull, Marilyn. *English Romanticism: The Human Context.* New York: Norton, 1988.

Gies, Frances, and Joseph Gies. *Women in the Middle Ages.* New York: Harper, 1978.

Gilbert, Sandra M., and Susan Gubar. *The Madwoman in the Attic: The Woman Writer and the Nineteenth-Century Literary Imagination.* New Haven: Yale UP, 1979.

Goldberg, M. A. *The Poetics of Romanticism: Toward a Reading of John Keats.* Yellow Springs, OH: Antioch, 1969.

Heilbrun, Caroline. *Reinventing Womanhood.* New York: Norton, 1979.

Hirst, Wolf Z. *John Keats.* Boston: Twayne, 1981.

Hollander, John. *The Figure of Echo: A Mode of Allusion in Milton and After.* Berkeley: U of California P, 1981.

Homans, Margaret. *Women Writers and Poetic Identity.* Princeton, NJ: Princeton UP, 1980.

Janeway, Elizabeth. *Between Myth and Mourning: Women Awakening.* New York: Morrow, 1974.

Keats, John. *John Keats: Selected Poems and Letters.* Ed. Douglas Bush. Boston: Houghton, 1959.

———. *The Letters of John Keats.* Ed. Hyder Edward Rollins. 2 vols. Cambridge, MA: Harvard UP, 1958.

———. *The Poems of John Keats.* Ed. Jack Stillinger. Cambridge, MA: Harvard UP, 1978.

———. *The Poetical Works of John Keats.* Ed. H. W. Garrod. Oxford: Clarendon, 1939.

Lau, Beth. "Keats's Mature Goddesses." *Philological Quarterly* 63 (1984): 323–41.

Lemprière, John. *Lemprière's Classical Dictionary.* London: Cadell and Davies, 1818. Rev. F. A. Wright. London: Bracken, 1984.

Levinson, Marjorie. *Keats's Life of Allegory: The Origins of a Style.* Oxford: Basil Blackwell, 1988.

———. *The Romantic Fragment Poem: A Critique of Form.* Chapel Hill: U of North Carolina P, 1986.

Louis, M. K. "Emily Dickinson's Sacrament of Starvation." *Nineteenth-Century Literature* 43.3 (1988): 346–60.

Millett, Kate. *Sexual Politics*. New York: Doubleday, 1970.

Pagels, Elaine. *Adam, Eve, and the Serpent*. New York: Random, 1988.

Paglia, Camille. *Sexual Personae: Art and Decadence from Nefertiti to Emily Dickinson*. New York: Random, 1990.

Patterson, Charles I., Jr. *The Daemonic in the Poetry of John Keats*. Urbana: U of Illinois P, 1970.

Praz, Mario. *The Romantic Agony*. Trans. Angus Davidson. London: Oxford UP, 1951.

Rajan, Tilottama. *Dark Interpreter: The Discourse of Romanticism*. Ithaca, NY: Cornell UP, 1980.

Reiman, Donald H. "Keats and the Humanistic Paradox: Mythological History in 'Lamia.' " *Studies in English Literature* 11 (1971): 659–69.

Ricks, Christopher. *Keats and Embarrassment*. Oxford: Clarendon, 1984.

Ridley, M. R. *Keats' Craftsmanship: A Study in Poetic Development*. 1933. Rpt. Lincoln, NE: U of Nebraska P, 1963.

Ross, Marlon. "Beyond the Fragmented Word: Keats at the Limits of Patrilineal Language." *Out of Bounds: Male Writers and Gender[ed] Criticism*. Eds. Laura Claridge and Elizabeth Langland. Amherst, MA: U of Massachusetts P, 1990. 110–31.

———. "Romantic Quest and Conquest: Troping Masculine Power in the Crisis of Poetic Identity." *Romanticism and Feminism*. Ed. Anne K. Mellor. Bloomington and Indianapolis: Indiana UP, 1988. 26–51.

Rzepka, Charles J. *The Self as Mind: Vision and Identity in Wordsworth, Coleridge, and Keats*. Cambridge, MA: Harvard UP, 1986.

Schapiro, Barbara. *The Romantic Mother: Narcissistic Patterns in Romantic Poetry*. Baltimore: Johns Hopkins UP, 1983.

Shelley, Percy Bysshe. *Poetical Works*. Ed. Thomas Hutchinson. 1905. Rev. G. M. Matthews. Oxford: Oxford UP, 1970.

Showalter, Elaine. *A Literature of Their Own: British Women Novelists from Bronte to Lessing*. Princeton, NJ: Princeton UP, 1977.

Simpson, David. *Irony and Authority in Romantic Poetry*. Totowa, NJ: Rowman, 1979.

Sinson, Janice C. *John Keats and the Anatomy of Melancholy*. London: Keats-Shelley Memorial Association, 1971.

Spenser, Edmund. *The Faerie Queene*. Ed. A. C. Hamilton. New York: Longman, 1977.

Sperry, Stuart M. *Keats the Poet*. Princeton, NJ: Princeton UP, 1973.

Stillinger, Jack. *The Hoodwinking of Madeline and Other Essays on Keats's Poems*. Urbana: U of Illinois P, 1971.

Stone, Merlin. *When God Was a Woman*. New York: Harcourt, 1976.

Swann, Karen. "Harassing the Muse." *Romanticism and Feminism*. Ed. Anne K. Mellor. Bloomington: Indiana UP, 1988. 81–92.

Trilling, Lionel. "The Poet as Hero: Keats in His Letters." *The Opposing Self*. New York: Viking, 1955.

Van Ghent, Dorothy. *Keats: The Myth of the Hero*. Ed. Jeffrey Cane Robinson. Princeton, NJ: Princeton UP, 1983.

Vendler, Helen. *The Odes of John Keats*. Cambridge, MA: Harvard UP, 1983.

Waldoff, Leon. *Keats and the Silent Work of Imagination*. Urbana: U of Illinois P, 1985.

Ward, Aileen. *John Keats: The Making of a Poet*. 1963. Rpt. New York: Viking, 1967.

Woolf, Virginia. *A Room of One's Own*. New York: Harcourt, 1957.

Wordsworth, William. *Poetical Works*. Ed. Thomas Hutchinson. 1904. Rev. Ernest de Selincourt. Rpt. Oxford: Oxford UP, 1988.

Yaeger, Patricia. *Honey-Mad Women: Emancipatory Strategies in Women's Writing*. New York: Columbia UP, 1988.

Index

Allott, Miriam, 144
Amor. *See* Psyche, myth of
Anatomy of Melancholy, The (Burton), 139–41, 147, 180
Ancient Mariner, The (character), 61, 109, 111, 192n.11
Apollo (character): androgynous, 8, 103, 174; birth of, 39, 91, 98–102, 148, 163; compared to Hermes in "Lamia," 147; and Delphic priestesses, 31; immortality of, 117, 142; as Keats's alter-ego, 16–17; and misogyny, 4–5; Mnemosyne and, 116, 148, 165; myth of, 4–5, 16, 22, 23, 29–30, 38, 185n.2; successor to Hyperion, 161–62, 191–92n.6; youthful, 95, 109. *See also* Imagination, Apollonian
Apollonius (character). *See* Keats: works, "Lamia"
Apuleius, Lucius, 15
Ariadne: myth of, 150, 195n.2
Auerbach, Nina, 3, 195–96n.3

Bacchus: myth of, 56–57, 195n.2
Bailey, Benjamin: Keats's letters to, 3, 31, 64, 72, 153
Baker, Jeffrey, 76
Bate, Walter Jackson, 92, 131, 169
Beaty, Frederick, 188n.7
Beauvoir, Simone de, 1–2
Bertha (character). *See* Keats: works, "Eve of St. Mark, The"

"Beyond the Fragmented Word" (Ross), 97, 98, 99, 164
Blake, William, 53, 199n.11
Brawne, Frances (Fanny), 69; and Keats as ghost of Lorenzo, 74, 75; and Keats's "private self," 197–98n.7; Keats's tragic relationship with, 6, 199n.9; and "Lamia," 145–47, 152, 153, 157. *See also* Cressida, Fanny Brawne as "the Cressid"
Bronte, Charlotte, 196n.4
Brown, Charles, 13, 161, 186n.2
Bullough, Vern L., 196n.3
Burton, Robert, 139–41, 147, 180
Bush, Douglas, 147
Butler, Marilyn, 145
Byron, Lord George Gordon, 189n.3, 196n.4
Byronic hero, 153

Calidore (character), 40, 108
Ceres, 176, 197n.3
Chase, Karen, 104, 119, 152, 196n.4
"Christabel" (Coleridge), 196n.3
Circe: myth of. *See* Keats: works, *Endymion*
Coleridge, Samuel Taylor, 61, 192n.11, 196n.3
Courtly love: 187n.6; in "La Belle Dame sans Merci," 107
Cowden Clarke, Charles, 26, 30
Cox, Jane, 181, 185n.1
Cressida: Cresseid (Burton), 140;

Karla Alwes is an associate professor of English at the State University of New York College at Cortland. Her work has appeared in *Nineteenth-Century Literature*, in the *Encyclopedia of Romanticism: Culture in Britain, 1780s–1850s*, and in anthologies on misogyny in literature and on women and violence in literature.